Hitchcock
à la Carte

Hitchcock
à la Carte

Jan Olsson

Duke University Press   Durham and London   2015

Printed in the United States of America on acid-free paper ∞
Designed by Natalie F. Smith
Typeset in Quadraat by Copperline Book Services, Inc.

Library of Congress Cataloging-in-Publication Data
Olsson, Jan, 1952–
Hitchcock à la carte / Jan Olsson.
pages cm
Includes bibliographical references and index.
ISBN 978-0-8223-5790-2 (hardcover : alk. paper)
ISBN 978-0-8223-5804-6 (pbk. : alk. paper)
ISBN 978-0-8223-7602-6 (e-book)
1. Hitchcock, Alfred, 1899–1980—Criticism and
interpretation. 2. Human body in motion pictures.
3. Human body on television. I. Title.
PN1998.3.H58O47 2015
791.4302'33092—dc23
2014032512

Cover: Photograph by Jim Miller for Los Angeles
Magazine (cover, August 1974). Courtesy of the
Academy of Motion Picture Arts and Sciences.

CONTENTS

ACKNOWLEDGMENTS

From first fancy to final form, fabulous facilitators and formidable sparring partners have been highly influential for my attempt at serving up the Hitchcock brand. Lynn Spigel got me under way when she invited me to teach a Hitchcock seminar at Northwestern University. Throughout, she has acted as a veritable champion for the project. Ken Wissoker at Duke University Press discreetly steered the process from first pitch to book design with unfailing elegance. For the masterminding of the final hands-on process and copyediting, I'm beyond grateful for having had Liz Smith in my corner. Her unfailing sense of style and graceful attention to matters big and small are nothing short of superb. During the cumbersome process of securing rights for the book's figures, Elizabeth Ault was a rock when I needed one.

The resources at Northwestern University, especially the efficient Interlibrary Loan Division and the many digital resources on campus, have been essential for my research. In the triangulation of Hitchcock beyond Evanston, the fantastic staff of the Margaret Herrick Library at the Academy of Motion Picture Arts and Sciences, especially Barbara Hall (during her tenure) and Faye Thompson, have been model archivists—as always—and the New York Public Library, particularly the cheerful young staff in the Microforms Reading Room, as well as their colleagues at the branch for the Performing Arts at Lincoln Center, went beyond the call of duty to gratify my scholarly appetite.

From my perspective, no one can write a film book without regularly consulting Ned Comstock at the Cinematic Arts Library at the University of Southern California. He cannot be praised enough for pertinently sharing his vast knowledge of the collections and film culture at large. I have also benefited immensely from his colleague Dace Taube and her unrivaled command of the regional history collections at USC. Francisca Folch at the Harry Ransom Center, University of Texas at Austin, patiently helped me to dig out rare Hitchcockiana—and not only from the Selznick Collection. Jane Branfield at the Roald Dahl Museum and Story Centre in Buckinghamshire, England, generously gave me access to unique source materials from the production of "Lamb to the Slaughter," the Hitchcock franchise's most famous teleplay. The knowledgeable staff of the Prints and Photographs Division at the Library of Congress maximized my payoff from the wealth of imagery in the collections. At the British Film Institute, Dave McCall went out of his way to assist me in ransacking the rich collection of Hitchcock stills. Michael Shulman at Magnum Photos worked miracles in the late stages of photograph hunting. I am particularly indebted to Howard Mandelbaum and his colleagues at Photofest for their willingness to take even the most eccentric requests in stride.

Will Schmenner, during his time at the Block Museum, Evanston, commissioned my very first draft for this project in conjunction with an exhibition in 2007. His infectious enthusiasm and energy were important for the future of the project. I'm also much indebted to Jeffrey Sconce, Northwestern University; Bart van der Gaag, Stockholm University; and Jan-Christopher Horak and Mark Quigley, both at the University of California, Los Angeles, Film and Television Archive, for all kinds of assistance and support.

Input from Steve Wilder was key in the early stages of drafting, while Anitra Grisales proved absolutely indispensable down the stretch. I cannot thank my readers enough; one of them, especially, exerted a truly formative influence during the manuscript's revision phase. Jakob Olsson has lent his professional eyes and dexterous hands to optimize the visual materials. The Lauritzen Foundation for Film Historical Research, Stockholm, has once again provided much-needed funding.

I want to express my sincere appreciation to Norman Lloyd, the Hitchcock franchise's stellar producer, actor, and director, for inviting me to his home and eloquently discussing his work. Similarly, James (Jim) Allardice took time to talk to me about his father, James B. (Jimmie) Allardice, and to ferret out materials from the family vaults bearing on the ingenious scripting of Hitchcock's on-tube segments and more.

If Marina Dahlquist is fed up with Hitchcock reflections, she lovingly manages to turn them into creative observations and astute advice. Daily life apart, joint research trips for our separate projects have turned into marvelous adventures irrespective of the long hours in the archives.

This is for my late father, Bertil, and my still spry mother, Sonja. Without them . . .

INTRODUCTION

A BODY FOR ALL SEASONS

"But I'm Alfred Hitchcock, I am, I can prove it."
"Sure, sure everybody is."
"I am, I insist."

Alfred Hitchcock's double when removed by the orderlies, as scripted
by James B. Allardice for *Alfred Hitchcock Presents*

"Goooood eve-en-ing," and welcome to a study of the intertwined strands of
Alfred Hitchcock's creative world. As Hitchcock's trademark television greeting suggests, this is predominantly a foray into TV territory, where Hitchcock's famously rotund profile ushered in a teleplay per week for ten seasons,
summer reruns included. Though they were most obviously paraded in his
television hosting, Hitchcock's impish designs and voluble conceits spread
across a vast body of work that is inseparable from Hitchcock's commanding
physical form. Scaling one of the most written-about bodies in the twentieth
century as a matter of course, countless texts equated Hitchcock's poundage
with excessive fat. Through such slanted, unblushing stabs, and the sheer volume of these ink ruses—mainly found in gossip columns—blots, patterns,
and identity markers were affixed to a body that fronted for the franchise.

Take this "portrait" from the *New York Times*, for example, offered as a
lead-in to an exchange around Hitchcock's film poetics, which the director
outlined in a series of talking points while eating lamb chops:

If you look at Alfred Hitchcock obliquely, which is the way he likes to
look at things, he appears absolutely the same from any angle—as nearly
spheroid as a man can be. Push him gently and he might rock on his
axis like a humpty-dumpty. Reaching their greatest girth at approximate

equator, Mr. Hitchcock's 290 pounds taper off evenly to both extremities. Beyond the undulating chin, the immense jowls, the dome of his head glistens like an inaccessible summit. His small buffoon's eyes twinkle beneath high brows in the vast expanse of his face, and the sagging lower lip is permanently compressed between the heavy cheeks on either side of which the immense lobes of his indented ears sprout incongruously like pink buds. Mr. Hitchcock, in short, resembles a baroque cherub.[1]

This flippant style illustrates a prevalent mode of writing that pivoted around outlandish descriptions of Hitchcock's body, like the derogatory remarks one associates with a demeaning variety of private gossip. In the public genre of gossip columns in the 1940s and '50s, it is hard to find similar unflattering inventories of bodily traits in regard to anyone else.

Not merely an abstract logo or cameo figure, Hitchcock created his franchise via bodies or embodiments in a variety of ways. He began by playing up and using his own body—fat by default, except after crash dieting, and English by design. Strategies of multiplicity, doubling, and surrogacy—both textually and in a production sense—were also key. Actors' bodies, not just his own, also became brand signifiers on and off the screen, while his production team conjured up stylistic earmarking in his name. And of course, there are the countless bodies that were strangled, poisoned, bludgeoned, stabbed to death, and buried under his macabre trademark. Over the years and through this corporeal prism, audiences, critics, scholars, and the talkative biographical legend himself partook in cooking up the discourse on a public figure tantamount to a brand: Hitchcock. Thus, as one writer explains, "for many years he was known as fat man, a description that never particularly troubled him. In a sense it was his trade mark."[2]

Television turned Hitchcock into a star, and the trappings of television marketing shaped his public performance all the way to his last film. In this book, Hitchcock's cinema will play second fiddle for a change, in spite of the celebrity status the director managed to stir up around his films and his persona. Hosting the television series Alfred Hitchcock Presents (AHP, 1955–1962) and The Alfred Hitchcock Hour (AHH, 1962–1965) for a decade gave Hitchcock a novel scope of visibility, ample screen time, and a reverberating voice in a medium with a deeper cultural penetration than cinema. As Hitchcock spiritedly performed Hitchcock on television, the convergence of art, commerce, and ingenious brand building formed "a multi-million dollar suspense factory turning out feature-length films, a weekly television series, and a line of books and magazines."[3] The media confabulation around the versatile Hitchcock figure resulted from a calculated strategy of staging and performing starting in the mid-1930s, as he began perfecting his recipe for stardom during his transition from England to Hollywood.

On the threshold of his television tenure, Alfred Hitchcock was the consummate purveyor of ritzy consumerism, flight of fancy, and ultra-elegant fashion. Off frame and in public print, he was an enigmatic, eloquent figure with a conspicuous appetite and a perennially discussed and photo-friendly body. His film fame, food reputation, and fabulous physicality were supreme assets when he signed up for AHP in 1955, on the cusp of Hollywood's television era. Hitchcock television, designed for the suburban living room—a symbolic site of media consumption indicative of 1950s middle-class ideals—and elsewhere, dished out stories with humorous subtexts about dysfunctional domestic life that was often cut short by murder at the dinner table.[4] At the time, black-and-white television images came with less lustrous connotations than did Hollywood movies, but Hitchcock was able to bring star charisma and Hollywood glamour to the home screen as he straddled two forms of moving images. Similarly, he traversed the cultural divide between England and America, mainly by standing apart and quizzically observing and reflecting on both societies with a cool eye and glib tongue.

Eye and tongue apart, I argue that the enduring success of the Hitchcock franchise hinged on embodiment in all senses of the term: Hitchcock's own sensational English figure and how he performed it for American media; hosting a television series with his own body as mediator; inserting himself in the frame through strategic body doubling via cameos and surrogates; and, not least, manipulating audience bodies by creating suspense and fear that swirled around imperiled character bodies. Combined, these brand-building strategies distanced him from the run-of-the-mill role of mere film director. Hitchcock's tactic from the beginning was to ceaselessly draw attention to his larger-than-life persona and pose as the only true star of the franchise. His pert comment comparing actors to cattle took the spotlight away from the movie stars in his productions by repurposing screen dazzle as an effect of his own storyboarding—actors were mere afterthoughts and "dummies" articulated by the master ventriloquist.[5] From a related vantage point, a set of weighty film characters figured readily as Hitchcock stand-ins or surrogates of sorts. In such convoluted processes, the ventriloquist has total command and crafts the characters he controls. The impression of a singular Hitchcock experience across the production process, created by his role as host for the series, bracketed the formidable team in charge of the day-to-day operations of the television franchise. As I will show, the spin and marketing efforts, the hosting and directing, the intricate presence through cameos and surrogates, and the palpable fingerprints on the stylistic manipulation of screen content (irrespective of hand and screen size) ushered in the generic quality labeled "Hitchcockian."

American journalists were taken aback when encountering the incongruous figure behind the stylish story worlds. Hitchcock cleverly capitalized on this shock and quickly turned his "real" grotesque body into the embodiment of the suspense thriller. This conflation was created by his super-visibility and talent for generating copy, as he blended himself with his genre through witty talking points, cultural observations, and outlandish pranks. John Belton has perceptively theorized the stakes of Hitchcock's relation to classic filmmaking: "Hitchcock's visibility tends to function in a somewhat paradoxical fashion. It undermines the invisibility of the classical paradigm while harnessing his own authorial visibility as a dominant feature of the narrative experience, as that which makes it 'Hitchcockian.'"[6] As I will make evident, excessive "authorial visibility" goes way beyond his literal visibility in cameos, for example, to the inescapable but somewhat nebulous identity markers associated with the term "Hitchcockian." I begin, in chapter 1, with the mise-en-scène of the Hitchcock figure in the transition from England to Hollywood.

Before taking on television, Hitchcock had indeed marketed himself in table talks, promotional contexts, and photo-essays. His celebrity, still not fully flourished, relied heavily on an appropriation of the grotesque as he stuffed himself, dieted, and cheerfully talked about his embonpoint while journalists tried to outdo both each other and Hitchcock in whipping up grotesque, often belittling physical cracks. This discourse was partly the result of a novel type of gossipy celebrity journalism bent on producing slangy barbs and pointed lampooning. The pioneer and unrivaled master of this was the legendary columnist Walter Winchell. The vilification of Hitchcock in America, however friendly and benign, is directly connected to the type of columns Winchell and his colleagues Leonard Lyons, Hedda Hopper, and Louella Parsons—to mention only the stars—excelled in. Evidencing his allegiance with leading columnists, on several occasions Hitchcock stepped in as a temp for journalists on a break from typewriter duties. More important, this style existed alongside a somewhat more sober focus on personalities that animated magazines like *Time*, *Life*, and *Look*.[7] Hitchcock ingeniously straddled this discourse when posing as master craftsman and prankster in one magnetic package. One of Hitchcock's associates summed up the penchant for showmanship in paradoxical terms: "Hitch is . . . painfully shy, but a genius of self-promotion. For all his enormous dignity, he'll still lend himself to corny publicity layouts that would embarrass a burlesque comic."[8] This "corny" buildup of the Hitchcock persona in the United States was the result of his little-discussed role as a fixture for leading American photo journals alongside the Hitchcock prose in public print from his first visit to America in 1937 up to the mid-1950s. To fully appreciate the inventive consolidation of Hitchcock's detached, mischievously playful yet very formal English persona for television we need to walk through the period of full-blown grotesque and the lampooning of Hitchcock by columnists, which began when the director disembarked in New York City in 1937 and continued as he gradually moved west.

Hitchcock's first American boss, the legendary film mogul David O. Selznick, was one of the earliest to elaborate on Hitchcock's role as a cultural fixture beyond the frames. By 1943 Hitchcock had already established himself as a linguistic entity, according to his producer, who expanded on the adjectival Hitchcock in a perceptive memo:

> Hitch loves publicity, has been made into one of the most important figures in his field in the industry, and indeed into a figure known throughout the world by publicity, and he has a real genius for it himself. I am sure you will agree that Hitchcock has practically come into the language as not merely a name but an adjective, as is demonstrated by the use of his name in hundreds of stories and articles every year, and by such references as appear in book advertising almost every week: "As thrilling as a Hitchcock movie, et cetera."[9]

In 1949, in an off-the-cuff aside in a syndicated piece commenting on Hitchcock's recent weight loss, Walter Winchell also tersely weighed in on the meaning of the adjective "Hitchcockian," pronouncing it "synonymous with suspense." It had, Winchell opined, "been an adjective for good melodramas for years."[10] Much later, in the release material for *Marnie* (Universal Pictures, 1964), it was reported that the term "Hitchcockian" had found its way into modern American slang and that the term's domain had expanded somewhat to denote something macabre, bizarre, and suspenseful. Paula Marantz Cohen puts it well in terms of the television context: "But more than the idea of the man was the idea of the Hitchcockian experience, a composite of elements associated with the films, the thriller genre, and cinema itself."[11]

Hitchcock was an instant hit on television in 1955, and his performance as host was sensational and very cleverly crafted. I elucidate this process in chapter 2, with an emphasis on the hosting rather than the teleplays. Critics raved about the playful irreverence in the way he always chided the sponsor, and they celebrated the absurd pontifications regarding the meaning and afterlife of story events. James B. (Jimmie) Allardice is the unsung presence behind the franchise's distinctive hosting. He was the scriptwriter for the prologues and epilogues during all ten seasons of the show, and a ghostwriter for many of Hitchcock's public performances during the show's tenure.[12] Allardice's genius was in finding a truly unique style for Hitchcock's television performance. And it was the Hitchcock franchise's genius to sense the value of marrying Allardice's oblique creative mind to Hitchcock's curious performance range.

The core context for this study of the Hitchcock brand is the popular reception of his persona in newspapers, general-interest magazines, and photographic periodicals; this mise-en-scène served as a prism for creativity throughout Hitchcock's American career. Here salient aspects of his self-styled identity as food connoisseur, fatso, and film director were inimitably intertwined and rhetorically set off in exchanges across high-end tables and in the Hitchcock family kitchen. In this spirit, the two television episodes discussed as interludes between the chapters feature fine dining and murder with food-related twists.

Hitchcock's already intense marketing mode culminated with the television show during its decade on the air. The fame Hitchcock had managed to stir up as an integral part of his cinema was a prerequisite for the television engagement, which in turn had repercussions for his cinema and particularly its marketing. This media strategy turned the already showy Hitchcock into a full-fledged celebrity. In the transition from cinema to television and back, the Hitchcock figure underwent considerable tweaking. The series names, *Alfred Hitchcock Presents* and *The Alfred Hitchcock Hour*, clearly put premium on presenting and hosting. In this quaintly framed role, Hitchcock became an icon on American television, and soon across the globe, while the teleplays offered refracted perspectives on both English and American culture. I therefore give the prologues and epilogues for AHP and AHH as much attention as, if not more than, the crime stories. As paratexts, they are tucked into and channel the text proper, in this case the stories, while regularly flogging the commercials in between.[13]

Over the years, Hitchcock's talking points and appearances across media formed a poetics in fragments by providing interpretations for salient scenes, singling out the most important films and teleplays, and in general reinforcing the director's mastery of his oeuvre. In the late 1950s, with a mystery magazine in his own name, edited book collections, and television ventures going strong, the Hitchcock figure became increasingly cross-medial, permeable, and ubiquitous.

Intro.1. Stroboscopic exposures by Gjon Mili. Courtesy of Getty Images.

A set of unpublished photographs from a photo session for *Life* magazine in conjunction with the shooting of *Shadow of a Doubt* (Skirball Productions / Universal Pictures, 1943) perfectly captures Hitchcock's figurative multiplicity on a metaphorical level (fig. Intro.1). Gjon Mili later published one of them in his *Photographs and Recollections*, adding the telling caption comment that Hitchcock "found the idea of being directed very amusing and behaved accordingly."[14]

This convoluted doubling, or serializing, of the multimediated Hitchcock figure provides the critical focus for this book. Hitchcock's own body and his figure at large offer the grounding and rationale for expanding him into a franchise. He enlisted a phalanx of other bodies as surrogates to bolster the brand together with his own cameo figures, his hammy marketing efforts, and his friendly interaction with journalists, all under the marquee of a style that was read and experienced as Hitchcockian.

Mili's photographic technique captures this multiplicity by bringing together fragments in suspended motion into an imaginary bigger picture—a stroboscopic poetics featuring malleable bodies summed up under Hitchcock's logotype, if you will. Similarly, this book moves across printers' ink, photographs and photo-essays, big and small screens, and big and small plates when analyzing the ingredients and recipes for this multiple-body-centered branding. Symbolically, Hitchcock's body, in different postures and by way of complex forms of surrogacy, is splendidly alone on the stage. In chapter 3 I track down traces of Hitchcock's corporeal specter and multiple modes of surrogacy in both his television stories and some exemplary films.

In the way that so many critics, including Hitchcock himself, have used the term, I refer to his "figure" to highlight the constructed nature and multiplicity of this renegotiated, refashioned, and paradoxical Hitchcock as a discipline and identity in motion, across a body of works and with many working bodies. The figure came with a conspicuous physical frame that became a logotype for the brand, yet it was highly malleable and fraught with anxieties and constant scrutiny and supervision. Seemingly, there was always an extra Hitchcock figure to mobilize for a brand obsessed with doubling in a multitude of constellations, some vertiginous, uncanny, and abyss-like, others playful, upbeat, and jolly.

During the first season of AHP, this doppelganger (or "multiganger") motif had its thematic counterpart on television in a story cleverly labeled "The Case of Mr. Pelham" (AHP 10). Mr. Pelham (first name Albert) is removed from his humdrum life in a hostile takeover when a doubling copycat begins showing up everywhere in his place. Tom Ewell played both Pelhams. Exasperated, the first/original/real Mr. Pelham fatally tries to distance himself from the intruder/copy by sporting an out-of-character tie. The tie tactic backfires and is used as evidence against him, making him seem like the impostor.[15] In the epilogue to this Hitchcock-directed episode—and indicative of Allardice's scripting style—Hitchcock doubles the spoof by turning it on himself when he encounters a second Hitchcock, complete with gaudy tie, and is forcefully taken by orderlies to a mental ward. The discursive Hitchcock personages and look-alikes function much like rotund *matryoshka* nesting dolls, but without the progressively shrinking size. Although his physical format fluctuated dramatically over the years, the dark-suit uniforms were tailored to fit all imaginable Hitchcock sizes. The gaudy tie, fatal in Mr. Pelham's case, later became a signature article of clothing for Hitchcock's imaginary brother, a frequent guest in the host segment's identity game and substitution play.[16]

My interpretation of Hitchcock's multiplicity follows Thomas M. Leitch's perceptive analysis of Hitchcock's work for television. To authorship theory's three concentric circles as developed by Andrew Sarris—technique, personal style, and interior meaning—Leitch productively adds a fourth: the director as a celebrity spreading his name beyond the confines of his own creative work to a franchise.[17] Leitch's fourth circle either encloses the three others or is at the very core of the enterprise, if not oscillating between them all. Leitch performs an inspired critical twist by moving the outer celebrity circle into the very core of the authorship project via the assumption that the television episodes, mainly those that Hitchcock directed, "are as typical of his work, as revealing of his range and his preoccupations, and as constitutive for our image of Hitchcock as his feature films."[18] For Leitch, the outer and inner circles function as mutually reinforcing fields of criticism blending with marketing spins, depending on the angles from which Hitchcock's figures are perceived. The all-embracing figure, or the deck of multiple figures à la Mili, is fully aligned with the adjectival form "Hitchcockian," which encircles not only the films and the Hitchcock-directed teleplays but also the franchise's overall story universe and the photo-essays featuring Hitchcock. Television, arguably, is at the top of the food chain in the feeding process for the franchise.

Critical standards and unflattering physical barbs aside, commentators invariably noticed a novel type of Hitchcock marketing across popular media during the combined run of AHP and AHH from 1955 to 1965. Hitchcock directed episodes quite regularly during the first seasons, then progressively less often as time passed—though he still put his indelible stamp on the show and bracketed others' contributions with his wit, whimsy, and overpowering screen command as host. Where to place Alfred Hitchcock's television work in relation to his cinema within this rich cocktail of artistry and self-serving promotion still poses a critical dilemma. In this sweep of media, with a magazine in his name (*Alfred Hitchcock's Mystery Magazine*, 1956–) and a phalanx of book anthologies, all elements feed off each other. The lack of scholarly attention to small-screen Alfred—with the exception of excellent contributions from Robert E. Kapsis, Thomas M. Leitch, and some minor overviews and ambitious documentation volumes[19]—seems to indicate that the television venture stands thematically decoupled from Hitchcock's cinema and at best resides among the footnotes to his film work. I argue that rather than just an intertwined strand in the larger fabric of the Hitchcock oeuvre, it represents a resounding echo chamber for reception and reputation. For marketing and global brand recognition the television work was truly paramount and served Hitchcock well all the way to *Family Plot* (Universal Pictures, 1976).

Hitchcock's television kitchen cooked up lethal fare 24/7. A morning omelet spiked with ground glass eliminated the need for lunch. For those who survived breakfast, lunch was no picnic owing to premeditated aftereffects. The nice cup of tea or coffee in the afternoon could be fatal for anyone still around, as arsenic lurked in many a pot or was mixed into the sugar bowl. Next trial: the cocktail hour, featuring an array of killing concoctions. And then the dinner specials: not only was murder committed with the famous frozen leg of lamb, but prepared food also came fraught with murderous designs, and the truly devious chefs even cooked up their dinner guests. When a dinner dish went around for the second time, some husbands, as an inspired afterthought, penciled botulinum bacteria on the leftover ham for the benefit of their wives. Desserts, too, reaped victims, while some killers preferred to strike during the after-dinner liqueur. Late-night cocoa or tea was particularly perilous, as wives poisoned husbands, husbands wives, and daughters their mothers. The truly clever operators duped spouses trying to poison them with bedtime cocoa by siphoning away the beverage and playing dead, thus turning the game around come breakfast time. Around the clock and across the menu, Hitchcock's television world was a culinary ordeal running in tandem with the marketing of the host as a prandial authority.

The ubiquity of on-screen food reflects a brand built around a Hitchcock who was perennially at the table, expounding on food culture in between his observations on screen culture. Sizing him up for his poundage and perplexing prowess, journalists joined Hitchcock in his element at the very best table. Meanwhile, his characters sometimes celebrated food frugality to a fault. An illustrative tidbit in the latter register seems in order before we turn to Hitchcock's trendsetting table riches in New York City in 1937. "Cheap Is Cheap" (AHP 143) is a witty, original gem featuring Dennis Day as a supreme penny-pincher.[20] The teleplay was scripted by the writing duo Albert E. Lewin and Burt Styler, who formed as a team for radio and wrote primarily for Bob Hope before their long television career. The premise is immediately set up in the inner monologue, as Day's character, Alexander Gifford, comes home to his dreary apartment, disappointed about not receiving a Christmas bonus. For him, life is all about saving money—and so is death, as it turns out. In the absence of a bonus, he is too depressed to even sneak-read the neighbor's evening paper. From this sorry state of affairs things turn even worse, as his wife, Jennifer (Alice Backes in her first of many roles for the show), has found Alexander's six hidden bankbooks holding a grand total of $33,000. After discovering the couple's relative affluence, she wants a divorce to escape their gloomy life. She reveals her find when she serves dinner that night. To Alexander's horror, his wife replaces the cheap stew meat he habitually eats with an expensive steak for herself. Later, as they once more sit down for a shared dinner, again with separate dishes, the teleplay approaches its "happy" but one-sided resolution.

In between the dinner scenes, Alexander enterprisingly explores all kinds of options for killing off Jennifer, since a divorce would rob him of half the money. He ponders the situation in voice-over, eliminating one alternative after the next as being too costly a solution to his dilemma. Inspiration from crime novels takes him nowhere, but then a visit to the county jail puts him in touch with a contract killer. The gun for hire is far too expensive for Alexander, but he is a family man himself and very sympathetic, so he offers numerous helpful suggestions. The wittiest, perhaps, is a method he has seen on television (and we all know on which show): "A dame did it, she clobbered her husband with a frozen leg of lamb." At fifty-nine cents a pound, the meaty murder weapon is unthinkable for the cheapskate. Finally, a perfect method virtually presents itself: food poisoning. Alexander even manages to steal botulinum bacteria from a lab, putting it on the leftover ham Jennifer eats for dinner while he cautiously sticks to a hamburger. Predictably, she gets sick, but after the doctor's prognosis that she might in fact recover, Alexander feels obligated to secure the hoped-for outcome. He suffocates her with a pillow embroidered with the cheerful but misplaced adage "Home Sweet Home." As the doctor signs the death certificate, the next chilling cost dawns on Alexander: the funeral. Once again, a happy solution rescues him. Alexander sells Jennifer's body to a medical institution and turns a threatening cost point into a healthy seventy-five-dollar profit.

The Lewin-Styler brand of humor, predicated on a low-key acting style with absurd inflections, bizarre plot premises, and characters carrying out nutty schemes in vignette style, worked splendidly in the AHP context of merry murders, not least owing to the producers' inspired casting of Day. This episode ingeniously blends the Hitchcock brand's prime features: murder in the family circle executed in a food context, here delectably humorous; a modicum of suspense; and ingenious casting that takes advantage of, and sometimes tweaks, established roles, often in highly intricate ways—all in the hands of a capable production team, with Hitchcock on the sideline as "mere" host. Here the outsourcing of the Hitchcock experience to the producers and the director, Bretaigne Windust, featured an original script with a Hitchcockian in-joke: the sly reference to one of the most classic episodes, "Lamb to the Slaughter" (AHP 106), a veritable master recipe for the show. Otherwise, the series overwhelmingly favored published material, much of it English. Hitchcock's macabre, often self-deprecating humor as scripted by Allardice took hosting to an unprecedented level of creativity. In "Cheap Is Cheap" the prologue is cut in half on the screen, with half the screen blackened out. Hitchcock, too, has to economize in one of the show's many televisual jokes, always in tune with the upcoming teleplay and with sly commentary concerning the sponsor. As often was the case, murderous accomplishments are absurdly punished by an off-hand comment. In the epilogue, Hitchcock returns with most of the screen blackened out, telling the audience that Alexander did not live happily ever after: "He was caught and paid the supreme penalty. In his case, a heavy fine." Furthermore, "the perfect murder should also include a happy funeral and a decent burial." Jolly interments, at times serialized or performed in impromptu fashion, were closely associated with the franchise and its focus on bodies—dead and alive—and body approximations. This particular host commentary neatly illustrates the tenet of this study: that Hitchcock, by way of his television hosting, reclaimed the body discourse—set in motion during his 1937 gastronomic holiday in New York City—for his own purposes and on his own terms. By the time the suspense factory was going strong in the late 1950s, Hitchcock had found a template for his performance and a perfect rapport between television and cinema, with added support from photojournalism and print media. The Hitchcock brand, propelled by the success of his television show, turned the Hitchcock figure into a global household name, eponym, and legend.

1. FEEDING THE LEGEND

Setting the Table

On 23 August 1937, among other news items, the *New York Journal American* carried the report that "Alfred Hitchcock, English director of the famous 'Thirty-nine Steps' and other classic examples of dramatic suspense, came over for what he termed a 'gastronomic holiday.' He gave his weight as 282 pounds and has no intention of losing an ounce of it while here."[1] As an East Coast overture to Hollywood, the Hitchcock family came to New York City to do a marketing tour for a director too big for British cinema. Alfred Hitchcock clearly had a game plan from the moment he set foot on American soil: to entertain journalists while eating and turn his culinary propensities into a prime selling point for his creative persona. Topping their entertainment menu was a systematic and very public mapping of the city's best eateries.

The chronicling in the New York City dailies of this long, busy week earmarked the public image of Hitchcock for decades to come. The flourishing British body jokes in the London press, fueled by Hitchcock's own grotesqueries, can be read as mere appetizers for the meatier entrées cooked up by Manhattan pens in dialogue over dinner with the new man in town. When Hitchcock moved to Hollywood a few years later, the local columnists effortlessly tapped into and further promulgated the discourse.

Alfred Hitchcock was by no means unknown upon arriving in New York. His prominent cinematic reputation was underpinned by a series of articles he had recently written for the *New York World-Telegram*.[2] Hitchcock enjoyed a strong following among U.S. critics as a director of first-rate thrillers, and he would be honored by New York critics in 1938 as best director for *The Lady*

1.1. The Hitchcocks sharing a meal at their London apartment, c. 1928. Photograph courtesy of Getty Images.

Vanishes (Gainsborough Pictures, 1938). When he arrived in the considerable flesh, his accomplishments on the screen were for a time overshadowed by his gastronomic ventures and commanding physicality.

In the first round of American press accounts Hitchcock was invariably painted as vivacious, vagarious, voracious—and voluminous. The marketing strategy worked, probably even better than he expected, insofar as the mise-en-scène of the Hitchcock figure generated a set of bodacious reference points that were impossible to ignore in future promotion and reception contexts. As he had previously in London (fig. 1.1), Hitchcock held court in private-public settings, preferably entertaining one journalist at a time. In lieu of a home, he used New York City's most renowned tables as venues for gargantuan exploits while displaying his mischievous personality and vulpine humor. At restaurants and in his suite at the St. Regis Hitchcock relied on his conspicuous embonpoint, which, according to the reports from August 1937, was growing by the minute since he was putting away his signature meal—steaks and ice cream—with gusto while renouncing exercise (fig. 1.2).

On his arrival in the United States, as Hitchcock told an interviewer after returning to England, reporters "took one look at my shape when I came

1.2. Hitchcock in his element in New York, 1937, together with his wife, Alma, daughter, Pat, and assistant, Joan Harrison. New York World-Telegram and Sun Newspaper Photograph Collection (NYWT&S), courtesy of the Library of Congress, Prints and Photographs Division, NYWT&S Collection, LC-USZ62–138471. This photograph was also published in *Newsweek*, 6 September 1937, 25. A cropped version featuring Alfred only was published twice in London in 1938. The first English caption was "Having hit his weight down from 21 stone to a mere 19 on a diet that prescribes no real drinks, but champagne . . . he now 'boasts' he is 'only twice as fat as Charles Laughton'" (*Daily Express*, 20 September 1938, 8). The altered version was used again when New York critics chose *The Lady Vanishes* as the best film of 1938. The *Daily Mirror* opined that it was the "best film that Alfred Hitchcock, fat and famous director, ever made." It was further mentioned that "after thrills, Mr. Hitchcock is most fond of food" (*Daily Mirror*, 7 October 1938, 26).

down the gangplank and started interviewing me on food. I told them my favorite dish was steak *à la mode*."[3] After having his extraordinary prowess as gourmet-cum-gourmand chronicled by the New York dailies, Hitchcock had to run the not-unfamiliar print gauntlet of cutting body jokes. In the wake of the reported displays of wondrous gluttony in action, his physique became an inescapable topic in the American press. The most famous and trendsetting of the articles from Hitchcock's inaugural visit was served up with verve from inside the renowned Jack and Charlie's 21 Club. This restaurant soon became a prime Hitchcockian haunt, for both Hitchcock and his screen characters. Dr. Edwardes in *Spellbound* (Selznick International Pictures / Vanguard Films, 1945) habitually dines there; the restaurant's famous chefs prepare the gourmet takeout dinner Lisa Fremont orders in *Rear Window* (Paramount Pictures / Patron Inc., 1954); and later Hitchcock posed there for photo-essays printed in upscale magazines. The witty journalist H. Allen Smith had dinner with Hitchcock at the club in 1937. Smith's account of Hitchcock's repast is classic, a veritable ur-scene for the director's then-uninhibited approach to eating. Hitchcock ordered two servings of steak, both followed by ice cream, before rounding out his meal with tea and brandy. According to Smith, Hitchcock generally started his day in New York City with ice cream flavored with a dash of brandy for breakfast and invariably had a sizable steak for lunch.[4] In an interview with Janet White a couple of days later Hitchcock said, "I refuse to diet or take any exercise. It makes me disgruntled." He explained, "I never walk when I can ride. My exertion is from the neck up. I watch."[5] By 1919, when he turned twenty, he had already described himself as very fat and very ambitious, and at twenty-seven, when he married the petite Alma, he was five foot seven and the scales registered two hundred pounds. A couple of years later he had reached three hundred pounds, and in 1935 he was well over that and was considered "grotesquely obese."[6] According to his collaborator Charles Bennett, he had by then developed "a monstrous ego that matched his appetite."[7]

According to Hitchcock, the ice cream at the Waldorf was heavenly and the T-bone steak at Gallagher's a masterpiece, but American tea was a total letdown.[8] Wine, in contrast, proved a pleasant surprise for someone fearing that America could serve only something fit "for a fountain pen."[9] Summing up the accounts of Hitch's ten gastronomic days in the United States in 1937, a trade columnist quipped, "In view of all the publicity Alfred Hitchcock has been receiving on his food preferences in the town's cabareateries, [the name of his company should] be changed to GOURMAND-BRITISH."[10]

When Hitchcock stopped over in New York City the following year, on his way to visit Hollywood for the first time to negotiate with David O. Selznick and other producers, dieting dominated the conversation over prime beef. When dining with the World-Telegram's George Ross at Jack and Charlie's 21 Club, Hitchcock pledged to reduce to "a meager 260 pounds" by riveting his attention solely to steaks.[11] A few days later the same paper's William Boehnel outlined Hitchcock's dieting regime in nutritional terms, once again as explained over juicy steaks at 21: "The idea . . . is to eat only proteins and let them do all the work. No starches, of course, because the proteins are supposed to eat up all the starch in the body."[12] This is the Atkins diet avant la lettre, or an emulation of William Banting's regime from Letter on Corpulence (1863).

Capitalizing on the director's presence, New York movie houses staged a small film festival featuring Hitchcock's recent thrillers. Ezra Goodman described the event from the perspective of Hitchcock's reputation: "When

Alfred Hitchcock, internationally renowned English gourmet who dabbles in shadowy psychoses on the side, arrived for a short stay in New York some time ago, a score of Gotham's movie houses took advantage of the occasion."[13]

The first major U.S. magazine article devoted to Alfred Hitchcock, Russell Maloney's portrait essay, was published in the *New Yorker* in 1938. This was after Hitchcock had visited Hollywood and signed with the Selznick studio, but before he moved to the West Coast. Maloney could not, of course, avoid the food and body discourse or Hitchcock's recent dieting. He came up with his own spin by comparing Hitchcock to a "Macy balloon," a reference point that others used later. According to Maloney:

> The ship-news reporters, for all their notorious industry, seem to have gleaned only one story about Hitchcock; he likes to eat steak and ice cream—ice cream first. They keep asking him about the steak and ice cream and he keeps confirming the story. . . . He cheerfully perpetuates the steak-and-ice-cream canard: in spite of the fact that for the past six months he has been on a diet—has, in fact, whittled some twenty-five pounds from last winter's all-time high of two hundred and ninety.
>
> His fatness seems to buoy him up. Spiritually and physically, he might be kin to a Macy balloon. His large, close-set ears, bright-blue eyes, scrubby hair, and double chin give him the air of one of his own likeable cinematic villains.[14]

The food discourse, firmly in place in Britain before Hitchcock came to New York City, was set in full motion as Hitchcock discreetly negotiated his future in an opening gambit with studio representatives from MGM, RKO, and Selznick between meals.

On the Gangplank between Cultures

In the late 1920s Hitchcock emerged as a cinematic wunderkind. A decade later, his public persona and showmanship were as riveting as his films, and Hollywood slowly emerged on his radar. Embarking on a career in the film industry, he started out in a British extension of Famous Players-Lasky's Hollywood studio designing title cards. After shifting studios, to Gainsborough, he quickly learned the tricks of the trade at large, working himself up through the ranks until he was entrusted with directing. In the late 1930s, then at Gaumont-British, he was Britain's unrivaled star director and had found his cinematic niche: the suspense thriller. When first visiting the United States and New York City in 1937, he arrived as a renowned director with multiple hit films on his résumé. The inaugural visit ushered in a Hitchcock persona with opportunities for endless spin as his culinary propensities and wondrous table largesse became a blueprint for his future studio biographies well in advance of his being hired by Hollywood.

Early in 1938, Hitchcock formally acquired an American agent, Myron Selznick (David's brother), to take care of his transatlantic affairs. The Selznick agency had hounded Hitchcock via Harry Ham, a former actor turned scout and liaison for Myron Selznick, and convinced him that they could secure a more favorable Hollywood deal than any Hitchcock himself could negotiate. Representation was a novelty; in London Hitchcock had no agent, only a business manager, J. G. Saunders, while Hitchcock Baker Productions Ltd. took care of marketing. Hitchcock had informally enlisted Ham's services in 1935, sensing that his future was in Hollywood rather than in the lean British studios. Still, in 1937 Albert Margolies, Gaumont-British's man in New York, helped set up most of Hitchcock's New York arrangements, not least the introduction to Katherine (Kay) Brown, who was in charge of David O. Selznick's East Coast operations, as well as "Jock" Whitney, a major investor and chairman of the board for the Selznick studio, and later U.S. ambassador to the United Kingdom. In a memo to Brown on 23 August Selznick stated his position: "I'm definitely interested in Hitchcock as a director and think it might be wise for you to meet and chat with him. In particular I would like to get a clear picture as to who, if anyone, is representing him and what he has in mind in the way of salary; also whether he is dealing with MGM."[15] Through Benny Thau, MGM was indeed the leading contender at this stage for signing Hitchcock. The studio's British wing was closely affiliated with Hitchcock's London producer, Michael Balcon, which from Hitchcock's perspective was something of an impediment. An MGM option was on the table until October. Kay Brown then reported to Dan Winkler at the Myron Selznick agency that the Metro deal was dead.[16] After the first deal fell through, Myron Selznick was confident that another one with his brother's studio would materialize. Even Fox was mentioned, but Fox seemed to prefer to have the director working for them based in England, as had MGM, while Hitchcock wanted to move over to Hollywood, and ideally to the Selznick studio.

Uncertainty lingered, as is reflected in David O. Selznick's memos from November 1937. Selznick wrote to Kay Brown on 6 November 1937: "MGM has no interest whatsoever at this time in Hitchcock and have decided they do not want him." A couple of weeks later (29 November 1937), Selznick returned to the topic: "I do not want to proceed further with Hitchcock negotiations until I see his last picture [Young and Innocent, Gaumont-British Picture Corporation,

1937] and check on Metro's opinion."[17] The initial Selznick strategy was seemingly to pick up Hitchcock in a parallel deal should he sign with Metro. With no offers on the table from other studios, there was no urgency for Selznick. Hitchcock could be plucked in due course. Hitchcock was, for the time being, stuck in England, but he now had proper representation in Hollywood via the relentless Myron Selznick.

Hitchcock felt restless after having finished *The Lady Vanishes*, and when he learned that a deal with David O. Selznick was "off for the present" he elected to take matters into his own hands.[18] He and his family again boarded the *Queen Mary* for New York, but this time Hollywood was the final destination, for face-to-face negotiations with studios. Selznick had by then bought the rights for Daphne du Maurier's not-yet-published novel *Rebecca*, but the producer was still vacillating on the issue of a contract for Hitchcock and was mired in the day-to-day (and night) production of *Gone with the Wind* (Selznick International Pictures / Metro-Goldwyn-Mayer, 1939). After a stopover on the East Coast, a perturbed Hitchcock was dragged around Hollywood by his agency for talks with not only Selznick but also several other producers. Eventually David O. Selznick, seemingly strong-armed by his brother, presented an offer. Hitchcock eagerly signed, even though the terms were flimsier than what he had hoped for.[19]

During the Hitchcocks' visit to Hollywood in 1938, the journalist Molly Castle, without an accompanying photographer, found the couple at the Brown Derby. By way of introduction in her resulting article, Castle reeled off the default portrait: "The plumpest, palliest English director, only one of his trade ever to reach top fame-and-fortune rungs by staying in England, had just arrived in the Metro-Goldwyn-opolis for the first time with his half-pint missus, Alma."[20] Hitchcock got a chance to show off his gourmet savvy by comparing French and English mustards, headlined for the article, while Alma, in preparation to take up residence, was heading for the "swank section of Bel Air" to house hunt. The blueprint in her mind's eye, minus a swimming pool, matched what she eventually got: "I want a house . . . with a big room in which Hitch can pace up and down, a house with furniture that won't break when he sits on it. At least three double bedrooms. And . . . a swimming pool would be nice."[21] Her scouting inspired her husband a few years later, after they had been residing in apartment hotels and temporary rentals, to present her with a gold key to the abode at the top of her desiderata list. This, the only house the Hitchcocks owned in Los Angeles, provided a backdrop for a multitude of encounters with journalists, predominantly with a culinary slant.

Mission accomplished, Hitchcock returned to England with a signed contract, but the date for moving to Hollywood was still not set. To keep himself busy Hitchcock accepted a job directing Charles Laughton in *Jamaica Inn* (1939) for Mayflower Pictures Corporation, a company Laughton had formed together with the émigré producer Erich Pommer. Puritan associations apart, Hitchcock could hardly have found a more aptly named company at a time when he desperately wanted to sail away from his native country for the promises of the New World. In spite of Hitchcock's jesting claim to double fatness vis-à-vis his star and coproducer, handling Charles Laughton proved to be a rocky, nerve-racking venture. Afloat on the waves of his comrade's Mayflower shenanigans during shooting, Hitchcock later described the assignment as refereeing rather than directing.[22]

Hitchcock scholars seldom engage with *Jamaica Inn*. Peter Conrad's reading is the most appreciative and, in fact, predicated on a brotherhood in fat, among other affinities between Hitchcock and Laughton. According to Conrad, Laughton was configured as a surrogate for Hitchcock twice—the second time around in *The Paradine Case* (Vanguard Films / Selznick Studio, 1947). "Laughton too," Conrad eloquently explains, "was a fat man, a figure of plaintive grotesquerie whose own body derided him."[23] Abundant fat was not the sole common denominator for Laughton and Hitchcock. They were weekend neighbors in Shamley Green, and Laughton "[dropped] in often to talk things over and listen to Hitch's fund of jokes."[24]

Finally, Selznick cabled his go-ahead, and the Hitchcock family plus entourage climbed the gangplank onto the ship bound for New York City, from where they would journey onward to Hollywood. Here Hitchcock was up against a producer of stature with an impressive record of achievements and no awe whatsoever for any aspects of Hitchcock's British style. The production relationship was not without friction, and over the years mutual resentments developed. After the success of *Rebecca* (Selznick International Pictures, 1940) and yet another Academy Award for Selznick as producer, Hitchcock was farmed out to direct for other companies, mainly on stories set in England or written in Britain. This highly lucrative arrangement for Selznick became a bone of contention between the studio and its star director, whose high standing after *Rebecca* was, in the producer's opinion, the result of his supervision—verging on makeover—of Hitchcock's style, especially compared to the lack of success experienced by most European directors in Hollywood, including Jean Renoir.

Patrick McGilligan's *Alfred Hitchcock: A Life in Darkness and Light* is the most dili-gent and reliable biography of the director's career. It is, however, off the mark in its claim concerning the British press's account of Hitchcock's physique: "It would be unheard of in 1937 for the British to dwell on a physical description of Hitchcock, or to sling gibes about his weight."[25] This is true only for a so-ber paper like *The Times*; the London press otherwise brims with unflattering grotesqueries much as America's does. The genre was seemingly irresistible.[26]

Evidence of this writing style can be found even earlier in the British press, in an unsigned *Observer* article from 1935 authored by a friend of Hitchcock's, C. A. Lejeune. Her play on the grotesque functions as a segue to the American drolleries and connects the discursive dots in fascinating ways. The article is especially momentous in light of McGilligan's discussion of Hitchcock's first days in Manhattan. Lejeune writes that Hitchcock's thriller fame has turned him into a national institution alongside "'Cheshire Cheese' and the Savoy Grill for incoming American journalists." Here the two countries' press tra-ditions blend revealingly as Lejeune proceeds to recount her wicked pleasure at thwarting the American preconceptions of Hitchcock when introducing incoming journalists to the man behind *The 39 Steps* (Gaumont-British Picture Corporation, 1935). "Oddly enough," she writes,

> they all seem to approach him with the same figure in mind. They expect to find a lean, tough, grim fellow, compound of Dashiell Hammett, Sherlock Holmes, and Perry Mason. It is one of my major professional pleasures to lead up some transatlantic colleague, unprepared, to the genial "Hitch," and watch him as his hand is engulfed in the vast directorial paw.
>
> During my ten-year friendship with Hitch—the full name is unthinkable to anyone who knows him—I have never known him fail to impress strangers with a start of surprise. He has always been chubby, but to-day he is a mellow, exuberant mountain of a man in the late thirties, whose passion is music, whose pleasure is good living, and whose genius is for visual imagery. He is a man who visualises both by instinct and training. He cannot help drawing. As he talks to you his broad, draughtsman's pencil sneaks out, and he blocks in groups and figures on the napkin or table top. When he signs his name to a letter the flourish under the signature slips into a cartoon. His Christmas cards are self-portraits, broadly saline.[27]

This template with its cutting body slings was further promulgated by Hitchcock himself, as he talked about his own reflected images as piggish and porky while stuffing himself for observing newspaper chroniclers. This modus operandi was obviously slyly calculated for marketing and for building a brand around an aberrant body that inspired an endless string of corporeal wit, first as Hitchcock disposed of gourmet food aplenty while critically appraising the dishes, and then in a second round when the conversation segued to dieting.

When Hitchcock, in his English glory and with his Manhattan reputation, finally reached Hollywood in 1939 to direct for Selznick, the San Francisco columnist Paul Speegle also highlighted the incongruous mismatch between Hitchcock's body and what viewers imagined the English director to look like: "One would picture Alfred Hitchcock, the eminent English director, as a tall, hawk-faced man, slim of build, whose long fingers, when they are not toying with the stem of a cocktail glass, are gliding deftly over the still-warm body of a corpse, searching for clues." In stark contrast to "the image we conjured up . . . Mr. Hitchcock is actually a round, roly-poly man, possessed of several chins which lie in chuckling folds upon a non-existent neck."[28] In his column in the *San Francisco Chronicle*, Speegle offered a bona fide blueprint for the American write-up of Hitchcock along the axis of the grotesque. The elegance of Hitchcock's implied world is here pitted against its fleshy opposite in the real world. The corpulent glutton responsible for cooking up pictures overwrites the perception of the lean authorship suggested by his exquisite brand of gourmet cinema. Speegle tapped into the discursive domain generated out of the New York City dailies after Hitchcock's gastronomic adventures of 1937. The journalist's cunning intervention plays up a mode of gentlemanly detection reminiscent of dandyesque sleuths à la Lord Peter Wimsey, only to have the image collide head-on with the nearly grotesque persona Hitchcock had devised for himself in London and brought with him as his American marketing model.

This rhetorical flourish gradually petered out as Hitchcock became a household image and thereby too visually familiar to play around with for mismatching discursive coups. Or, to phrase it differently, his body gradually reframed the physicality of the suspenseful and the macabre by turning both his abstract and concrete profiles into a bodily logotype for the genre, most famously for the television show. The incongruous conflation with or incorporation into the register of the grotesque was at the core of his marketing strategy and visual profiling. Speegle's figurative extraction of a Hitchcock from inside the British films sketches a classic bodily conception of pure intelligence and refined taste, with a body that serves as a mannequin for sartorial splendor. This imaginary conceptualization clashes with the grotesque body that overflows with physicality, expanding and protruding in all directions.

Once Hitchcock's physical body was established as the logo for Hitchcock's body of work, there was no more room for springing Speegle-like surprises on unwitting audiences or readers.[29] Lejeune continued to sport physical adjectives in passing when writing on Hitchcock in England, and Hedda Hopper, for one, took up the baton after the director's move to Hollywood. The endurance of the press's interest in his image is a testament to Hitchcock's successful strategies for setting bodily brand descriptors in motion.

Fat Cemented

In the spirit of the London and Gotham reports, the gossip queen Hedda Hopper, perhaps now best known for playing herself in *Sunset Blvd.* (Paramount Pictures, 1950), found three opportunities in the fall of 1940 to remind her *Los Angeles Times* readers that Alfred Hitchcock was "rotund," as well as two in 1942. Hopper then shifted to "plump" in 1943 for a report from the shooting of *Shadow of a Doubt* (Skirball Productions / Universal Pictures, 1943).[30] In a more digressive mode, Hopper wrote about the shooting of *Suspicion* (RKO Radio Pictures, 1941), featuring Cary Grant, when the film had the working title "Before the Fact": "With obese practical joker Alfred Hitchcock telling them how to do it in 'Before the Fact,' some of the actors think [the] picture should be titled 'Before the Fat!'"[31] On a similar note, Hopper gleefully reported the following story: "Alfred Hitchcock loves to watch surprise on other people's faces. Well, the expression on his was funny when the chair on the set collapsed beneath his weight. He huffed and puffed, and finally, getting to his feet, yelled: 'Sabotage!'"[32] Clever indeed, since this was the subject of the current production, *Saboteur* (Frank Lloyd Productions / Universal Pictures, 1942). Hopper's pieces illustrate how commonplace it was to juggle physical epithets when writing about Hitchcock. Her reporting does not address his famous eating habits per se, which otherwise was standard procedure instigated by the man himself and his publicity folks.

As Alfred Hitchcock created sensations at American tables, the United States, with its puritan tradition, had not yet experienced the postwar abundance of inexpensive industrial food that gradually encouraged overeating and put obesity on the fast track, almost as a default cultural value, and that in turn inspired an industrialization of health food, novel forms of food awareness, and alimentary and bodily discipline among the elite. Hitchcock was thus an exponent of the old, excessive English food culture at a time when phenomenal indulgence was a rarity in the United States. Consequently, journalists writing about Hitchcock's table prowess associated it with figures from

English literature. From a puritan tradition, a vibrant cultural undercurrent in the United States, gluttony, as a cardinal sin, harbored elements bordering on the pathological. The uninhibited, regressive love of ice cream in particular was not expected of adults. In this respect Hitchcock's repasts were depicted as alien in several ways against the backdrop of an American culture of food sobriety, puritanism, and health consciousness, which eventually, as in England, was connected to class distinctions.

Peter N. Stearns has analyzed the discourse on fat in American culture from a historical perspective. His materials evidence an ongoing policing of fat, foremost for women, from the 1890s onward as body norms were redefined by fashion and puritan ideals of self-discipline coupled with novel nutritional and medical insights. The emerging advertising market, in tandem with popular media, further fueled this discourse, making fatness grotesque and aberrant and thus fair game for ridicule. The many reports on phenomenal dieting results and the shedding of staggering accumulations of poundage were a staple of this discourse. Hitchcock willingly and creatively fashioned himself for crash-diet reporting on multiple occasions. The unblushing stabs at Hitchcock's bulk in the press had their background in this American policing of fat and a perception of plumpness as comical and the result of a lack of moral fiber. Hitchcock's gluttony and initial dismissal of dieting and exercise were aligned with his exotic Englishness and were thus somewhat foreign in relation to American culture and its body norms. Despite the intense cultural policing of fat, however, Americans grew progressively heavier during the twentieth century.[33]

Hopper's comments evidence what William Banting observed in his mid-Victorian *Letter on Corpulence*: "Any one so afflicted is often subject to public remark."[34] Within the realm of fat studies, Banting's text is a pioneering work that outlines a dietary regime and contains reflections on the psychological and cultural meaning of corpulence, which has given his pamphlet a place on the websites of low-carb dieting programs. From the 1930s to the 1960s hardly anyone was publicly subjected to fat's rich cluster of meaning—and its cultural (and often gendered) applications—more often than Alfred Hitchcock. The Hitchcock discourse is replete with all the features and fixtures of fat theory: the obsession with figures on the scale, the ideal of body norms tightening dietary regimes, and the comedic discourses slighting fat people as deviant. In his case, however, his corpulence also served as a marketing device for brand recognition, which was eventually reduced to the fat silhouette.

Early on, the comedy of fatness turned into a subgenre of its own in vaudeville, as well as a gendered billing item, such as fat ladies in "freak shows" and at circuses (which Hitchcock included in *Saboteur*). And a whole gamut of heavy male comedians have paraded across the screen, from the famous fat quartet led by Oscar Stribolt in early Danish cinema to Hollywood actors such as Roscoe "Fatty" Arbuckle, in addition, of course, to several comedy teams formed in the body-polar manner of Laurel and Hardy.[35] More than anybody, Alfred Hitchcock inserted himself into this roster by playing heavily in the register of the grotesque, which is predicated on a celebration of culture's fat underbelly, so to speak. His brazen display of fat was as aberrant as the paeans to perfect murders, and when combined they were soon heralded as salient components of the Hitchcockian. Catching the drift, a generation of writers in popular media ushered in and excelled at fat Hitchcock jokes and references, as Hopper's writing illustrates. Fat joking functioned as a tie-in to the brand of sly humor, pranks, and practical joking that enveloped Hitchcock's biographical legend. Back in England, before the director subscribed to Banting's carb-less dieting, a more playful regime had been attributed to Hitchcock. The method apparently had its drawbacks: "Britain's heavy-weight champion film director, has gone on a diet. It works like this:—Monday: Soup and liquids. Tuesday: Lean chop and pineapple. Wednesday: Anything he likes. No change in weight yet. Too many Wednesdays."[36]

In a much later interview, Jimmie Allardice, scriptwriter for Hitchcock's on-screen segments for *Alfred Hitchcock Presents* (AHP) and *The Alfred Hitchcock Hour* (AHH), jestingly mentioned the difficulties of devising jokes for television shows eight weeks ahead of time not knowing whether a new diet would have taken its toll on Hitchcock's body when it was time to shoot the introductions. In Allardice's hands the fat discourse took on novel, playful forms. In the prologue to "Man with a Problem" (AHP 124) we find Hitchcock seated and giving instructions to someone who, when the shot widens, proves to be an exercising skeleton. The setup is indicative of the absurd spins and adroit reframing that became a trademark of Hitchcock's televisual on-screen persona. The skeleton, Mr. Webster, could be read as a Hitchcock look-alike of sorts within a franchise that pivoted on doubling. "When Mr. Webster first came to me," the host explains, "he weighed nearly three hundred pounds. He was sluggish and run down and was the object of ridicule because of his obesity." However, the latter stage of intense dieting has its drawbacks for Mr. Webster, as "the dogs keep carrying him off and burying him." Fortunately Hitchcock's own diet, in the absence of an exercise regime, was less efficient. Still, he was not quite tasty enough for discriminating chefs. While coming to a slow boil in one of the most bizarre of the host segments, the prologue for "The Last Request" (AHP 86), Hitchcock, fully dressed, explains his strange position from inside a large kettle. Allardice's text opens with a critical question after Hitchcock greets us as "fellow gourmets." Here is Allardice at his wittiest:

> Have you ever been in a position where the success or failure depends entirely on you? Of course, all this is not without its compensations. It is always reassuring to learn that other human beings still find you desirable . . . and I am the main course. It would be horrible to go through this and be nothing but an hors d'oeuvre. . . . It seems that one of the natives was condemned to death and as a last request was granted the right to indulge in a hearty meal. I'm proud to say I was his first choice.

In the epilogue Hitchcock has to face a truly embarrassing situation: being substituted with another dish—a young woman. Apparently the chef had intervened and dropped Alfred from the menu for being insufficiently tender. A young woman wearing nothing but spectacles and reading a book has taken the host's place in the pot. This was sad for the prospective dish, of course, but the outcome meant that Hitchcock could return in full form the following week.

From the morgue of Hitchcock's texts a few years into his Hollywood career, one particular piece serves as a template for how, when writers set their mind to it, the grotesque body discourse could be spelled out in fuller format than in Hopper's asides and slings. In 1943 Alva Johnston, a Pulitzer Prize winner and author of several biographies, treated Alfred Hitchcock to a lengthy portrait in the *Saturday Evening Post*; the reportage came amply illustrated with photographs from the Hitchcock home. The piece, in its pointed headline, calls attention to Hitchcock's body, which is described in exemplary but unflattering detail. Hitchcock's weight is advertised in the essay's title, "300-Pound Prophet Comes to Hollywood"; the epithet "the fat director" then introduces the full-figure portrait:

> Hitchcock's physique made a greater impression on the film capital than his English reputation. Three hundred pounds distributed around five feet, nine inches of height are not to be ignored. The newcomer was a sensation with his cycloramic torso, setting-sun complexions, round, wonder-struck eyes, and cheeks inflated as if blowing an invisible bugle. People reacted to him like children at [the] sight of balloon giants in Macy's parade. . . . Against the 300-pound background everything relating to Hitchcock attracted attention. He drove about a tiny Austin which fitted him like a bathing suit [the car and its owner were photographed for the

piece]. He was reported to have the appetite of a lion farm, although, in reality, he is not an immoderate eater.[37]

Johnston's article echoes the reports from his New York City visit in 1937, as well as Maloney's balloon metaphor from the *New Yorker* in 1938, albeit focusing on the effects, rather than the act, of eating. By the 1940s, however, Hitchcock's moderate consumption in public, invariably at Chasen's, was far from the uninhibited feasts he had enjoyed back in New York.

Weight-wise, 1943 was a watershed year for Hitchcock and for his own version of waxing fat. Starting out at way over three hundred pounds, as Johnston reported, after the making of *Shadow of a Doubt* Hitchcock put himself on a strenuous dietary regime, which downsized him to slightly more than two hundred pounds by the end of the year. Selznick was worried and made sure that a physician did regular check-ups of his property. Philip K. Scheuer picked up on Johnston's "balloon" article as a segue to *Lifeboat* (Twentieth Century Fox Film Corporation, 1944) and reported that the actual weight was down to 246 pounds, continuing: "In line with his own diminishing perspective, the director's next picture will take place in its entirety in a 26 foot lifeboat. When you consider that he usually requires a couple of continents to move around in, this would seem to be the reductio ad absurdum for fair."[38]

The cameo in *Lifeboat* presents Hitchcock in a printed ad for a dietary potion, Reduco, "the obesity slayer," which shows him before and after dieting, while *Life* highlighted the actual process in a series of snapshots (fig. 1.3). Reminiscing about his cameos, Hitchcock singled out the one in *Lifeboat* as his favorite. After he appeared in the ad for the fictive weight-loss drug, he said, "letters literally poured in from fat people, asking where they could buy Reduco, the miracle drug that had helped me lose 100 pounds. Maybe I shouldn't admit it, but I got a certain satisfaction from writing back that the drug didn't exist, and adding smugly that the best way to lose weight was to go on a strenuous diet, as I had done."[39] Hitchcock's dieting ran as a parallel strand to the body grotesque and accompanied any and every news item bearing on the director, including the copy his studios produced.

According to Frank Nugent, Hitchcock had for "most of his life been taunted by ovicular descriptives" and in "public print" was pegged as "globular, ovoid, roly-poly, rotund, egg shaped, Humpty Dumpty, balloonlike, and so on." Nugent related this discourse to Hitchcock's recent hardcore dieting. Writing when Hitchcock had just finished *Spellbound*, Nugent offers a lightning sketch of the director's personality with a psychoanalytical slant that includes

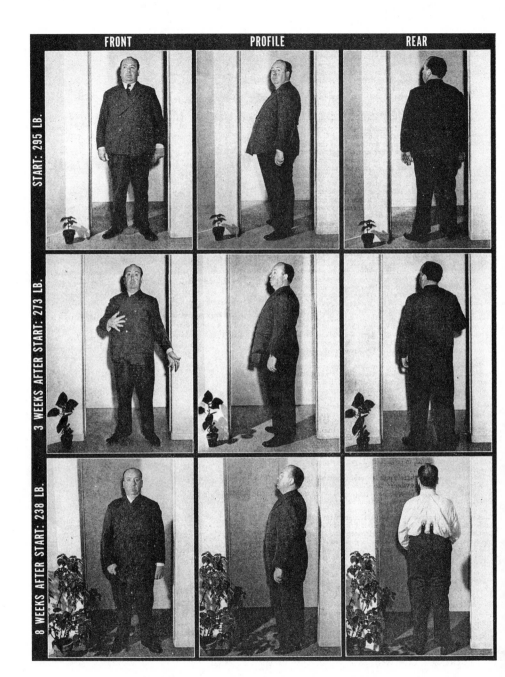

Hitchcock's brief imprisonment as a child, as requested by his father. Untroubled, it seems, Hitchcock turned the physical barbs to his own advantage.[40]

On at least one occasion Hitchcock was asked about his reactions to being described in terms of "physical indignities," as "your nose has been called pendulous [and] your lower lip has been compared with a sugar scoop." This interviewer then asked Hitchcock to describe himself physically. Hitchcock replied: "A New York doctor once told me that I'm an adrenal type. . . . That apparently means that I'm all body and only vestigial legs. But since I'm neither a mile runner nor a dancer and my present interest in my body is almost altogether from the waist up, that didn't bother me much."[41] The attention to "physical indignities" followed Hitchcock all the way to the obituaries. "Resembling a pixieish gargoyle, the rotund director had a pudgy basset-hound face with heavy jowls and pouting lips," Peter Flint wrote in the *New York Times*.[42]

In his less majestic stages, just after the shooting of *Shadow of a Doubt* in Santa Rosa, Hitchcock tried to counteract the fat discourse and exert damage control—or, perhaps, slyly further promulgate the buzz from 1937. As a guest columnist in the *New York Post* in 1943 Hitchcock wrote: "Ever since I began directing pictures, people have been told about a Hitchcock who eats steaks with alternate mouthfuls of ice cream three times a day. . . . To begin with, take that business about the steaks. I haven't the slightest notion where it started or who started it, but it has gained currency as Washington's cherry tree, by sheer force of repetition and for lack of denial. I suppose because I have bulk on my side, somebody came to the all-too-obvious conclusion that I must simply stuff myself with beefsteaks."[43]

The director himself had cemented his biographical legend by entertaining reporters with small talk on cinema and culinary matters while ingesting mammoth servings of steak and ice cream. Since the predilection for this food combination emerged out of the Manhattan tablehopping, it is surprising that Hitchcock here frames the discourse across his whole career, as if he had begun directing in the United States.[44] In a studio biography signed by Don King, the director of publicity at the Selznick studio, around 1946, the food

1.3. (*facing*) In health-conscious Hollywood, Hitchcock's obesity was constantly joked about, especially prior to his first dramatic weight loss after the making of *Shadow of a Doubt* (1943), which was ingeniously documented in a photo-essay featuring a plant growing bigger next to the progressively shrinking body. "Speaking of Pictures: Alfred Hitchcock Reduces as Plant Expands," *Life*, 27 December 1943, 12–14. Photographs by John Florea, courtesy of Fahey / Klein Gallery, Los Angeles.

discourse took center stage in formulations that would appear verbatim in multiple installments of Paramount biographies in the late 1950s.[45] According to King, the foundational food story was apocryphal, a "fable" no less:

> Out of a New York interview rose the typical fable that Hitchcock eats only beef-steak and ice-cream in this country because he lacks confidence in the ability of American chefs to create other viands. This, he now admits, was a culinary canard. "I'm not really a heavy eater," Hitch puts it, "unless you mean that I'm heavy, and I eat."
>
> While Hitch is not the enormous figure he used to be, he retains the double chin and round face which, with his bright blue eyes and bristly black hair, give him the appearance of an alert and intelligent cherub.[46]

Apparent attempts to write off the discourse gave it additional longevity. Even decades after the gastronomic excursion to New York City, and multiple diets later, the pervasiveness of the food grotesque prompted Hitchcock's studio to address the matter with explicit reference to the first round of texts from 1937, writing them off as fable. The fable proper, the "ur-scene" recounted by H. Allen Smith, eventually faded, but traces of it lingered even in a CBS bio from 1962, when the network again took on the Hitchcock show after a couple of seasons at NBC, though in a new format and as The Alfred Hitchcock Hour. According to the bio, "the director's reputation for drollery preceded him and his good humor has helped to build certain legends about him, particularly regarding his gastronomic prowess. These were credible in view of his former 290-pound weight, now reduced by more than 100 pounds."[47]

Self-serving pranks and outlandish gimmickry were part of a strategy for conquering British cinema and later Hollywood. In the United States the reading frame became convoluted and blurred, as Hitchcock first and foremost was perceived as quintessentially English in his demeanor and delivery, and the nuanced traces of English class and culture in his mannerisms were ignored. In the British press, however, Hitchcock never escaped the world of the gents and the lower middle class he was born into. In class-conscious London, even when Hitchcock was recognized in New York City in the late 1930s, he was invariably cast as a gent and the "son of fruiterer Bill Hitchcock."[48] When in 1971 he returned to London and the alimentary world of his childhood around Covent Garden to make Frenzy (Universal Pictures, 1972), he was still described, almost in a Dickensian manner, as "a portly little gent."[49]

A Bodily Imprimatur

For American highbrow critics in the 1950s and early 1960s, Hitchcock's cinema was too Hollywood and commercially successful, or outright absurd, as *The Trouble with Harry* (Alfred J. Hitchcock Productions / Paramount Pictures, 1955) and later, in a different register, *Vertigo* (Paramount Pictures / Alfred J. Hitchcock Productions, 1958) putatively evidenced.[50] These unimpressed critics considered the taut British thrillers to be his best efforts. For a later generation of scholars and arbiters, Hitchcock's constellation of objects, fabrics, settings, and bodies and their mise-en-scène stands out beyond conventional realism, thereby stretching the patterns of meaning toward a stylish modernism grounded in the seemingly or simulated "real," and eventually favors intertextual play with imagery over character exploration.[51] In the medium of television, Hitchcock acquired a distinct, tongue-in-cheek English drawl far removed the American advertising culture he spoofed in trademark style during the host segments. Television's flat characters offered a blueprint for Hitchcock's minimal concern with psychological development and rounded subjectivity in his postclassical films.

In a Swedish television interview from 1961, midway into his television tenure, Hitchcock was relegated to a position outside of the cinematic canon. He was in town to promote *Psycho* (Shamley Productions, 1960). According to the introductory capsule comment, "Alfred Hitchcock is not among the greatest geniuses of film art." Instead, the impudent film expert opines, he is "one of the most colorful individualists."[52] Pace the celebratory brouhaha from Paris surrounding Hitchcock at the cusp of the 1960s, the Swedish critic echoes Hitchcock-skeptical New York City highbrows at the *New Yorker*, *Nation*, and *Saturday Review* and their unflinching write-offs of films from *Rebecca* to *Psycho*, as Robert E. Kapsis demonstrated in his superb study of the shifting conjectures concerning the director's critical prestige.[53] The Swedish analysis operates on the traditional premise of two Hitchcocks, pitting the director and his cinematic oeuvre against the colorful, difficult-to-fathom public personage seen in guileful interviews, in irreverent marketing, and foremost in his role as television host. For some, the clowning performer reduced or overshadowed the artist; for others, this doubling represented puzzling parallel tracks that sometimes collided but mainly reinforced a remarkable franchise career writ progressively larger within the critical precincts of twentieth-century culture.[54]

Hollis Alpert's essay "Hitchcock as Humorist" from 1962 expands, as it were, on the succinct Swedish comment. Alpert's benchmark analysis is indicative of the stern policing of Hollywood Hitchcock among modernist critics in a text that affords praise only to *The 39 Steps* for eminently showing off Hitchcock's "matchless" handling of "humorous melodrama." Hitchcock is at his best, Alpert claims, when "his sense of humor is nicely in tune with his material."[55] The role of humor is key to his critical stance, which dismisses Hitchcock's attempts at seriousness—especially in *The Wrong Man* (Warner Bros., 1956), a film he reads as a reaction to the failed attempt at humor in *The Trouble with Harry*. Not fully succeeding in this refashioning, Hitchcock bounced back to his own genre in *Vertigo* and especially *North by Northwest* (Metro-Goldwyn-Mayer, 1959). For Alpert, Hitchcock comes across as a victim of his own humor: "it is impossible for him to be serious," and his suspense is "actually suspense being used for purposes of humor," as he manages to entertain with harebrained stories like *North by Northwest*. The side effect is that, in terms of content, many of his films pose at best an "enigma, at worst a vacuum." Thus, "throughout his long, successful career he has entertained and surprised, but he has said nothing." Searching for depth in Hitchcock is pointless, as "you will find only clues to his own personality," while he mobilizes his humor as a "form of defense." Hitchcock's personality seemingly permeates his films: "He is a droll man personally, and it is his drollery that is mainly expressed in his cinema."[56]

In passing, Alpert chides the European admirers who have hailed Hitchcock as "much more than a trickster and a purveyor of suspense tales to the populace." This is a cinema where "the joke itself is the raison d'être," and "like all jokesters," Hitchcock "is an exaggerator"—for example, in the closing carousel scene in *Strangers on a Train* (Warner Bros., 1951) or the overstretched sequence on Mount Rushmore in *North by Northwest*. Often "the joke becomes stale, the running gags run thin, and garishness is the effect," and, not least in *Vertigo*, "there is usually this straining that vitiates the humor." Alpert relates this straining to AHP and the "television comedian who must expose himself week after week with material that grows thin. To compensate he will put greater effort into the 'business.' He will roll his eyes, double-take, ham it up, make 'funny' faces." In sum, Hitchcock is a "clever man indeed, but perhaps the joke is also on Hitchcock, for he has outsmarted himself by being taken as a mechanic and a merchant of menace." For Alpert, this explains the absence of Academy Awards for Hitchcock: "He is not serious enough, and sheer skill and craft are not enough to carry him over the line."[57]

If Alpert's criticism is representative of Hitchcock's ranking among American intellectuals in the early 1960s, when his filmic oeuvre was being reappraised elsewhere and the television show had put him on the fast track to worldwide fame, Hitchcock's approach to humor, almost invariably body tinged, took on novel and more complex layers of meaning for a later generation of academic critics. In a perceptive study, Susan Smith brings nuances and novel insights to the tonal registers of Hitchcock's cinematic humor.[58] Dana Polan, meanwhile, in a keen analysis of *Mr. and Mrs. Smith* (RKO Radio Pictures, 1941), has no beef with Alpert concerning the disregard for content, message, and psychological depth in Hitchcock's approach to storytelling. For Polan, however, spirit and transcendence are not of critical significance for a cinema that, to his mind, approaches the self primarily as materiality, as an "all-too-earthy" body, and often ingeniously creates perceptual friction between mind and matter when siding with the body. Hence, writes Polan, Hitchcock's cinema displays "a whole concern with the need to turn people into bodies (for example, the protracted killing of a man dragged across the floor in *Torn Curtain* [Universal Pictures, 1966]), the need to dispose of cumbersome bodies (for example, the very premise of *The Trouble with Harry* [1955]), [and] the disposing of Marion Crane in the viscous muck of the swamp."[59]

Richard H. Millington, in a fine reading of *North by Northwest*, turns to the larger scope of the body cultural by defining Hitchcock's project as "an investigation into the kinds of bodies American culture characteristically manufactures."[60] Here, pace Polan, the lack of earthiness is the critical issue. The ad culture, cooked up by the likes of Roger O. Thornhill's attenuated character, somehow trapped everyone in Madison Avenue's lingo for wrapping commodities into desirable objects. Advertising culture emerged as the backbone of television, which to a large extent tuned out previously dominant media. Hitchcock's sly stabs at this particular mode of discourse as chubby television host offered a uniquely convoluted method for selling his own franchise, which was inextricably linked to the unmercifully chided sponsors.

The "weightless" American (advertising) bodies "mannequined" by Thornhill and Eve Kendall in Millington's reading accidentally stumble onto prospects of real grounding by way of romance.[61] Or take Lisa's (Grace Kelly's) model body in *Rear Window*, dismissed by Jimmy Stewart's character as out of place in his world of grit and grime. As it turns out, Lisa's quick-witted mind and resolute courage transcend Stewart's one-sided reading of her character in mere bodily terms as nothing but a superficial mannequin. The romantic odds have thus markedly improved when the film comes to its open-ended closure. One can take such turnabouts at face value owing to the artifice of Hitchcock's ironic fairytale style, in the manner of Lesley Brill's fine study of Hitchcock's miraculous romances.[62] Or one can turn skepticism up a notch to Richard Allen's "metaskepticism," a conceptual catchword for the illusory nature and ambiguous undermining of the romantic fables, however promising the prospects seemingly offered by the endings. "Encrypted in love," summarizes Allen, "are dark desires for and of annihilation, of both the self and the human."[63] Cary Grant's character in Suspicion is one of Allen's two templates for the doubt that shadows Hitchcock's romances.

Body disgust offers the premise for Charles Oakley's serial killing in Shadow of a Doubt. As tall and lanky as Grant, Joseph Cotten embodies Uncle Charlie. (Cotten later appeared in AHP on several occasions as a callous businessman.) Useless widows, to Uncle Charlie's mind, usurp the ideal of small-town domesticity and are thus his targets for ridding contemporary America of excessive female fat and collecting money in the process. William Rothman, in his analysis of Shadow of a Doubt, perceptively notes the ambiguity involved, as Charlie's contempt seemingly comes with an undercurrent of affection—for his victims' lost grace and beauty, if nothing else—in the form of inverted metaskepticism.[64] Older women in Hitchcock's world provide pointed caricatures vis-à-vis youthful beauty, which is always marked as fleeting. As Hitchcock with blushing bluntness phrased the connection when interviewed by Dick Cavett, "All breasts will eventually sag."[65]

In a perceptive but often overlooked article from 1973, Robert C. Cumbow outlines the contours of a tentative "fat theory" as a biographical foundation for Hitchcock's cinema. Claiming that Hitchcock "deals exclusively in situations of fear and suspense," Cumbow reads this attention as a result of "anxieties and discomforts peculiar to the fat person." Confinement, hydrophobia, and acrophobia are obvious sources of discomfort for fat people, he claims, and in this reading Hitchcock's mastery consists of his brilliant grafting of the fat person's fears onto extremely fit screen characters, which in turn excites in the "viewer of average build a sensation correlative to those which have aroused discomfort and fear in himself as a fat person."[66] This strategy, physical overlap apart, functions as a form of affective translation relaying fears and anxieties, though far removed from the default humor that defined Hitchcock for Alpert. Paradigmatic situations in this respect involve entering a phone booth or narrow train corridor and climbing steep stairs—not to mention the physical dexterity required to come out on top in chase scenes, no doubt the bread and butter of Hitchcock's brand of suspense.[67] Cumbow's argument obviously resonates in interesting ways with the "theory" concerning a real, slim Hitchcock trapped inside the obese body, which I discuss later, and Millington's focus on Cary Grant's advertising body in North by Northwest.

For Cumbow the ubiquity of food scenes and their connections to crime— the macabre intersection between dining à la française and murder à l'anglaise— is related to his claim that "any overweight person has an ambivalent view of food which reaches obsessive proportions." Food is loved and mistrusted and "viewed either with horror or with whimsy." In Hitchcock's body of works, eating and drinking are perennial plot points that juxtapose "food with situations involving fear, violence or death," but also with some comedy and whimsy. In Cumbow's analysis, Hitchcock as obese cameo figure provides virtually the only foil for "the physical attractiveness and ability of his heroes—they endure and accomplish things he can only have nightmares about."[68]

Cumbow here offers a psychological premise for a brand almost obsessed with corporeality by positing an inversion between the director's body and his characters. His line of reasoning addresses cinema only, but the embodiment of characters in the larger fabric of casting creates a complex network of intertextual meaning between the teleplays and Hitchcock's cinema, as well as drawing on typecasting and fixed acting signifiers at large. Without the consistent playing up of Hitchcock's body by the director himself, which in turn gave critics license to outwit him with similar cracks, Cumbow's comparative stance would not have been such an obvious point of departure. In accounts written in the late 1930s, when eating for Hitchcock entailed a gourmet-cum-gourmand stab at the best tables, the register of the grotesque was unavoidable. In later years, as television was added to the franchise, Allardice invented a much more complex set of Hitchcock figures to embody.

"Arse-about-Face" and the Grotesque

Hitchcock's penchant for one-on-one exchanges over food represents a supreme form of dialogism across high-class restaurant tables, which, following Hwa Yol Jung's analysis of Mikhail Bakhtin's work, is tantamount to "carnal hermeneutics." According to Jung, this neologism refers to "an 'application' of hermeneutics or interpretation theory and its procedures to the 'reading' of the body as social inscription in and of the world. It is an incorporation of conceptual categories concerning all the aspects, dimensions, levels, pivots, configurations, and representations, both verbal and nonverbal, of the body's diverse communicative performances."[69]

In the Hitchcock write-ups, and clearly in more accessible terms, culinary matters and table scenes ranging from festive gorging to melancholy dieting ran in tandem with observations on his craft and oscillating poundage. Hitchcock planted the fat seed when stuffing himself with double servings and dismissing physical exercise in all forms. Acting surprised and pretending to counteract the table reports when the alleged myth with its grotesque overtones gained traction further fueled its longevity rather than putting it to rest.[70]

Bakhtin introduced the grotesque in order to reinstate the body and carnal insights from the bottom up, in lieu of both abstract idealism and modernity's celebration of disembodied reason writ large. Carnivalizing strategies in the register of the grotesque best describe the Hitchcock figure's performance tone prior to television—irreverent and playful with an edgy, carnal energy—as well as the critical reception of his "specular pageantry," to borrow a felicitous expression from Hwa Yol Jung.[71] The term "specular" is key here, as the context for the grotesque is understood outside the carnival's democratic space of shared interaction, something to behold as carnal spectacle rather than to interact with. As Susan Stewart has shown, the grotesque body as spectacle "appears not in parts but in a whole that is an aberration." For her this goes back to the sideshow's showing off of physical deviants outside the range of "the normal," and especially the advertised "freakishness" of over- and undersized bodies.[72] Showcasing his at times extreme girth and extreme appetite aligned Hitchcock with grotesque display, particularly in the early stages of his career on both continents. For the Hitchcock figure, interest in sex took a backseat to remarkable food indulgence and the previously mentioned pleasures "from the waist up." Routinized family life was a prerequisite for Hitchcock's creativity, and the couple enjoyed a productive working relationship and a mutual interest in food culture, while other passions seemingly were less pronounced or to a large extent sublimated. Pointedly, Oriana Fallaci labeled Hitchcock "Mr. Chastity" in an excellent interview.[73]

By foregrounding his own bulky physique, Hitchcock shaped a bodily profile that spawned a headline-friendly reception genre. This discourse married unflattering descriptions of the director's allegedly grotesque carnal features with the suspense genre, as practiced by this heavier-than-life figure. The rich body of Hitchcock photographs in photo-essays and marketing materials has a similar point of departure. Yet the photographic representation of the Hitchcock figure and its enigmatic aura in glossy magazines cannot be fully divested of the glamorous strategies underpinning the way these journals showcased visually arresting personalities. Hitchcock's quizzical wit, photo-friendly demeanor, and unfaltering willingness to pose as a ham were godsends for this type of journalism. Hollywood was a mecca for style, and a focus on extraordinary personalities in public print was critical for the success of magazines like *Life* and *Look*.

Frenzy is the Hitchcock film that most heavily caters to the realm of the grotesque, but the film's murder victims are by no means of the variety Uncle Charlie singled out as obese and useless. Instead most of them are young and quite thin. The film is not, however, concerned with celebrating the mannequin qualities mentioned by Millington for a Cary Grant or Grace Kelly. If anything, the focus is on physical attraction that can be ushered in only by way of unsavory destruction, rape mixing lust and disgust, for an otherwise impotent killer. The film's sexual matrix is attuned to food- and cooking-inflected disgust that simmers around fragile bodies. In its representations and inversions, this mode and its bottom-up direction is riveted to what Bakhtin designates "the body's lower stratum."[74] The concept is substituted with "arse-about-face" in the off-color vernacular used in *Frenzy*. The sly killer in Hitchcock's perhaps "foodiest" film uses the colorful expression to describe the direction of the police investigation. The greasy pub fare in the film is associated with men and pitted against disgusting-looking and female-accented French gourmet dishes, while the necktie murderer enjoys fresh fruit and reels off fruity bon mots when not raping and strangling women.

Awry juxtapositions mobilized to bring down pomposity and strip away dignity—one's own and that of others—as in the charged arse-about-face expression, are at the core of the carnival spirit. In the carnival the powerful lose face, or hide face to fool around, while the powerless enjoy a momentary break from the hierarchies in daily life, as those at the top are fair game for ridicule. Social standing is degraded and inverted. The spiritual and noble are bracketed by the insight that all flesh harbors decay and death. Physicality is not only inextricably linked to birth, beauty, and spiritual life: in Bakhtin's analysis, the grotesque body is almost desperately connected to the world, and in the communal and tumultuous spirit of the carnival, the grounded body actively engages with culture, pompously inflated or not.[75] Outside carnivals proper, burlesque gestures and carnivalizing practices seek to destabilize static, hierarchic power relations and discourses by setting societal circulation in motion. The body in this perspective is in a perpetual act of becoming, never completed, constantly reauthored and refashioned—or even consumed in yet another arse-about-face twist. Hitchcock served up his own body in precisely this fashion and turned into a discursive package, as an open-ended project elaborated on by commentators, himself included, for decades, and most prominently in the television show.

Protruding physical features are the most significant connecting aspects of the grotesque body: bulging eyes, projecting nose, and prominent lips. All these were joined in Hitchcock's case by "a quite unmilitary protuberance at the belt line."[76] This ridiculing register of the grotesque was commonplace in the portraiture of the director and soon became its sine qua non. For Bakhtin, attention to the lower bodily stratum is critically significant, as bowels and genital organs are momentous for achieving a turnabout of the world's formal organization and power structure, which in terms of the body emanates from higher up. Bodily orifices function as passageways that overcome the split between world and body. Eating, drinking, defecation, other types of elimination, and copulation also take place on the border between the world and the body, Bakhtin writes.[77] The grotesque, consciously set in motion by Hitchcock, released a mischievous spirit of uncrowning and a disrespectful parody of self and others. This irreverent strategy of reversals amounts to arse-about-face, to stick with Frenzy's truly Bakhtinian phrase.

Concerning the tension between the carnivalizing and civilizing realms of food culture in relation to the social and political, Gwen Hyman situates her alimentary analysis in dialogue with the writings of Claude Lévi-Strauss and Norbert Elias on the cultures of food preparation, eating regimes, and table manners. In her literary case studies, as for Hitchcock's prandial practices, the table becomes a significant locus between self and the world, the prime site where practices are played out and negotiated on the bodily confines.[78] The table and its offerings were Hitchcock's arena of choice for dabbling in the grotesque, alongside his penchant for practical jokes, a highly irreverent practice.

Famous for his penchant for hoaxes and horseplay, Hitchcock, especially in the late 1930s, emerged as a veritable destabilizer by design, humorously attacking self-importance and officiousness, most often with "vulgar" overtones. Eventually the television sponsor turned into the preferred butt for this gambit. Its slinging playfulness had, however, been sanitized, the grotesque of old removed. The Hitchcock discourse is otherwise replete with accounts of jokes from his prankster days that were in tune with the grotesque direction of the lower stratum.[79] The most obvious aspect reinforcing this direction is, of course, the fixation on food.

Linguistically, the arse-about-face trope signifies not getting it right, a skewed perception or looking for something in the wrong place. I adopt the colloquialism here as a linguistic embodiment of the carnivalesque reversals and shifts of emphasis. For Hitchcock, arse-about-face, apart from showcasing his body as gateway to his work, could also be described as a creative, albeit furtive, working model with a grotesque underbelly. For example, when filming the protracted kissing scene in Notorious (Vanguard Films / RKO Radio Pictures, 1946) featuring Ingrid Bergman and Cary Grant, Hitchcock, according to John Russell Taylor, was imagining a parallel type of amorous scene: "He had an image in his mind of amorous obsession, derived from a scene he had once witnessed when his train stopped. He saw a couple standing near a great brick wall embracing while the boy was urinating against the wall. The girl occasionally looked down to see how he was progressing, then looked round, then down again, but never let go of his arm the whole time."[80]

This alleged private musing during shooting neatly illustrates the arse-about-face strategy. In regard to bodily features, nothing short of an erection could be more protruding and obtrusive than this urinating scene standing in for and decrowning a series of passionate kisses. Romance could not be more carnivalized, or pissed on. Alternatively, the gesture might be seen as amping up the eroticism by chasing away conventional romance to be replaced with a differently charged, lower-stratum fascination that does not shy away from elimination as an exciting carnal spectacle.

For the television team, in this spirit, Hitchcock was ready to take any type of self-decrowning bullet, as his detached figure, on and off the screen, always emerged from such shenanigans with unruffled dignity. Along this line, Hitchcock hosted a much publicized haunted-house party in New York City and a luncheon party in Beverly Hills. In the latter case, journalists invited to the Brown Derby were surprised to find themselves transported to a local jail for the meal.[81] A Psycho party in Australia came with a chorus line of widows who had limited bearing on the film. Vertigo was launched with a somewhat off-key burlesque party in a New York City skyscraper under construction, with attention riveted to nurses' showcased behinds as they alleviated symptoms of vertigo with the aid of oxygen tanks (fig. 1.4). The party had the full line of Charles Addams paraphernalia to boot: skeletons, coffins to rest in, eerie lighting, dummies to strangle, and macabre food.[82] In addition to the New York party, Hitchcock had hosted a guided tour of shooting sites in San Francisco in conjunction with the world premiere.[83]

Such brouhaha promulgated the public perception of Hitchcock as a prankster. At times, the ruses played against the tone of what was being promoted, as was the case with Vertigo and Psycho. The host segments for the television show reinforced the overarching frame for the series and cinema bearing his name; they fed off the circle of macabre stunts orchestrated offscreen for the benefit of the press, solidifying and promoting a brand by means of a variety of ruses. At parties in London in the early days of his career, in the spirit of full-blown grotesque, Hitchcock sometimes stripped to the waist and shook his flabby torso so that lipstick figures he had painted on his chest whirled around. This routine, known as "breast ballet," offers one of the best illustrations of his penchant for uninhibited, carnivalesque theatricality and a decrowning of his own dignity, as he offered his body for a spin to the lower stratum. In Donald Spoto's colorful description:

> Sometimes, after the liquor had flowed freely, Hitchcock could be persuaded to do his party piece, "The Whistling Sailor." He would leave the sitting

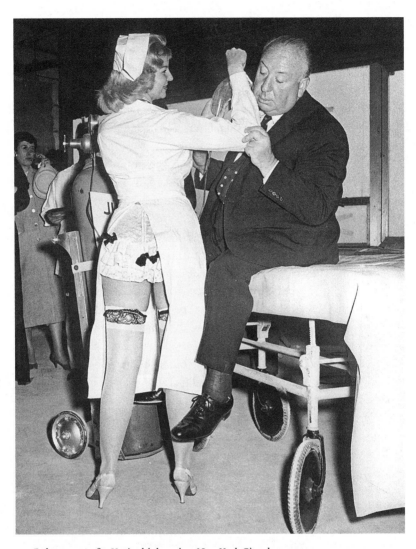

1.4. Release party for *Vertigo* high up in a New York City skyscraper.
Uncredited photograph, courtesy of Photofest.

room and return moments later, naked to the waist—a sight that, considering his almost three hundred pounds, must in itself have been in the realm of the comic-grotesque. On his chest and belly he had painted, with his wife's makeup, an enormous sailor's face, its lips rounded into an O as though whistling. Hitchcock himself then began to whistle a tune, at the same time wobbling and shaking his enormous paunch, and the big face below his own seemed not only to whistle but to dance a strangely exotic tango for the assembled guests' amusement.[84]

Such exploits were rare during the Hollywood years, but Patrick McGilligan, via Whitfield Cook, recounts a variation as Hitchcock boarded a train from his summer home back to Los Angeles: "Alma, Cook, and other guests saw him off at the train station. The director entered his sleeping car, drew up the shades, and started a striptease 'with all the mannerisms of burlesque.'"[85]

In a bicoastal article from the late 1940s, again based on a dinner-table interview in New York City that was followed up at the Hitchcock home in Bel Air, the photographer-reporter Mary Morris informed her readers that fat men come in two varieties: "repulsive ones and cute ones." Hitchcock, in her description "fatter than Santa Claus," still exuded the "right amount of charm, wit and taste" to qualify as one of the cuties. Furthermore, she reflected, he managed to hold the attention of the public, which "generally doesn't bother to remember the names of movie directors."[86] This obvious cultural capital had one of its foundations in the body discourse that Hitchcock had set in motion as soon as he touched down in the United States. Morris's circumspect article can be read as a harbinger for Hitchcock's television work and his performance as "cute" yet ironic impish host, instead of the grotesque self-stuffing glutton who provoked mordant body jokes.

The body discourse during the Selznick era wallowed in the grotesque aspects of Hitchcock's figure. Seemingly evidencing Morris's distinction between repulsive and cute fat men, the reporters wrote up Hitchcock as full of charm and wit, an enormously entertaining dinner raconteur, fat aside. In addition, he was highly photo-palatable, even glamorous, which inspired a slew of stylized photo-essays. The macabre slyness attributed to Hitchcock came with his cherubic side—a more frequent trope than Morris's Santa—albeit intertwined with dandyesque connotations. A formidable camera hog, Hitchcock was sought out by the best photographers of his generation. This aspect of Hitchcock's marketing and hammy role-playing has mainly gone unnoticed, but is critical to his branding.

Hitchcock in his sweep of guises was a frequent subject for leading American photo magazines during their cutting-edge era, which coincided with his relocation to Hollywood in the late 1930s. Over the years, the highly constructed idea of offscreen Hitchcock was marketed by studios and elaborated on in countless magazine and newspaper articles. Having secured regular attention by seeking out journalists, he and his studio explored novel options for keeping his persona visible at a time when photo-journals such as *Life* and *Look* had garnered an immense readership. Hitchcock's penchant for role-playing and practical jokes found a new outlet in photo-essays for these magazines and others. Many of these spins were attuned to the playful corporeal register Hitchcock had launched for himself. His unruly body and detection skills, indicative of his preoccupation with crime fiction, were cleverly married in one strand of photo-essays, while the contrast between the fraught world of criminality and his calm, even dull, domestic life operated on a parallel track.

The vivacious photo-essays from the years before the television engagement helped build a Hitchcock visibility that illustrated the cuteness Morris detected. These images evidenced Hitchcock's possession of entertainer qualities outside the limited job description of film director. In this respect the photo-essays were essential for brand recognition and brand dissemination. Once television became part of the franchise, Hitchcock was less dependent on photo-journalism, and when he did appear, the television hosting provided the template. In spite of the intense circulation of Hitchcock photographs, many of the pictures I will discuss are quite rare.

The first "domestic" reportage from Hollywood after the relocation was illustrated with, among other images, a full-page photograph of the director in slippers, pajamas, and a dressing gown at his suite at the Beverly Wilshire Hotel. The only family member here is Mr. Jenkins, a Sealyham terrier that resembled Hitchcock somewhat. Sealyham puppies are very active but have a tendency to become couch potatoes. Their weight is thus a consideration, and calorie management imperative, as for Hitchcock. (For a time Sealyhams were quite in vogue in Hollywood: Cary Grant, Bette Davis, and Elizabeth Taylor were all proud owners.) In the reportage featuring Mr. Jenkins, the transplanted director is described as "pudgy little Alfred Hitchcock," as well as "amiable, moon-faced roly-poly" and an "indefatigable gourmand."[87] The reportage primarily presented *Jamaica Inn* with multiple illustrations. Sandwiched into the text, and unrelated to the reportage on Hitchcock and his dog, was a full-page advertisement for "the bread diet," headlined "Help Your

Body Burn Up Its Ugly Fat Safely!" To corroborate its effectiveness, the ad shows off several slim couples in bathing suits. Inadvertently, the reportage, while waxing fat on English Hitchcock, simultaneously displays the policing of undesirable fat in American advertising culture.

Late in the fall of 1939 Life's Geoffrey T. Hellman visited Hitchcock, and in his extensive and profusely illustrated report we meet the entire family and the two dogs. The penchant for practical jokes receives liberal space in Hellman's write up, which also has a full account of the British career as well as some of the customary biographical tidbits, including a recent "preoccupation" with the big steaks at Dave Chasen's restaurant. At the time, the family had moved into an apartment building, Wilshire Palm, while still looking for a house with a good kitchen. For home cooking and to preserve a taste of the old home in diaspora, Hitchcock had already acquired storage space for food imported from England.[88]

After moving to Hollywood, Hitchcock publicly flaunted his eccentricities and penchant for posing. In conjunction with Hellman's profile, he gave a cocktail and dinner party at Chasen's to demonstrate that he invariably fell asleep right after a meal, which was photographically documented (fig. 1.5). The photograph did not make it into Life's pages, but the copy was played up in the Los Angeles Times and subsequently by Walter Winchell: "He's fast asleep at Chasen's while everyone around him is chattering noisily."[89]

In 1942, after the Hitchcock family had found their first and only house, they were featured in a House and Garden piece titled "Hitchcock Brews Thrillers Here." The house, modest for Bel Air, seemingly confirmed Hitchcock's simple taste in everything except "food and travel."[90] This two-page essay has only three paragraphs of text accompanying six photographs that show Alma and their daughter Pat setting a lunch table on the patio, Pat in her room with images of movie stars covering the walls, Alfred sitting on a sofa with Mr. Jenkins at his feet, the back garden with a large tree, the master bedroom, and an interior shot of the dining room. Though reticent about his private life, Hitchcock still regularly invited reporters to his Bel Air home, but the summer home outside Santa Cruz was apparently off limits. According to the house-hunting specifications, food culture was at the heart of the Hitchcocks' domestic life; culinary matters were therefore a predominant aspect of these "home" texts and their illustrations. Hitchcock soon turned into a fixture in Life, straddling multiple genres of photo-essayism at a time when the family was in the process of adapting to a life in Los Angeles and Hitchcock was working busily on Rebecca.

The inaugural photo-essay offering a plot in contrast to the reportage

1.5. "Last week [Hitchcock] staged a cocktail and dinner party at Dave Chasen's for the express purpose of having his picture taken while he was asleep" ("Tattletale," *Los Angeles Times*, 17 September 1939, D9). Around the table: Geoffrey T. Hellman, Alma Hitchcock, Alfred Hitchcock, and Joan Harrison. Photograph by Peter Stackpole, courtesy of Getty Images.

genre was published in *Life* in July 1942 as a spin-off from *Saboteur* and featured a Hitchcock cameo. This essayistic *Lehrstück*, titled "Have You Heard?," is documentarian in its approach and presented as a cautionary tale. The six-page story has eighteen captioned panels following an unnumbered establishing image of a gigantic ear. It depicts a disaster that involves a troopship going down after a submarine torpedo attack. The torpedoing is carried out after an Axis agent overhears rumors at a bar about when and where the troop transport is scheduled. Hitchcock is a bartender in one of the panels (fig. 1.6). The story closes with the submarine in the foreground of the full-page image, panel 18, and the troopship burning behind it as a result of the gossip. The idea was not Hitchcock's; he was hired to produce the story, which had been kicked around at the Selznick studio in preliminary form with a more frivolous setting (nightclubs) and the sabotage aimed at a dam, with the title "Have You Heard—Suggestions for Hitchcock Rumor Story."

"Have You Heard?" showed Hitchcock's commitment to the war effort, which was the thematic backdrop for both *Saboteur* and the earlier *Foreign Cor-*

1.6. Hitchcock cameos as a barman in the photo-drama "Have You Heard?," a story involving wartime rumors that he produced for *Life*, with photographs by Eliot Elisofon. *Life*, 13 July 1942, 68–73; this photograph is on p. 72. Photograph courtesy of Getty Images.

respondent (Walter Wanger Productions, 1940), which was presented as "Movie of the Week" in *Life*. *Life* returned to Hitchcock with another in-depth, war-related article in January 1943 in conjunction with the production of *Shadow of a Doubt*. The point of departure for the text was government restrictions on set expenditures, hence the rubric "$5,000 Production." It featured shooting on location in Newark, New Jersey, and Santa Rosa, California, and was richly illustrated with J. R. Eyerman's photographs from both coasts. In conjunction with the production, Gjon Mili photographed stroboscopic images of Hitchcock and the leading cast members in Hollywood (fig. Intro.1). For the published reportage from Hollywood, Mili replaced these images with stroboscopic series featuring other actors.

In December 1943 Hitchcock returned to *Life* in an inspired photo series photographed by John Florea, appearing alongside a plant that flourished as his own bulk diminished (fig. 1.3). *Life* was, however, not the only venue for spin-offs and mischief. In 1943, while Hitchcock was shooting *Lifeboat* for Fox, he produced a photo-essay for *Look* using actors from the studio, as he had previously done for the tie-in with *Saboteur*. In the *Look* piece Hitchcock was featured in his profession, and the premise was a murder in conjunction with a film shooting. Hitchcock directed the imaginary film and also solved the murder mystery. The essay resonates with a longstanding tradition at *Look* featuring a section called "Photocrimes" written by Austin Ripley. Ripley's work had been heavily syndicated when he devised his *Minute Mysteries* in the 1930s.[91] The photocrimes in *Look* fell into the same category, with concentrated plotting and a solution that the readers had to figure out, and often with a Hollywood connection in terms of players.

"The Murder of Monty Woolley," in seven panels, was written and directed by Hitchcock, according to the credits, and photographed by Earl Theisen. Monty Woolley, nicknamed "The Beard," was a colorful academic turned drama coach and stage actor before he successfully appeared in front of the film camera. He had recently been nominated for an Academy Award for *The Pied Piper* (Twentieth Century Fox Film Corporation, 1942). In the imaginary Hitchcock film "Death Wears a Beard" (Colossal Studios) Woolley has just received a threatening letter. While sitting in the makeup chair, he tells his costar Doris Merrick that he knows the writer's identity. Guy Pearce plays the makeup artist, and he in fact worked at Fox in that capacity. In panel 3 Woolley drives off the lot during lunch. As he fails to show up on the set (panel 4) when shooting is about to resume after lunch, Hitchcock suggests a break. Soon the makeup man comes running, shouting that Woolley is dead. Sleuth-savvy Hitchcock, of course, manages to solve the crime. This spin-off evidences that Hitchcock had established himself not only as a master of suspenseful film directing but also as an astute observer of crime. He regularly elaborated on famous murder cases, comparing the English and American criminal traditions, often in jest. Hitchcock had also published several crime anthologies and, as Selznick noted, marketed himself profusely. The photocrime genre intricately blended his profession with his hobby, thus illustrating a core aspect of the Hitchcockian.

Hitchcock did not return to the photocrime genre until 1955. In the meantime he enjoyed a few hammy appearances connected to movies in the making or recently released titles. Shortly after the opening of *Notorious*, Philippe Halsman's camera depicted Hitchcock playing Ingrid Bergman, or, rather, demonstrating a handful of captioned situations in a quite absurd fashion: for example, "Polite boredom" and "Standing up when someone enters the room." "Sitting down like a lady" was broken down into "Approach to chair," "Crossing legs," and finally "Formal sitting position" (figs. 1.7 and 1.8; see also figs. 1.9 and 1.10). Bergman was nowhere to be seen during Hitchcock's athletic exercises.[92]

Subsequently Hitchcock played around on the set with props for a *Life* report on the shooting of *Rope* (Warner Bros. / Transatlantic Pictures, 1948). The film features an experimental murder committed by two young men to test their self-proclaimed superiority. After strangling their allegedly less valuable friend, they hide the corpse in a chest. In one photo Hitchcock tries out the chest prior to the meal's being arranged on top of it in the film, and in another the director is enveloped in a cloud, looking positively angelic.[93] For *Dial M for Murder* (Warner Bros., 1954), also in *Life*, Hitchcock was actually labeled a ham when fidgeting with a supremely oversized telephone. In addition the director was "malignantly puffing a cigar, glowering over a script or grandly setting the stage" in images captured by Sanford Roth.[94] When Hitchcock returned to *Look* and photocrimes in 1955, shortly before the television series commenced, the players were picked up from *The Man Who Knew Too Much* (Paramount Pictures / Filwite Productions, 1956): Jimmy Stewart, Doris Day, and Daniel Gélin, plus Hitchcock. Later a property man, Neil Wheeler, is introduced after Gélin has been poisoned on the set. Wheeler had noticed a woman in Arab costume lurking around before the murder. In panel 1, tensions are about to turn into a fight between Stewart and Gélin over Doris before Hitchcock intervenes. After the murder we learn that Wheeler hated Gélin, Stewart was jealous of Gélin, and Gélin was blackmailing Doris. Hitchcock at first takes command of the investigation and accuses Stewart; Jimmy in turn accuses Hitchcock. "Under grilling, Hitchcock confesses" after Stewart discovers the Arab costume in Hitchcock's dressing room. Gélin was blackmailing not only Doris but Hitchcock too, and Hitchcock was jealous of Stewart in this intricate love triangle plus one. The director donned the Arab costume when administering the fatal drink, hoping to kill off Gélin and frame his rival, Stewart, for the murder in one bold stroke.[95] A fascinating stylistic element here is that Hitchcock is introduced in panel 1 in a mirror doubling (fig. 1.11), which in the films and teleplays signals duplicitous scheming, a personality split, or murderous designs. Reflective multiplicity was ubiquitous in AHP, where such mirror shots abounded.

This Week, sometimes called *This Week Magazine*, was syndicated widely in the 1940s and 1950s. Carried by more than thirty newspapers, its circulation reached nearly 12 million. Hitchcock was featured in two separate issues in 1957 as interrelated spin-offs from his television series, and in all likelihood produced by Young & Rubicam, his television sponsor's advertising agency. The first photo-thriller from August 1957, "Alfred Hitchcock Presents: The Great Hitchcock Murder Mystery," is perhaps the most convoluted and bizarre item in the roster of crime-detecting photo-essays and eminently in tune with the tweaking of Hitchcock for television.[96] Here Hitchcock plays eight out

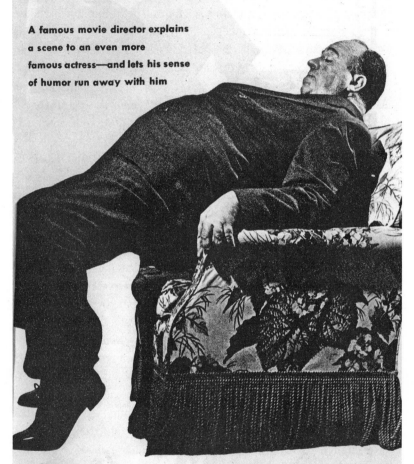

Standing up when someone enters the room is easy. All you do is crouch, grip the chair, bounce up like a Hitchcock-in-the-box, and there you are. Or are you?

1.7 (*facing*) and 1.8 (*above*). Hitchcock as Ingrid Bergman. "Ingrid Bergman—as played by Alfred Hitchcock," *Pageant* 2, no. 2 (March 1946): 38–41. Photographs by Philippe Halsman, courtesy of Magnum Photos.

of nine roles, foregoing the part of Lavender Mopeland. As he explained, "an accident of age and profile makes it impossible for me to counterfeit the charming young lady." The tale is set in "Merrie England," as are many of the stories in the television series, at Windblown Towers on the edge of Dartmoor. Here we encounter Lord Windblown, the victim of a stabbing; his widow, Lady Agatha; and her maid, Withers—all played by Hitchcock. The staff further consists of Small, the butler, and Cripps, the gardener, while Sir Roderic Gaines is a solicitor and weekend guest. To sort out the murder mystery, the none-too-bright Inspector Cranston has arrived together with Constable Bootle. One of the premises is that Lord Windblown, as guardian, has swindled money from Lavender Mopeland's estate. She is currently employed as a barmaid and enjoying the work. The story is told in first-person singular from the inspector's perspective; his first decision when arriving on the scene is to summon everybody into the library, but Lady Agatha is too upset and asks to be excused. As it turns out, she has killed her husband, and before being apprehended, she also knifes the gardener. She has been running a knife factory on the side for financial independence. This somewhat bizarre entrepreneurship distances the story from the otherwise Agatha Christie–like milieu. Alec Guinness's eight characters in *Kind Hearts and Coronets* (Ealing Studios, 1949) might have inspired Hitchcock's multiple roles: Guinness too played a Lady Agatha. The setup here draws on the Englishness cultivated as part of Hitchcock's trademark. His malleable body manages to incarnate the standard bevy of stock figures—minus the slim girl—that populate British murder mysteries (fig. 1.12).

For a function he hosted for NBC in 1957, Hitchcock appeared in a painting as Queen Victoria (fig. 1.13). The event took place around the time of postproduction work on *Vertigo*—a film in which painted portraits are significant story elements, one of them having a composite identity in the manner of Victoria and Alfred. As Hopper further reported: "Hitchcock had 20 beautiful girls dressed as widows, screaming like banshees, a corpse all ready to wheel through the drawing room. He abandoned the idea, since it was too crowded for a corpse." *Variety* offered some more details: "Dave Chasen [the

1.9 (*facing top*) and 1.10 (*facing bottom*). Philippe Halsman's photo series rubs shoulders with Ted O'Brien's photographs of Hitchcock in his specially designed chaise longue in the auditorium at the Hawaii Theatre, which opened on Hollywood Boulevard in 1940. The joke, labeled "Hitchcock Leviathan Lounge" at the Selznick studio, shows two young girls slim enough to share Hitchcock's push-back seat. Photographs courtesy of the David O. Selznick Collection, Harry Ransom Center, University of Texas at Austin.

1.11. The mirror shot and its doubling advertises Hitchcock's malicious intentions. "Photocrime," *Look*, 20 September 1955, 104–105, 114. Photograph by Robert Vose.

caterer] did some fancy scurrying to switch the festivities indoors when the rains came. . . . Visiting scribes were practically whisked from the airport directly to the party, planned as a belated Halloween event. NBC's John West, by the way, was bartender for the planeload of TV editors."[97] The widows were brought back for a *Psycho* party in 1960.

The television activities inspired additional spin-offs. A few months later, as Hitchcock took on the production responsibilities for some episodes of *Suspicion* (NBC, 1957–1958), *Look* hired him for a photocrime featuring a cast of characters from the show. In a knotted form of tie-in, the murder was an emulation of a story by Victor Canning, "The Mystery of Kela Ouai," published in the collection *This Week's Stories of Mystery and Suspense* and prefaced by Hitchcock.[98] A jealous host perpetrates the murder by lacing ice cubes with poison. Hitchcock, now back as sleuth, figures out the cocktail party scheme. A photo-essay published in the Canadian *Weekend Magazine* and syndicated in a multitude of local newspapers was actually set in Hitchcock's home, and again beverages were involved. The NBC actress Nan Leslie was invited so that Hitchcock could demonstrate for his interviewer, Stanley Handman, how to

1.12 and 1.13. Hitchcock in drag twice. For the photo-essay "The Great Hitchcock Murder Mystery" (*Los Angeles Times*, 4 August 1957, L8, 11) he appeared in eight different roles, here as Withers, the maid. Photograph by Maxwell Coplan, courtesy of the Academy of Motion Picture Arts and Sciences. The Queen Victoria portrait of Hitchcock was painted in conjunction with a party around the time of *Vertigo*. *New York Journal American*, 16 November 1957, 13. Photograph by Nat Dallinger, courtesy of University of Southern California, on behalf of the USC Libraries, Special Collections.

murder a blonde. It turns out that the preferred method in this case is to lace her champagne with peroxide, while Hitchcock shows off his art collection. He highlights his $15,000 Utrillo but does not mention a Charles Addams cartoon in the background depicting a Hitchcock figure in front of a film, or television, camera. William Read Woodfield, perhaps best known for his nude photos of Marilyn Monroe, shot the seemingly lost photos.[99] This session ties in with the photo track of food-related posing from inside the Hitchcock family kitchen run by Alma and designed by Alfred.

One of the last photographic dramatizations of the Hitchcock crime world was shot by Jeanloup Sieff at the Universal lot against the backdrop of the *Psycho* sets. For this session, Hitchcock flew down from San Francisco, where he was doing postproduction work on *The Birds* (Universal Pictures / Alfred J. Hitchcock Productions, 1963). Sieff was awarded forty-five minutes of the director's time, and he used it to have Hitchcock interact with the model Ina.

One of the photos was used in Sieff's reportage in *Harper's Bazaar*, "Hollywood Is . . . ," with Hitchcock chasing Ina outside the Bates mansion.[100] Hitchcock looks positively sinister when posing in this photo session, which is fully attuned to the violence in *Psycho*. At the same time, he carnivalizes the proceedings by means of hammy overacting that matches his stance concerning the humor in *Psycho*.[101] This again underscores the Hitchcock multiplicity and body play at the core of this study.

Kitchen Creativity

In the context of the photo-essays, Hitchcock enjoyed having the leeway to act out of line; to stand apart when quoting a film in production, such as *Rope*; or to carnivalize one of his favorite actresses, Ingrid Bergman, or his own oversized frame. The photo material offered one more gateway for Hitchcock, his producers, and their advertising agency to capitalize on the performance mode Hitchcock had set in motion from day one in America. Firmly in place as a cultural entity, as Selznick noted back in 1943,[102] the Hitchcockian brand that had been built up partly through the early photo-essays henceforth became a signifier readily available for further spin—with crime stories, domestic reportage, and film promotion dominating the materials here discussed. More than any Hollywood director, and this was the heart of the matter in Selznick's observation, Hitchcock had transcended the role of mere contract director and turned himself into a cultural commodity. By dramatizing himself for brand purposes and extracting elements from his individual films and his genre, he crested a seamless rapport between Hitchcock images and the Hitchcockian connotations. This was further cemented once his large figure moved onto the small screen and in the process substituted hamming for detached posing, often captured in a modernist style of photography.

Leaving behind the act of stuffing himself in public or sleeping at restaurants after dinner, in the television era Hitchcock adopted a slightly melancholy mode, facing very small portions while discussing dieting regimes or entertaining interviewers with recipes for his favorite dishes and considerable knowledge of Edwardian food culture. In 1958 Selma Robinson wrote the piece most indicative of this shift toward smaller portions and home cooking, in which Hitchcock talked candidly about the hardships of dieting, especially when entertaining at restaurants. The text is illustrated with an image of Hitchcock looking forlornly at a plate with a tiny portion. He was asked to compose his ideal dinner (if he were not on a diet), which led to a discussion of Edwardian cuisine and its many courses in the manner of a tasting menu—the emblematic chef was Georges-Auguste Escoffier—before the interview closed with Hitchcock's suggestions for "a good dinner on a diet."[103] In conjunction with Escoffier, Hitchcock wistfully recalled quail cooked with grapes, which is one of the gourmet dishes prepared by Mrs. Oxford for her unappreciative husband in Frenzy many years later.

For Hitchcock, the old food grotesque was sensual in the extreme, while home cooking during the television era, as demonstrated in photo-essays, removed the actual eating and upheld a professional aura concerning food preparation, with Alma as home chef in the family's remodeled kitchen. The modernist mise-en-scène of the kitchen was quite sparse and favored visual victuals and recipes for emulation. The seriousness of the food culture shown off chez Hitchcock marked the home as retreat and refuge, and eating as temperate, elegant, devoid of offensive abundance, and a point of convergence for cosmopolitan food items and wines flown in from choice locations. This rhymed with the conception of domestic life as a moderate, albeit exquisite, version of somewhat ostentatious Bel Air. The serious tone for home gastronomy removed both the grotesque and the playfulness of old—for example, when Hitchcock served only blue food for a dinner, mirroring, one presumes, Des Esseintes's black meal in J. K. Huysmans's À rebours.[104]

In a newspaper discussion a few years before Robinson's essay, dieting readers were invited to request copies of Hitchcock's favorite diets, the high-protein diet and the liquid diet.[105] Louella Parsons soon thereafter offered more details concerning the dietary regime with photographs of Hitchcock eating and inhaling the savory aroma from a chicken casserole Alma was preparing (fig. 1.14). This is one of the few reports featuring home cooking in action in the beginning of the television era that continues all the way to actual eating—from a time before the Hitchcocks' kitchen was redesigned in the early 1960s to better serve Alma's skills as chef. Rounding off Parsons's text, Hitchcock offered a recipe for steak and kidney pie, in line with the Englishness of his television show.[106]

The photograph showing Hitchcock eating in some versions of this syndicated piece is indicative of the reportage's transitional status. Somewhat ironically, the close-up of Hitchcock consuming food was captioned "Famed for film thrillers, Alfred Hitchcock has won praise for equally deft handling of food." The table photographs, posing with edible props, were soon thereafter theatricalized and detached from actual eating, at home as well as in public. The preparatory food culture–cum–small talk and culinary historiography connected to crafting films coincided with posing with birds—both inside and outside food contexts. After Philippe Halsman's promotional photog-

1.14. Chez Alfred: A visit to the Hitchcocks' kitchen. The photograph was used in Louella O. Parsons, "Kitchen No Mystery to the Master of Mystery," *Los Angeles Examiner*, 24 June 1956, Magazine Section. Courtesy of University of Southern California, on behalf of the USC Libraries, Special Collections.

raphy for The Birds, avian portraiture turned into prime references or "inter-images" for visual paraphrase as a form of signature or surrogate imagery for Hitchcock. The bird photographs sometimes referenced food as pretext for the macabre, often featuring blackbirds emerging from pies or pots. A parallel avian strand came with sexual overtones—for example, a cover portrait for Diners' Club Magazine in May 1963, the year The Birds was released. The illustration shows Hitchcock with two girls dolled up in outfits reminiscent of girlie magazines. In other contexts, an oversized cigar was sufficient for a sexual allusion, as in the Esquire photo-essay to be discussed below.

When the Hitchcocks dined with Wade H. Mosby of the Milwaukee Journal in the Ambassador East's Pump Room in Chicago in 1962, a time when eating with journalists was a rarity, diet talk was off the table. The venue was the hotel where Eve Kendall stays in North by Northwest. Mosby duly reported on what Hitchcock ordered, while the director spun an impromptu murder story built around characters with names made up from studio lingo: Pan Over, Dolly Shot, and so on. In the midst of the proceedings, Hitchcock pensively claimed that "restaurants are horrible places to eat. The things they do with food." Hitchcock's reflection prompted a parenthetical aside from Mosby: "Mrs. Hitchcock confided that she had a new kitchen in her home in Bel Air, Calif., and that Hitch liked everything she cooked—except shellfish." True to his current food moderation, Hitchcock had a fish for starters but did not finish his roast beef and even asked for a doggy bag to take away the remains for Stanley and Jeffrey, the Sealyhams.[107] The jest about dreadful restaurants segueing to Alma's new kitchen neatly illustrates the displacement of food enjoyment from restaurants to exquisite home cooking and moderate-sized portions. In this spirit, the food discourse predominantly moved from the public to the private sphere, Alfred and Alma's house, which was obviously designed for cooking and eating. The makeover of the kitchen mirrors the makeover of Hitchcock's persona, partly orchestrated by Allardice's scripting of Hitchcock for TV, talks, and public performances.

At the Hitchcocks' mansion the domestic routines revolved around food preparation. Hitchcock noted: "I designed the kitchen so madame can cook in the most elegant surroundings and serve those of us who patiently wait there, sipping good wine, for her to complete her culinary masterpieces."[108] As the conversation around eating turned more refined and erudite over the years, the Hitchcock figure and the food discourse became more complex and mediated in a broader context, especially in photo-essays. As food culture became theatricalized and abstracted, Hitchcock, with or without Alma, posed with food items before or during preparation, or carving, while mainly pushing

1.15. Alimentary modernism. "The Alfred Hitchcock Dinner Hour," Look, 27 August 1963, 42–44. Photograph by Cal Bernstein, courtesy of LOOK Magazine Photograph Collection, Library of Congress, Prints and Photographs Division, LC-L9O1A-63-1256, no. 1.

actual eating off frame, thus eliminating the critical stuffing element of the former grotesque.

The gourmet cooking at home reinforced this conceptualization, not least owing to the sleek style of photography deployed for a Look photo-essay from 1963, as a form of alimentary modernism displaying a sophisticated form of domestic food culture in matching visual style (fig. 1.15).[109] The early rounds of home reportage, in contrast, operated with a down-to-earth, realistic photo style culminating with Louella Parsons's visit and a close-up of Hitchcock eating. After the kitchen makeover, the style changed. Just as important, this retreat to the home underscored Hitchcock's lifelong partnership and collaborative ventures with Alma Reville Hitchcock. She cooked, Alfred ate; he directed, she was the perennial script supervisor. So from inside the kitchen, Alma enters the picture. When they were eating in public in the era of the grotesque, she was at the table, but mainly mentioned in passing as a silent, small, and birdlike accessory, often painted in amusing contrast to her husband's heft—for example, as "half-pint missus."[110]

Louella Parsons's reportage from 1956 offered a recipe for an English dish while the couple was preparing a French chicken specialty. The photo-essay in Look from 1963 came with three French recipes and was titled "The Alfred Hitchcock Dinner Hour"—a reference to the new television series. Here Alfred is written into the cooking sphere. Alma is, in fact, jestingly pegged as his sous chef, even though she is credited for her own contributions to the dishes being prepared, to which Alfred can lay claim in the name of California community property. Cal Bernstein's photographic style abstracted the alimentary sphere in a visual rhetoric, simultaneously playfully allegorical and hyper-realistic. The only full-page image is arranged as a Dutch still life, albeit with the Hitchcocks in the picture seemingly engaged in careful culinary deliberations indicative of their customary conversation at home. While he stands in the freezer, the "king-size chiller," Hitchcock's left hand gently squeezes the throat of one of the geese hanging along the wall. A Hitchcock quotation serves as lead-in by setting the tone for the intertwining of food and cinema: "Food, like pure cinema, is putting pieces together to create an emotion, . . . independently meaningless, together they mean something." Consequently, "in his home, dinner is perfection, conceived and created with the same care he puts into his distinctive thrillers." The remodeled home thus "provides the proper aesthetics and functional 'props' for their culinary productions." Turning the page, we find a medium shot of Alma Hitchcock preparing a vanilla soufflé. A second, high-angle photograph shows off the many fully

stocked racks of wine in the cellar. The heading for the recipes has a familiar but uncanny ring: "Recipes for specialties of the House of Hitchcock."[111]

As the television series came to a close in 1965, Hitchcock was less in demand, or more reluctant to pose for the magazines, while his films created considerably less buzz than they had during his television decade. The photo-essays did not disappear completely, but they remained on point and rehashed familiar topics—albeit at times imaginatively and by way of wonderful artwork—with food and his body as constants. In conjunction with *Family Plot* almost a decade later, Hitchcock was back on the marketing track. He posed as "distinguished guest gourmet" in *Harper's Bazaar* to present Alfred Hitchcock's Christmas Dinner Menu. The title of the piece written in Hitchcock's name gives away the main attraction: "Alfred Hitchcock Cooks His Own Goose." The instructions for preparing the goose were quite elaborate, as with the recipes in 1963, and not for the squeamish. They began with removal of the goose's head, in tune with the tenor of the carving piece. Two photos shot by Albert Watson featured Hitchcock and the goose before the preparations. Hitchcock again elaborated on Edwardian menus and Escoffier's dozen or so small courses.[112]

The very last instance of a journalist being entertained over dinner took place, appropriately, at Chasen's in 1976, at the table where the Hitchcocks had dined every Thursday, when in town, for more than thirty years. Gene Daniels photographed Hitchcock at the table, glass in hand, for the cover of *Holiday* magazine and up closer as an illustration for the article. Hitchcock told Sylvie Drake that he was a "mixed gourmet" in that he "liked fine yet simple food" like boeuf bourguignon and oxtails. This latter dish shifted the discussion to home cooking, as Alma, according to her husband, had a very good hand with oxtails. While ordering barley soup, breaded veal cutlet, and ice cream topped with a strawberry sauce, Hitchcock entertained Sylvie Drake with a list of favorite restaurants in London and Paris before turning the conversation to imports for the private wine cellar. As a preamble, as it were, to Pat Hitchcock's book about the woman behind the man, and as a holdover from the 1963 *Look* essay, the Chasen's report is rounded off with detailed recipes for quiche lorraine, pork and veal paté, and two versions of soufflé (cheese and sweet).[113] It also brought the couple back to where Hitchcock in 1939 demonstrated his habit of falling asleep after dinner (fig. 1.5).

When Hitchcock, very late in his career, received the American Film Insti-

---

1.16 (*facing*). Contact copies from a session for *Harper's Bazaar*. Photographs by and courtesy of Albert Watson. The photo-essay was published in *Harper's Bazaar*, no. 109 (December 1975): 132–133.

tute's Lifetime Achievement Award, his succinct acceptance speech underwrote the tenets of the kitchen creativity and dynamics explored here: "I beg
to mention by name only four people who have given me the most affection,
appreciation, encouragement and constant collaboration. The first of the four
is a film editor, the second is a scriptwriter, the third is the mother of my
daughter, Pat, and the fourth is as fine a cook as ever performed miracles in a
domestic kitchen. And their names are Alma Reville."[114]

Time now to slowly and gingerly step over the threshold and trespass inside Hitchcock's scary televisual story world. As is often the case in the teleplays, "Specialty of the House" (*Alfred Hitchcock Presents* [AHP] 165) is all about food, this time served behind a secluded door to a supper club, Spirro's. In this episode exquisite food is the members' sole desire. If ever granted, a visit to Spirro's mysterious kitchen, where the delicacies are cooked up, comes as a phenomenal bonus at the end of a trial membership period, followed by full membership, and then, ideally, lifelong membership—which, however, can be quite short. The protagonist in the story, Mr. Laffler, is played by Robert Morley, a witty, not very thin Englishman and food connoisseur in real life as well as in the teleplay.[1]

Lifelong membership at Spirro's and a visit to its kitchen are Mr. Laffler's top desires. As Mr. Laffler finally is granted the much anticipated visit, he is escorted into the meat freezer, where a sharp cleaver greets him. After proper marinating, he ends up on the other guests' plates as Lamb Armistran.

The vile subtext of cannibalism functions as an illustration of Hitchcock's penchant for the macabre in his body-obsessed franchise. Hitchcock, as predominantly was the case, appears only in the prologue and epilogue, having outsourced the directing to the versatile Robert Stevens (who was responsible for more series episodes than any other director). Variations of cannibalism abound in Hitchcock's work and references. For example, Lord Dunsany's short story "Two Bottles of Relish," which he mentions several times and even published in the collection *Alfred Hitchcock's Fireside Book of Suspense* (1947), features boiled-down bodies bottled as a condiment.[2] In a subsequent collection of stories marketed as too much to stomach for television, several contributions connect perfect murders to unblushing or furtive cannibalism. The collection's opening story, Arthur Williams's "Being a Murderer Myself," was later directed by Hitchcock as "Arthur" (AHP 154), while C. P. Donnel Jr.'s story in the same collection shared its title with a photo-essay marketing *Psycho*: "My Recipe for Murder."[3] Given this barrage of human flesh too close to the plates for comfort, one critic noted that Hitchcock "seemed obsessed with cannibalism and necrophilism."[4]

For this episode, based on an outrageously successful short story by Stanley Ellin—in fact his debut, published in 1948—Hitchcock's team, as it often did, settled for a primarily British cast, Robert Morley and Kenneth Haigh, alongside the New York nightclub queen Spivy Le Voe, who played Spirro. "Specialty of the House," one of eight episodes adapted by the franchise from an Ellin story, is set at Spirro's dinner club, a place reserved for men only (except for Spirro herself), and takes dining to an almost obsessive level. At Spirro's a mainly older clientele congregates every evening to savor the exquisite cooking, some even traveling from other continents several times a year for the sole purpose of dining there. Spirro's kitchen serves only one entrée per night, and the menu is composed according to her fancy, the availability of ingredients, and the offerings of the daily catch. What the members relish and eagerly await are the choice nights when the specialty of the house, Lamb Armistran, is served.

Unaware they are feasting on man marinated as lamb, the members are sheepishly united by their craving for that extraordinary dish, an obsession that proves lethal. Spirro conspires with the only young man in the club, Mr. Costain (Kenneth Haigh), who is brought to Spirro's by his employer, Mr. Laffler, as a guest and then becomes a member when the latter enters the freezer. As Mr. Laffler is being prepared for marinating, the young man brings his employer's photograph to be added to the gallery of retired members—all of them, we are led to believe, previously consumed in the conspiratorial game cooked up by Spirro and her all-male staff. The young man's role in all this remains enigmatic and, if nothing else, offers food for thought.

A fundamental change for the screen adaptation is the gender shift of its main character. Spirro is a man in the short story, but a woman in the show, and she runs her club in all respects: she sets the rules for membership, she entertains during the meal, she composes the menu, and she, as a rare treat only, can invite a guest to visit the kitchen. There are, however, many hurdles before a member is invited to enter this queendom. Such a long-desired invitation represents the climactic moment in a sexualized food economy; but,

Interlude I.1. In Spirro's kitchen. From "Specialty of the House" (AHP 165).

as our featured member learns, the entrance to the back room turns out to be a much colder affair than anticipated.

Spivy Le Voe, known professionally as Madame Spivy, ran a successful supper club or night club, Spivy's Roof, on East Fifty-Seventh Street throughout the 1940s. In her club she sang satirical off-color songs, some of them recorded on rare labels, while creating an offbeat, risqué atmosphere. Her lesbian aura added to the reputation of the venue. After losing the lease, Spivy opened clubs in Rome, Paris, and London with mixed success. Following her club years she acted in small parts, first on Broadway and later in Hollywood.[5] Le Voe was thus surrounded by a choice set of transgressing signifiers when she became Spirro for the Hitchcock episode. And she acted the part with macabre delight.

"Specialty of the House," as mentioned, was not directed by Hitchcock: he only supervised. Similarly, Spirro explains her role in the kitchen thus: "I only supervise; the only dish I personally prepare is Lamb Armistran." The gender switch has profound symbolic implications if we want to go that route. In addition Spivy's brand of sexuality offers opportunities for multiple readings. Whether or not she eats the men she occasionally serves up remains unclear. The maternal power is, however, absolute when it comes to food. As Mr. Laffler explains to his young associate apropos Spirro's dictatorial eating regime:

"My mother used to say, we eat what is set before us and we like it." This associates Spirro with the maternal, and the power she wields over the young man might represent a form of motherly affection when she recruits him as accessory to her lamb preparation. Costain in a sense participates in the slaying of a father figure, and besides eventually eating Laffler, he takes over his office, removing his former employer's framed photograph and giving it to Spirro to add to the gallery, or menu, of resigned members.

Judging from the table reception, human flesh masquerading as lamb is a much more palate-friendly dish than the symbolic cannibal menu served by Mrs. Oxford in Hitchcock's Frenzy. In Tania Modleski's keen discussion, Mrs. Oxford's home cooking is read as repugnant and associated with defiled female flesh, or, rather, bare bones.[6] The male flesh served as lamb at Spirro's, in pointed contrast, is deliciously tender and boneless, but offered too seldom and in undersized portions, according to the guests. There is no food moderation on their part as they scramble for more. Spirro's cooking camouflages the raw nature of cannibalism, while the elaborate cooking à la française in Mrs. Oxford's haute cuisine apparently only serves to underscore the raw, and thus revolting, aspects of the bony dishes her husband chokes on; hence his surreptitious feasting on pub fare away from home.

Frenzy pits traditional English grub against virtually inedible foreign dishes, and Mrs. Oxford even serves a margarita cocktail to her husband's flustered colleague, which prompts his quick exit after a small sip, leaving the bartender to finish the drink in a resigned swig. The sexless marriage, Mrs. Oxford hints, offers a premise for her exotic cooking frenzy. Her husband seems to prefer to suffer silently at the home table—and take care of his food needs at the office—rather than return to bed with her. Hitchcock, with his penchant for French cuisine and pleasure from the neck up, would have been more appreciative at Mrs. Oxford's table, where the bread sticks crack in precise rhythm with the discussion of breaking fingers frozen in rigor mortis.

In Spirro's capable hands the marinated human flesh is cooked to perfection and greeted as the ultimate dish, residing at the very apex of delectable food, at least when advertised as lamb. Spirro seemingly orchestrates the ultimate revenge on patriarchy by organizing a club where the members excitedly feast on each other's flesh unbeknownst. One can perhaps read this as a female, lesbian-tinged conspiracy feeding on Spivy's offscreen reputation. In addition, an exotic code is in play: the only server with dialogue has an accent that might be French; Spirro herself comes with an undetermined cosmopolitan aura; the only vice president of the club is a gentleman from Singapore; and the location is liminal, in San Francisco's nondescript harbor area. In sum, this particular show, supervised solely by Hitchcock, strongly resonates with choice concerns running through both his cinema and his offscreen proclivities regarding practical jokes. The grisly one played on the members here is quite something.[7]

In the grander scheme of the Hitchcockian and a franchise predicated on body play, cannibalism takes body obsession to its absolute extreme. In a refined setting, the cooking up of the members' flesh provides the classic twist ending that the teleplays often served up. A shocking twist was a key criterion for story scouting, but even more important to the series was the signature host segment. As the presenter of his own television show, Hitchcock became a legend. The novel scope for dishing out the Hitchcockian each week wrapped his profile and figure in trappings that impacted the franchise and preset his performance mode for the rest of his career.

2. SMALLER SCREEN, BIGGER BRAND
HOSTING "HITCHCOCK"

TV in the Making

When Hitchcock's contract with Selznick expired after *The Paradine Case* (1947), and with the brand firmly in place, as his producer had noted already in a memo in 1943,[1] Hitchcock was free at last to explore other options. He elected to set up and operate under Transatlantic Pictures, which he co-owned together with the British exhibitor Sidney Bernstein (the Granada Group), with Warner Bros. as distributors (and sometimes producers). Although he was still operating from America, the partial retreat to a British-based business constellation guaranteed a higher level of independence for Hitchcock after his seven itchy years under contract with Selznick. The Transatlantic titles (*Rope* [1948] and *Under Capricorn* [1949]) were no smash hits, and neither were the Warner films, with the exception of *Strangers on a Train* (1951). In 1953 Hitchcock shelved Transatlantic Pictures and embarked on a fresh start in Hollywood, now under contract with Paramount and with *Rear Window* (1954) as the first venture. Hitchcock's public persona was still regularly showcased, not least owing to Hedda Hopper and her colleagues' levity in the columns, and fueled by the man himself as the mash-up of photo-essays evidences.

Parallel to the move to Paramount, Lew Wasserman, Hitchcock's agent at the Music Corporation of America (MCA) and later studio head at Universal (and perhaps the last Hollywood mogul), with his customary foresight, managed to talk his client into broadening the media repertoire to include work for television.[2] Myron Selznick, Hitchcock's first agent and the man who paved the way for his relocation to Hollywood, had prematurely died of a stroke in 1944; he was born the same year as his client, 1899.

After protracted negotiations, the premiere of *Alfred Hitchcock Presents* (AHP) was formally announced in a January 1955 press release that outlined all the components of the show. There would be thirty-nine installments during the 1955–1956 season, all produced by Hitchcock or someone he would assign, and the sponsorship was picked up by the Bristol-Myers Company, a pharmaceutical behemoth with a high stake in radio and television. The Sunday slot at 9:30 p.m. on CBS was already set for the broadcast, and mystery, suspense, and humor were advertised as the program's signature ingredients.[3] The sponsor was represented during the negotiations by Young & Rubicam, its advertising agency. By way of further embellishment, Hitchcock, in an interview for the *New York Times* during the summer, outlined the plot of Roald Dahl's short story "Lamb to the Slaughter" as ideal for the type of half-hour show he envisioned. Directing six episodes himself and hiring young directors for the remainder, he would, in addition, "supervise their work and also narrate all of the subjects." Filming was to commence in August at the Republic lot, at a time when Hitchcock expected to have *The Man Who Knew Too Much* (1956) in the can. Tellingly, the entry on Hitchcock in Thomas M. Pryor's condensed column of notes from Hollywood is labeled "Joker"; this alludes to Hitchcock's penchant for buffoonery and dramatization of his persona as a sideshow for his films.[4]

In another advance notice, Emily Belser displayed her familiarity with the discursive framing when she wrote, "Hitch, who has gone from 300 pounds to a sylph-like 195, is venturing into the realms of TV at the prodding of his agents who think it's about time he spreads out—his talents, that is. Naturally, the Hitchcock dramas will be exciting, insidious, and hair-raising."[5] When the show opened, the tongue-in-cheek ad in *TV Guide* promised a "tasty dish of thrills served up in the inimitable Hitchcock sauce."[6] Regardless of screen size, the Hitchcock brand inspired and resorted to bodily descriptors and culinary metaphors.

Hitchcock had been reluctant, but tempted by a singularly lucrative contract, he signed.[7] His picking up the full rights to the material as his personal property after the first airing sweetened the deal. As a domestic syndication market began to develop parallel to the global spread of television, such controlling rights proved to be lucrative assets. In the summer of 1955 Hitchcock announced that his former assistant, Joan Harrison, had been hired for the television show's production team (fig. 2.1). A member of the Hitchcock entourage when it had left England for the Selznick studio, she worked for him in Hollywood as an assistant and scriptwriter before beginning a career as a film producer and later a producer of a television series, *Janet Dean, Registered*

2.1. Joan Harrison (1907–1994) in a script conference with Alfred Hitchcock in 1957. Photograph by Robert Vose, courtesy of LOOK Magazine Photograph Collection, Library of Congress, Prints and Photographs Division, LC-L9-57-4269-H, no. 10.

Nurse, starring Ella Raines.[8] It was on this show, shot in New York and lasting only one season (1954–1955), that Joan Harrison cut her teeth as a television producer. Some of the people she worked with resurfaced in the Hitchcock show—for example, the director James Neilson.[9]

When Harrison was hired, Hitchcock had already enlisted his British story scout from the Transatlantic days, Mary Elsom, to dig up material suitable for the television format he fancied. According to an oft-quoted letter he wrote to Elsom, the template should be "short stories by well-known authors . . . definitely of the suspense, or thriller, type. . . . One important factor that should be common to all of them . . . is that the ending should have a 'twist' almost to a point of shock in either the last line or the last situation."[10] It was not by happenstance that the search for material was conducted out of England, as the explicit model was Dahl's "Lamb to the Slaughter." Later Pat Hitchcock, in addition to her involvement with *Alfred Hitchcock's Mystery Magazine*, "help[ed] her father hunt for suitable TV material. He accept[ed] about 90 percent of her suggestions."[11]

In bare figures, Hitchcock's production company, Shamley, produced more than 370 television episodes from the fall of 1955 to the 1964–1965 season. Of those ten seasons, seven featured AHP in half-hour format, for a total of 268 episodes; Hitchcock directed 17 of these teleplays. CBS aired the show's first

2.2. The gloomy host reaps revenue from the sponsor's products. Among those that Bristol-Myers advertised were Bufferin (an aspirin preparation), Vitalis (hair tonic for men), Ipana (toothpaste), and Ban (deodorant). Publicity still. Photograph courtesy of Photofest.

five seasons, and NBC the last two. Of the subsequent three seasons, comprising 93 episodes of *The Alfred Hitchcock Hour* (AHH), the first two were broadcasted by CBS and the last one was picked up by NBC; Hitchcock directed only one show for AHH, "I Saw the Whole Thing" (AHH 4). While AHH had multiple sponsors, the half-hour show at CBS was carried by the customary model of single sponsorship: Bristol-Myers for the first four seasons and Bristol-Myers and Clairol in season five (Bristol-Myers acquired Clairol in 1957). When AHP moved over to NBC, Ford Motors and Revlon shared the sponsor role.[12] In addition, the Hitchcock franchise produced ten hour-long episodes in the series *Suspicion* for NBC during the 1957–1958 season. Hitchcock directed the series premiere, "Four O'Clock," featuring E. G. Marshall. He also directed one show for *Ford Startime* in 1960, "Incident at a Corner." Finally, the franchise produced one show for *Alcoa Premiere* in 1962, "The Jail," directed by Norman Lloyd and featuring John Gavin, known from *Psycho* (Shamley's sole feature film production).

Apart from its inimitable host, the format for AHP was no novelty: CBS had broadcasted its mystery and crime series, *Suspense*, live from New York for six seasons commencing in 1949. Hitchcock took the format to Hollywood and to film stock. Many performers, directors, and writers overlapped between the two series. More interesting is that the Hitchcock series, in addition to those Elsom, Pat Hitchcock, and the producing team might have brought in, produced a number of stories that had previously featured in *Suspense*—for example, "Revenge" (AHP 1), "Help Wanted" (AHP 27), "The Creeper" (AHP 38), "De Mortuis" (AHP 42), "Alibi Me" (AHP 46), "The Rose Garden" (AHP 51), "The Hands of Mr. Ottermole" (AHP 71), "Listen, Listen" (AHP 110), "Post Mortem" (AHP 111), "The Kiss-Off" (AHP 212), and "The Monkey's Paw—a Retelling" (AHH 90). And writers like Francis Cockrell and directors like Robert Stevens were credited for their work on *Suspense* before Harrison recruited them for AHP. *Suspense* was a television show with a longstanding radio pedigree going back to the early 1940s; Hitchcock was keen on appearing on radio in the early 1940s, but his studio and agency dissuaded him.

Wasserman's pitch came at a time when MCA's subsidiary company, Revue, was gradually turning into a force to be reckoned with in Hollywood television, as analyzed by Christopher Anderson.[13] Apart from packaging an array of pedestrian, bread-and-butter shows, Revue garnered cultural prestige with the *General Electric Theater* (CBS, 1953–1962), hosted by Ronald Reagan at a time when live, New York–produced dramatic shows were being increasingly supplanted by telefilm productions from Hollywood. This process was spearheaded by Revue alongside the Desilu franchise and its successful *I Love Lucy*

(CBS, 1951–1961). With Hitchcock on the MCA-Revue roster, the company hoped for significant profits and critical cachet. In the fall of 1955, after hesitating, several film studios began producing their own shows for television — Warner Bros. in September and Fox in October, both for ABC, a network with limited resources of their own for expensive anthology productions or spectaculars, the latter a staple at NBC.

Alfred Hitchcock Presents began airing on Sunday, 2 October 1955. In a column published that very morning, Jack Gould, the *New York Times'* renowned television critic, unfavorably compared American commercial television to the recently inaugurated British version. Independent Television (ITV) began broadcasting in September 1955 parallel to the longstanding public-service network, the British Broadcasting Corporation (BBC). The ITV network would broadcast AHP from 1957.

The following day Gould reviewed the opening installment of AHP on CBS. He described it as "routine Hitchcock" but added that "the director's personal appearance was something not to be missed." The host's "superb disdain for the usual TV amenities" endeared him to the critic. In conclusion, Gould claimed that the "sardonic introduction to the commercials should gain [Hitchcock] a Peabody Award with no trouble at all." From the very outset, Gould and the critical establishment at large struck a chord that would permeate the reception throughout the series' run: a split between the innovative frame featuring Alfred Hitchcock and the occasionally unoriginal stories leading to the more or less imaginative twist endings. In regard to the director's stature — whether it was Hitchcock himself or someone he supervised — they were no "match for Hitchcock, the maître d'."[14] This split and its further branches are critical for our discussion of Hitchcock's showmanship and role-playing — and eminently in tune with Gjon Mili's chorus line of stroboscopic Hitchcocks (fig. Intro.1).

The figure Hitchcock performed as television host was decidedly English. Joan Harrison's background and the recruiting of Elsom further evidence the penchant for British stories and settings. And across seasons a steady stream of actors were British — from John Williams, a fixture on the show, to Roger Moore's single performance. Detecting an American inspiration among the overwhelming Englishness, Don Page, a few years later, called Hitchcock the host "television's lardy O. Henry."[15] Fat, twists, British wit, and a bit of re-framed O. Henry were thus the main ingredients for Hitchcock's television discourse and the brand's body politics. Or, as the scriptwriter for the show's prologues and epilogues, Jimmie Allardice, directly stated: "With a comic like Hitch . . . I have three things to bounce the humor from — his disdain for the commercials, his weight and his sense of the macabre."[16] "Comic" is a singularly important category here, one drawing on a multitude of traditions and styles and in tune with Hollis Alpert's "autopsy" of Hitchcock's body of work.[17]

In the very first television prologue Hitchcock described the genre of the show as "stories of suspense and mystery" and his own role as "an accessory after the fact." He introduced the sponsor without much of an edge, as someone (anthropomorphically referred to as a "gentleman") who filled out the time until the actors were ready, as if the show were broadcast live. Over the years, format and media jokes were prevalent in the host segments. After the chilling episode titled "Revenge," about a trailer-park rape and the subsequent murder of a misidentified perpetrator, Hitchcock returns to round out. This time the irony vis-à-vis the sponsor comes with more pointed references, as "certain quarters" protested the original title, "Death of a Salesman." Furthermore, since "crime doesn't pay, not even on television," a sponsor is called for, which segues to the last of the three commercial blocks, after which Hitchcock closes with a snide comment on Bristol-Myers's commercial for its laxative product, Sal Hepatica: "That was beautifully put."

Tersely summing up the television month of October 1955, Jack Gould remained as unimpressed by Hitchcock as with the abundance of filmed anthology series in general, opining, "The master isn't trying very hard."[18] Ironically, Gould received a Personal Peabody in 1956 "for his outstanding contribution to radio and television criticism through his New York Times writings," while Hitchcock never received the award, which Gould predicted as a sure thing. Hitchcock was nominated for an Emmy as presenter for 1955 but lost to Perry Como and in fact never received this honor. Tellingly, Robert Stevens, the show's go-to director, was the only one to get an Emmy Award for AHP: he won Best Direction for the 1957 episode "The Glass Eye" (AHP 79). The series won the Golden Globe twice, in 1957 and 1958, and racked up three Look Awards, one for the directing and two for the series, plus a bunch of minor awards. And as for the big screen, Oscar famously eluded Hitchcock in the directing category.[19]

Gould, an ardent proponent of the original New York–based television model predicated on live broadcasting and drama as the quintessential material, was no friend of canned shows from the Hollywood studios and hence wasted precious few words on Alfred Hitchcock over the next ten years.[20] He was thus fully in tune with the comedian George Gobel's self-conscious quip introducing his show—"This comes to you dead from Hollywood," referring to Hollywood's nonlive, canned television—and added one of his own: "The films especially made for TV? A sorry lot, by and large."[21]

Regardless of the popular recognition of Hitchcock's cinema and his television hosting over the years, the critical reception of AHP remained mixed, as many television critics like Gould disliked Hollywood television on principle. The Hitchcock figure's prefatory and concluding on-screen appearances, in contrast, inspired undiluted critical awe and became iconic in the very process of emerging, as Gould and the critical establishment noted, with Alpert as a sole dissident.

As an expatriate film director nursing a carefully cultivated English persona in Hollywood, Hitchcock had sworn allegiance to the flag shortly before the television show opened. When he signed on for the project, Hitchcock was a winning proposition, highbrow skepticism aside. Just a couple of weeks after AHP opened was the premiere of the film *The Trouble with Harry* (1955)—this "curiously whimsical thing," as Gould's renowned colleague Bosley Crowther perceptively put it.[22] With writers seemingly at a loss for a catchy descriptor, the marketing campaign for this out-of-character nonthriller was carried out under the bland sales banner of "unexpected" for Hitchcock, the otherwise perennial master of the thriller genre. Penelope Houston likewise notes that one Hitchcock film "stands apart" when she refers to *The Trouble with Harry* as "that conversation piece and divertissement."[23] More than any other of his films, however, its whimsies and upbeat mode resonate with the focus on merry murdering that runs through Hitchcock discourse as a macabre thread. Whimsical or not, *The Trouble with Harry*, an enduring favorite with Hitchcock, was, in fact, screened for Allardice as exemplary in tone for sought-after scripting of the director's television appearance.

Allardice single-handedly authored a decade's worth of Hitchcock's ingenious lead-ins and postscripts. He also won an Emmy in March 1955 for his contribution as comedy cowriter of NBC's popular *George Gobel Show* (NBC, 1954–1959; CBS, 1959–1960), which gives an indication of the digressive, self-conscious comedic style that Hitchcock and his people opted for. As Hitchcock explained: "The style comes from one of my pictures, *The Trouble With Harry*, the man who writes them so expertly is James Allardice, who used to create some of the George Gobel humor."[24] In a televised interview in 1962, Ralph Story asked Hitchcock about Allardice's contributions:

Story: Where did you get these ideas, the lead-ins? Who thinks them up?
Hitchcock: I have a very fine man who collaborates in the writing of them, a Mr. James Allardice.
Story: One might think you're keeping Mr. Allardice down in the vault like Jack Benny's.
Hitchcock: Oh, no. Mr. Allardice is alive because I've seen him eat.[25]

2.3. James B. Allardice (1919–1966), the man behind Hitchcock's on-tube performances. Photograph courtesy of Jim Allardice.

That same year, besides eating, Allardice was scripting the radio spots for the reissue of *Rear Window*. However, he never got any on-screen credit for his scripting of the host segments.

The combination of Allardice's facetious scripts and Hitchcock's peerless delivery proved to be a perfect fit for television. As one headline tersely but pointedly described the division of labor: "The Face, Hitchcock—The Words, Allardyce [sic]."[26] Even outside the show, Allardice contributed to many of Hitchcock's public performances over the years—later scripting trailers featuring Hitchcock for *North by Northwest* (1959), *Psycho* (1960), and *The Birds* (1963)—up until the writer's premature death shortly after the end of the television run. Not until scripted by Allardice for television were the lingering signifiers of the grotesque supplanted by a richer character palette, tinted with low-key absurdist wit and delivered in a wily, mischievous British drawl. Television thus turned the figure of Alfred Hitchcock into a very different type of commodity from just an overweight director of genre films with a penchant for somewhat coarse stunts, like telling scatological jokes to leading ladies just before shooting.[27]

Hitchcock entered the television world as an internationally renowned master of suspenseful films and a bona fide franchise star. The recasting of the Hitchcock persona in the television context is critical for its open, head-on play with the body discourse. In spite of the character "upgrade," Hitchcock's performance and how it was received continued to be focused on his body. He also continued to develop what became the show's most consistent and distinctive carnivalizing device: "knocking" the sponsor, for the purpose of cutting him down to size. On television, Hitchcock, posing as a suffering artist in cahoots with his fellow victims, the audience, strikes back by dragging the sponsor's dignity and the commercial world in general through the mud. The term "gentleman" in reference to the sponsor is fraught with ironic insolence. Irrespective of his heckling of the hawker, Hitchcock had, in fact, lent his name to sell products back in London, for Lux Soaps.[28]

As the creative backbone for Hitchcock's on-screen hosting, this is a preeminent version of Bakhtinian carnivalizing in the form of degrading, decrowning, or dethroning a potentate, which reverses the direction of the usual fawning and sucking-up to corporate interests television hosts had to endure.[29] A leading magazine on the advertising business aptly described the arrangement from the sponsor's point of view: "B-M [Bristol-Myers] acquired the 'plus' of Hitchcock cynicism. As program host, Hitchcock introduces the commercials with disdain and as a necessary interruption."[30] The witty barbs aimed at the sponsor gave the Hitchcock figure an air of superciliousness in tune with his detachment on the threshold of the story world, in a nondescript host space. Critiquing the sponsor had a lean but discernible broadcast tradition, however, with preeminent "knockers" such as Ed Wynn, Henry Morgan, and Fred Allen on radio, and Arthur Godfrey successfully crossing over from radio to television, as did Jack Benny.

Discussing the television show's business plan before the premiere in 1955, and fully aligned with Hitchcock's own critical tenet, Cecil Smith declared that "for the first time in TV history, the director is the star." According to the well-established model for press interaction, Smith interviewed Hitchcock over a "massive slab of broiled steak," which the director disposed of while again outlining the macabre plot of Dahl's story as a little shocker with a meaty twist ending.[31] Surprisingly, 105 episodes were produced before "Lamb to the Slaughter" finally aired.

Hitchcock's mise-en-scène for the interview with Smith, combining quizzical small talk with conspicuous eating, sets the tone for the brand. The show's historical reception was forged around suspenseful murder stories with a macabre twist under the auspices of a star host with a pixieish acting style. Coupled with this were alimentary excesses, dieting, and body talk à la grotesque with, paradoxically, a dazzling dose of glamour included in the mix. Gargantuan repasts, witnessed and embellished by journalists, formed a prolonged chain of identity-formation performances as Hitchcock renegotiated his own brand of Englishness and filmmaking while eating. Fine dining coupled with phenomenal overindulgence almost beyond comprehension defies the sobriety associated with the figure of the gentleman, instead evoking elements of the grotesque. Hitchcock's cheerful "alimentary exploits," to borrow a phrase from Gwen Hyman's fascinating book on gentlemen in nineteenth-century British fiction, placed and simultaneously displaced him in relation to the gent/gentleman distinction.[32] For Hitchcock, the endless string of haute-table performances showcased and reconfirmed a fluid body politics and an enigmatic identity with multiple overtones, many of them read as English.

English Murders

After two decades in Hollywood, Hitchcock was still "invariably referred to as a British director but," as Hedda Hopper explained, "actually learned his craft from Americans as script writer and art director" in London in the 1920s.[33] Donald Spoto, as does Charles Barr, emphasizes the importance of Hitchcock's Englishness as a frame of reference in diaspora, both for his craft and for his persona.[34]

The English ripples and its deeper undercurrents propelled AHP, and not least the conundrum posed by the key tenor of Catholicism—sin is an inescapable human condition—combined with a class-based conviction concerning what "nice people" do and do not do. As it turns out, gentlemen can be murderers, which came as no surprise for Hitchcock, an irreverent critic of polite society and traditional manners with a "cockney defiance of social convention," as Spoto pointedly phrases it.[35] Upping the game half a notch in terms of class, some scholars would label the defiance roguish. Citing Hitchcock's remarks during a discussion at the American Film Institute's Center for Advanced Film Studies in Beverly Hills in 1970, Spoto summed up the director's mode of harnessing content and technique as "devoted to tearing apart the English canonization of manners" due to a form of "schizophrenia" caused by tensions between "Englishness and Catholicism." Refinement and niceness apart, "there's a devil in every one of us," according to Hitchcock, who was brought up in the Jesuit tradition.[36]

Never an ambassador for England (the burly aura of Englishness apart), Hitchcock had signed on as an American, seemingly in preparation for his television series, which was otherwise a highly English endeavor, given team, tone, themes, story scouting, and Hitchcock's on-screen demeanor. Hitchcock repeatedly ventured cross-cultural observations concerning his two countries, primarily as a form of pragmatics in regard to murders both inside and outside fiction. As John Crosby reported concerning Hitchcock's eloquent crime enthusiasm, "Hitchcock speaks with the relish of a gourmet talking about pressed duck." His conversation with Hitchcock then drifted to Hitchcock's old country, with the director stating: "The British treat crime on a much higher plane. . . . We English have the classic approach. I think it all started with Shakespeare." Combining his predilections for strangling with the tasking matter of body disposal, Hitchcock recounted elements from two cases. In the first, the judge asked, "'Were your hands around her neck at the time?' The man said: 'I think so!' Delicious! Another wonderful case was that of a man who put his victims in vats of sulphuric acid."[37]

In an article written for the *New York Times* during the early days of his television tenure and devised as a neighborly conversation across the hedges at his Bel Air home, Hitchcock ponders the peculiar taste Americans have for, as the title puts it, "Murder—with English on It."[38] Murders in the United States are, he explains, infinitely more common than in Great Britain—seven thousand compared to three hundred per annum. The Brits' preferences for homely homicides result from a combined of lack of space to dispose of corpses and escape plus the premium they put on privacy and politeness, which allows killers to stay clear of unwelcome interference from nosy neighbors. When crimes eventually are unearthed, the Brits are more enterprising in squeezing the juice out of what they have—"making do" with a domestic flavor. Once the court proceedings commence, Hitchcock elaborates, the press coverage becomes intensely detailed. In addition, just one opportunity for appealing a verdict is available, and such appeals are handled with dispatch within weeks (as was the execution of sentences, until capital punishment was abolished in 1965). Together, the in-depth coverage and high-pitched drama during concentrated judicial proceedings are sufficient to propel the cases across the Atlantic, where homicides, according to Hitchcock, are drab and commonplace, and the legal machinery drags out the process for many years, not to mention the time span between final verdict and execution. In an interview a year later, Hitchcock again deplored "unoriginal crimes" and the lack of charm characterizing U.S. murders. It is too easy to obtain firearms and too easy to get a divorce, he claims, while "murders in England are less

2.4. Hitchcock body-tagged as Made in England. From "Design for Loving" (AHP 123).

bang-bang-bang-and-run than here."[39] Similarly, he noted in 1972, "divorce is not easy in England, hence the need to murder. You really get some of the most bizarre cases. Arsenical poisoning is one of my favorites. It's so clean, so sadistic and there are no traces. All the man has is a sick wife on his hands."[40]

Interviewed by Larry Wolters, Hitchcock offered one of his most elaborated profiles of the English relish for the macabre:

It is the view of Hitchcock that the British, so law-abiding in themselves in contrast to the hot-blooded Latins, get a vicarious thrill out of murders, especially murders that are gory.

"The enjoyment of the macabre is very high in Britain," said Hitch. "You have a limited audience appreciating Charles Addams' cartoons in America. All that sort of thing that he extols in his drawings would go great in London. They love the grisly. Of course, we've had the writing experts in the macabre from Shakespeare to Conan Doyle.

They love Mme. Tussauds' 'Chamber of Horrors' on which scenes in wax of notorious murders may be viewed and studied. They love to recall the story of that necrophile, Christie, a gentle-appearing man, who murdered and buried eight women in his home."[41]

Hitchcock's analysis and historiography of English murders, of singular importance for his teleplays and some of his films, partly echoes and overlaps with George Orwell's essay "The Decline of the English Murders" (1946).[42] Orwell similarly identifies an English golden age of homicide between 1850 and 1925 and a series of spectacular murders that received intense coverage, both in the press and by novelists, and thus continued to stir the imagination on both sides of the Atlantic. The bulk of the cases shared common features: money played a limited role, with sex and a desire for untarnished respectability instead providing the prime motives; the murders were committed in a middle-class context, predominantly by way of poison; the culprit was exposed only gradually and by accident, owing to unforeseeable circumstances; and the background "was essentially domestic." Of ten or so cases, Orwell, like Hitchcock, highlights the one committed by Dr. Crippen. The doctor killed his wife, stepped on the gangplank, and left for the United States with his new love. She carelessly wore Mrs. Crippen's jewelry aboard the ship, which led to the couple's apprehension in transit between the two countries. Orwell bemoans a current decadence for English murders, which he attributes to the influence of popular culture, movies, and dancehalls, interpreting it as an unfortunate Americanization.

It was this golden age of English homicides that Hitchcock tapped into with his television show, and some of the most spectacular tales came with a patina of actual cases. Given Orwell's analysis, an escalating Americanization of murder, and Hitchcock's paradoxical relationships with his two countries, it makes sense that the English murder legacy, with the home as the preferred location, became the prime source of inspiration for a Hollywood television series produced by an expatriate Londoner turned American.[43]

The Framing of the Show

Structurally, AHP consisted of three types of slots: Hitchcock's Allardice-scripted comments in the prologue and epilogue; three commercials (before the story, in the middle of the episode, and the final one cut into the epilogue); and the story proper. The format was slightly modified for AHH. Following the main title and opening billboard came Hitchcock's introduction, leading to the first of six commercials, each a minute long. The first commercial preceded credits for producer, writer, and director; then came act one, the second commercial, act two, and a third commercial. Hitchcock then announced the station break (thirty seconds for local commercials) and returned after it. Following Hitchcock was the fourth commercial, act three, the fifth commercial, act four, and then Hitchcock's epilogue segueing to the sixth commercial, which was followed by a trailer for the next week's episode and closing credits.

Hitchcock's hosting is the glue that holds the segments together while positioning the sponsor's messages as unwanted, intrusive salesmanship that annoyingly interrupts a smooth passage into the show—in addition to lacking any redeeming qualities. Even so, in one prologue Hitchcock jestingly clarifies the differences between the segments, in case the viewers are not quite sure: "I repeat, you will first see the commercial, then our story" ("Shopping for Death," AHP 18). Attacking the sponsor was a shrewd attempt at severing the ties to the overall television format and taking the program to a higher artistic level. Channeling and slyly mouthing the stories through Hitchcock's body and making them part of his overall body of work and macabre persona placed Hitchcock apart from the sponsor's realm in a besieged creative zone within commercial television. The host most memorably describes the ads in one prologue as "boring, repetitive, noisy, tedious, soporific, juvenile, dull, ridiculous . . ." ("The Monkey's Paw—a Retelling," AHH 90).[44]

This mise-en-scène of the hosting—being locked in an agon-like feud with the sponsor and the world of commerce—apparently sold more products than praises for them did. As an advertising journal put it, "B-M feels this [Hitchcock's disdain] sets its commercials off, calls attention to them, and wins viewer 'affection for the underdog.'"[45] On an edgier, more colorful note, *Time* described the conflict between the host and the sponsor as "the equivalent of a fastidious man brushing a particularly repellent caterpillar off of his lapel." "Still," the writer noted, "for a rating that high [29.5 Nielsen rating], Sponsor Bristol-Myers is more than happy to put up with the quips about its commercials."[46] Stinging sarcasm vis-à-vis hucksterism offered a more effective commercial strategy than run-of-the-mill hosts who merely functioned as dummies for the sponsors' ventriloquism acts. Arguably, the agon was merely rhetorical posturing, as Hitchcock and the sponsor were undercover partners in a mock discourse, not foes. In this sense, the agon was a subterfuge for the engagement between two aligned and locked-in brands, both on the receiving end of consumerism. Hitchcock phrased it best in a syndicated piece, after he had taken on the role of producer for *Suspicion*: "'We are now virtually a part of the sponsor's company,' he said proudly, referring to the firm he has sometimes kidded unmercifully on TV."[47]

Hitchcock invariably opens with "Good evening," albeit sometimes a bit delayed, in which case its "Oh, good evening," as if he is just noticing the audience. In his nondescript studio space Hitchcock's own talkative body functioned as the plaything supreme and butt of constant negotiations. The wacky business and discourse in the prologues often had only metaphorical, if any, bearing on the story that followed, while the epilogue added more or less absurd off-story information or pontificating, especially when killers seemingly got away with murder. "Paratexts" or "parasegments" are accompaniments—Hitchcock would probably say condiments—for the text and the whole battery of significations framing it. These accompaniments function as zones of "transition and transaction" in relation to the master text. In his influential study of paratexts, Gérard Genette describes the literary preface as "a threshold" and, borrowing a spatial metaphor from Jorge Luis Borges, a "'vestibule' that offers the world at large the possibility of either stepping inside or turning back."[48] As ceremonial television host, Hitchcock resided in a televisual vestibule, a naked studio space outfitted with only a few bizarre props, while occasionally a stray assistant would parade by on the threshold to the text. A bland studio space is an eminent instance of what Michel Foucault has called "heterotopias," or an "other place." Potentially, such places are capable of standing in as an experiential equivalent for any other space or place. Such threshold places/spaces—real or imagined—are between stages, a position that Foucault associates with crises, negotiations, rites of passage, refashioning, and illusion.[49] (Not that Hitchcock ever literally crossed over—except by way of surrogates.)

In Foucault's tentative discussion of heterotopias, temporal principles intersect with spatial practices, while corporeality is under severe scrutiny. In fact the heterotopical function is primarily a consequence of how bodies are acted upon—physically, via detached monitoring, or discursively. Cleansed after sweating in saunas; corrected in prisons; mentally transported in heterotopias of illusion (theaters and cinemas, for example) and shifted in time (museums); on the verge of being physically transported when passing through airports (after qualifying for passenger status by making it through the processes of inspection and screening); maturing after visits in heterotopias of rituals; and so on. These "other spaces" have a transient, nondescript quality as well as a stand-in, surrogate, or secondary function representing or offering gateways to other spaces beyond them. Simultaneously, in a multilayered fashion, they invoke several spaces, real or imagined. Heterotopias are cultural laboratories for bodies in transit, on the verge of crossing thresholds or reaching out to spaces elsewhere, again real or imagined, as the case may be. Connecting back to Bakhtin, the carnival is a preeminent form of heterotopia as a performance site where grotesque aspects of bodies take center stage as relays to another space or a social utopia beyond the given. The corporeal aspects of heterotopias rhyme with the analysis of Hitchcock's cinema as riveted to bodies and physicality. And Hitchcock's body and identity were at the core of the host segments. The television host playfully fashioned himself for the anthology format as a malleable body engaged in a process of transaction and transition playing out in a many-layered space reserved for weekly rituals. As bookends, prologues and epilogues contain the text or discursive body, simultaneously sticking out and connecting as cultural relays in the manner of the grotesque body.

As host, Hitchcock always remained firmly outside the fiction, in contrast to Rod Serling in *The Twilight Zone* (CBS, 1959–1965), who often walked into the story's setting or in front of a back projection, not always as a cameo figure within the diegetic world. Hitchcock, instead, consciously played with the quizzical distance from story matters and sponsor. Of course, there is no rule without exceptions, as Hitchcock once showed up in the story's setting for the epilogue to "The Perfect Crime" (AHP 81). Hitchcock directed this episode, and its title defined a dilemma addressed in the discourse on repeated occasions. After strangling a man who knew too much (errors made by a detective, played by Vincent Price, had cost the life of an innocent man), the accuser (played by James Gregory) ends up strangled himself, and Price's character then incinerates the dead body in his kiln to preserve an impeccable record. In the epilogue Hitchcock plays around with a figurine containing incriminating gold fillings from the murdered man's teeth. *Variety*'s critic detected "a pattern which seems to fascinate Hitchcock in his telefilm format. That is, the proponent, in this case Vincent Price, gets away with murder in the body of the story, but is brought to justice in a more-or-less whimsical postscript by Hitchcock himself."[50]

If Hitchcock stood firmly apart from the stories, other hosts straddled the divide. Loretta Young in *The Loretta Young Show* (NBC, 1953–1961) dressed in the high-end register of fashion as hostess. She introduced her show by reading a letter as a bridge to the episode's story, a device familiar from the early days of serial films in the 1910s, most prominently the Hearst serial *Beatrice Fairfax* (International Film Service, 1916).[51] Young's role as presenter distinctly connected the opening of the show with the story proper via the letter of impetus, and she often played the lead. James Gregory's introductions for *The*

Lawless Years (NBC, 1959–1961) also broke down the barrier between prologue and story. Adolph Menjou, always a gentleman, even asked his audience for permission before segueing from host to character in Your Favorite Story (ZIV Television, 1953–1955). Without asking permission, Henry Fonda in "his" series The Deputy (NBC, 1959–1961) now and then expanded his role as narrator to character. A notable star presenter and one who often crossed over from master of ceremonies to actor in the series was Boris Karloff, for Thriller (NBC, 1960–1962). Karloff never taunted the sponsor, but he often added story information post-closure, as Hitchcock did.

The hour-long, short-lived Thriller shared many traits with AHP, and several writers, directors, and actors bounced between the two shows. When Thriller was shut down, Hitchcock took over the hour-long format at a time when several other shows were being stretched out. The Hitchcock team had tested the format already with installments of NBC's Suspicion. Rick Du Brow had a theory concerning Karloff's failure: "I think part of the reason definitely stems from the fact that Hitchcock is fat and Karloff is not. Thin fellows, with their lean hungry looks, are too obvious in such surroundings; whereas there is an implicit humor in a jolly fat man being involved in such allegedly romantic goings-on."[52]

After leaving CBS to go to NBC for season six of AHP and in the process acquiring new sponsors, Ford and Revlon, Hitchcock talked about the nature of his show in the prologue for "Mrs. Bixby and the Colonel's Coat" (AHP 192). "As has been our custom," he claimed, vouching for continuity, "we shall present homey little stories of an unusual nature. We shall continue to give the little man, or woman, his due. When crime is occasionally dealt with, it will be crime as practiced by ordinary people, like the fellow next door."[53] Two seasons later, when his television show expanded from the half-hour format of Alfred Hitchcock Presents to The Alfred Hitchcock Hour in the fall of 1962, Hitchcock commented on the change as a guest columnist in the Morning Telegraph, in his customary jocular tone: "It is not literally true that television viewers, during the coming season, will see twice as much Alfred Hitchcock as before. My diet forbids such a ghastly eventuality. At the same time that I am determined to remain a sylph of my former self, it is decidedly true that the Alfred Hitchcock Hour, as the title rather plainly implies, will endure for 60 minutes."[54] "Why the longer show?" asked Larry Wolters when interviewing Hitchcock in 1963. "I'm getting tired of doing an anecdote with a twist," Hitchcock replied. "So we're going to do novels, novellas, and remakes of famous pictures. Thereby I'm inviting the problems of condense and cut. But I'd rather do that than pad."[55] Hal Humphrey's comments sum up the general consensus regarding

Hitchcock's new format: "In Hitchcock's case his production company has to sacrifice much of the humor and suspense usually prevalent in the 30-minute series. Even Hitchcock's own little comedy vignettes, used so effectively to introduce the half-hour and its middle commercial, lose their luster among the plethora of commercials inserted during the hour show."[56]

Hitchcock's performance mode, predicated on taunting the sponsor, differed from the run-of-the-mill host discourse on the small screen in terms of key, style, and self-consciousness. Predominantly, critics described its distinctiveness in three intertwined registers by highlighting the performance style, the institutional critique, and the genre assumptions. A number of recurring adjectives were mobilized as prime descriptors for each register: "sly," owing to the mischievous delivery; "mordant," for the gibes directed at the intrusive sponsor; and "macabre," for the lighthearted small talk about murder plots as a commonplace aspect of domestic life.

In his sponsor-bashing mode of hosting, Hitchcock differed from the subordinating model that was fully aligned with the sponsor and thus echoed and underwrote the value of "his" products. With his extratelevisual auteur prestige, Hitchcock instead elected to play with television and its inartistic hawking protocols and, by way of smart-alecky pranks, posed as a victim as long as the model generated high ratings and hence profit for the flogged party. The host's lofty detachment from the sponsor's wares, acknowledged in negative terms only, offers a stark contrast to, for example, Ronald Reagan's role of product spokesperson for *General Electric Theater*.

Identity Games

The host's fluid identity, corporeal and otherwise, played a crucial role for scaffolding the segments featuring Alfred Hitchcock. In perhaps the most involved of these strands, Hitchcock was recurrently paired with look-alikes and relatives, or turned into quite unexpected forms or versions of himself. This, in a sense, harks back to the trick films from the silent era and their many modes of transformation, while it also reinforces the bodily insecurities and unstable identities swirling around the Hitchcock figure. The very first identity game bore directly on the story in the episode "The Case of Mr. Pelham" (AHP 10). The strategy for toying with the host's identity in the epilogue, by means of cloning, clearly demonstrates Jimmie Allardice's scripting technique—namely, picking up cues from the stories or their titles and adapting them with a twist within the cultural preconception of the Hitchcock figure. His knack for twisted spins became the signature strategy for the show.

In one prologue Hitchcock's identity was reeled off with a mock résumé comprising a string of his film titles, which are listed as the reason for his being apprehended for trespassing into television. As an identity game, consider this succinct, highly charged version from the prologue to "Number Twenty-Two" (AHP 60) read out as a television dialogue between a police officer and a booked culprit in a lineup, identified and named as

"Hitchcock, comma, Alfred. Height: five foot six. Weight: prisoner refuses to make a statement. Here's his record: 1940 picked up on 'Suspicion,' 1942 'Spellbound,' 1944 'Notorious,' 1955 'Rear Window,' 1956 'The Man Who Knew Too Much.' Anything to say, Hitchcock?"

"Well, sir, I admit it ain't a good record, but I'm trying to do better."

"Better? Do you call this latest charge doing better? Appearing on television."

"I'm sorry, Sir, but my family was hungry."

Characteristically and cleverly, this playful prologue mixes televisual skepticism with film records that are slyly spelled out as identity matters, while papering over the sensitive and pervasive weight conundrum and its relation to food. Not much dignity for the apprehended Hitchcock here, stripped of the formality of his suit uniform, which in the lineup is substituted for garb that matches his cockney demeanor. An alternative version in paper form from half a year later, dated 8 August 1957, is a fake FBI record card that lists the crime as "provoking panic" and the culprit's criminal specialty as "suspense" (fig. 2.5).[57] Contrary to fact, Hitchcock's nationality is noted as British only. As in the prologue, a criminal history is outlined in the form of film titles, though the charge here records some different titles, namely *Rebecca*, *Lifeboat*, *Spellbound*, and *Rear Window*.

This was not the only time the host faced the law. Being ticketed for blocking a supermarket aisle in "Lamb to the Slaughter" (AHP 106) was a misdemeanor at worst, but the situation for which Hitchcock's face appeared on a Wanted poster seems more serious. In line with the episode's title, "Outlaw in Town" (AHP 198), Hitchcock was wanted "for everything," and the reward was $1,000,000. The host is represented in the poster both in close-up profile and facing and talking to us from a cut-out "window." The description of him seems a bit off the mark, though, as Hitchcock protests in the epilogue: "Slim, attractive, dark wavy hair, no visible scars, age 29, rich brown eyes." Hitchcock admired himself on another type of Wanted poster on a cover of *Alfred Hitchcock's Mystery Magazine*. As he explained in the editorial, here he was "WANTED in the fullest and most flattering sense," as his old network, CBS,

FEDERAL BUREAU OF INVESTIGATION, UNITED STATES DEPARTMENT OF JUSTICE
WASHINGTON, D. C.

Record from .... Address ....
(On the above line please state whether Police Department, Sheriff's Office, or County Jail)

Date of arrest .... August 8, 1957
Charge .... Provoking Panic
Disposition of case ....

Residence .... Hollywood, Calif.
Place of birth .... London, England
Nationality .... British
Criminal specialty .... SUSPENSE

F. B. I. NO. 40876

Age .... 57 .... Date of birth ....
Height .... Comp. .... Hair ....
Weight .... Eyes .... Build ....
Scars and marks ....

CRIMINAL HISTORY

NAME	NUMBER	CITY OR INSTITUTION	DATE	CHARGE	DISPOSITION OR SENTENCE
A. Hitchcock	40876	Hollywood, Cal.	1940	Rebecca	
		"	1944	Lifeboat	
		"	1945	Spellbound	
		"	1954	Rear Window	

ACCOMPLICES

NAME	NUMBER	NAME	NUMBER	NAME	NUMBER
CBS-TV					

(Please furnish all additional criminal history and police record on separate sheet)   16—53306-1

2.5. Fake FBI card. Courtesy of the Academy of Motion Picture Arts and Sciences.

was bringing him back in the new full-hour format after a few seasons of AHP at NBC.[58]

Television provided Hitchcock with ample opportunities for serialized toying with his plastic identity. The host segments offered space for an intricate process of molding his figure into slightly different Hitchcock characters or novel versions of his figure. In "The Gentleman Caller" (AHH 57) the prologue comes with a look-alike contest for the host and three identical versions of Hitchcock presented by a young girl. After the story, when all the votes are in, the winner signs off the epilogue. Surprisingly, it turns out to be the young girl. Hitchcock "himself" did not even qualify for the final round, claiming he was unable to make the weight in the first.

During season two a somewhat younger Hitchcock-like stand-in is introduced, a full-fledged cockney version no less, in "Jonathan" (AHP 49). The cockney version of Alfred will fill in for Hitchcock when a second company is sent out on the road. An even younger Hitchcock, allegedly a version from back when he joined "the firm," is presented in "Profit-Sharing Plan" (AHP 252); this one has little resemblance to his current self. The youngest imaginable Alfred emerges after the host imbibes excessively from the fountain of youth in "The Pearl Necklace" (AHP 220). Here Hitchcock is truly rejuvenated and ends up in a baby carriage; the viewers are not, however, granted a peek into it, as the nurse delivers the closing on the toddler's behalf.

Televisual multiplicity is key for "Festive Season" (AHP 109), which features a Hitchcock duo. Here he is embedded both on the screen and off, seated in front of a television set watching his host persona. The offscreen Hitchcock fights his televisual other, the "obnoxious fellow" on the tube, for the sponsor. The oversized remote control used to blow the screen up in the epilogue smacks of a science-fiction gadget in a time long before the era of remotes. One hundred episodes later, in "The Greatest Monster of Them All" (AHP 209), revenge is meted out in a harem (for no apparent reason other than to offer a different setting from the horror-film one in the story) when the host is blown to smithereens. After the smoke clears, one of the girls, the perpetrator, takes over Hitchcock's role in rounding off the episode. Sexy girls intermittently dethrone the host, taking over as host or replacing him in the kettle as dinner.

An unnamed brother substituted for Hitchcock on several occasions to further negotiate identity politics and doubling, often with a bit of vengeance. Alfred's brother is first introduced in "Little White Frock" (AHP 117). When we encounter him, dressed in a loud costume and sporting a moustache, he is putting heavy objects into a coffin that he explains will be sunk into the river. He tells the viewer that Alfred is indisposed and cannot be found, and then uses Alfred's notes to introduce the episode, though he skips the "too frank" language concerning the commercials. The brother figure is always much more sponsor-friendly than Alfred. As is customary, the epilogue is bisected by the final commercial. Here the brother struggles with the coffin's lid as someone is apparently trying to get out of it. Could it be Alfred? Before the struggle, the brother announces the commercial: "Now I believe it is time for another of those splendid little commercial messages, which my uncouth brother detests so, but which I like very much." After the break, Hitchcock is back and busy cementing. He explains: "I don't believe my brother will be bothering you anymore. Oh, he was a nice enough fellow if he just hadn't been such a stickler for form. He was that way to the end. The last thing I heard him say was, 'Really Alfred, with an axe.'" Incidentally, an image of Hitchcock holding an axe next to his own bald pate was used on the cover of the LP *Alfred Hitchcock Presents Music to Be Murdered By* (1958).

Ninety episodes later, in "A Crime for Mothers" (AHP 207), a brother shows up again. This time Hitchcock is on vacation, and his brother, complete with moustache and gaudy tie, harbors ill will and murderous designs, made evident by a series of vignettes titled "The Best of Hitchcock." The brother claims, as the family allegedly has always known, that he is the best of the Hitchcock line. In the first of his favorite film clips Alfred stands tied to a telephone pole, surrounded by a large pyre. After lighting his cigarette and dropping the match, the brother is blown out of the frame by an explosion. In the second clip Alfred is tied to a log on a band saw conveyor; a girl in a bathing suit stands nearby as the saw comes to a halt in the nick of time. As the brother claims, this one "stopped just short of perfection." In the following two clips Hitchcock is tied to railroad tracks and blown up in a laboratory. Miraculously, Alfred reappears in the epilogue, with his customary tie and clean-shaven face—and with his own selections for "The Best of Hitchcock." In the first clip Alfred picks up a good bottle from the wine cellar and in a voice-over announces that this is "truly vintage Hitchcock." The shot looks as if the host had been transported to the wine cellar from *Notorious* and its far-from-innocent bottles. The voice-over leads directly to the next clip, in which four girls in bathing suits surround a flustered Alfred, measuring tape in hand. Seemingly a bit confused on how to size up the beauties, he comments on the scene as being "without the violence my brother seems to admire."

The feuds with his corporeal double—distinguishable from the genuine article only by way of costume—provided a unique form of self-reflexive interaction in that the brother addressed the audience on occasion in the host's absence. Other figures in the paratexts were merely functional props with only the most minimal of dialogue to set up a host spin, and only on rare occasions.

"Ten O'Clock Tiger" (AHP 255) features the next brotherly appearance on the show, and again he sports his customary outfit. Here both brothers are present, though not quite fully visible at the same time. Alfred's brother is literally on top of him, standing on his shoulders as they share delivery of the introductory remarks. As the camera pans down, Alfred explains the setup: "I agreed to take part in this absurd charade only because I was assured it would get us booking on a certain Sunday night variety show. However, I'm not sure

2.6. Alfred's brother uses the host as marionette. From "See the Monkey Dance" (AHH 69). Photograph courtesy of the British Film Institute.

it's worth it, since watching us is a rather limited form of amusement." In the epilogue the feud between the siblings continues as Alfred lights a match to give his brother a hot foot and to end the fight once and for all. Putting a match to someone's shoelaces was a well-established comedy routine in vaudeville.[59] The act here functions as a rehearsal for a later episode, and a much more ingenious attraction in the host segment for "See the Monkey Dance" (AHH 69), which featured the final brotherly routine (fig. 2.6). For this act Alfred appears as his brother's marionette. No top-down pan here;

instead, the camera cuts to Alfred with the brother's legs in the top frame. Allardice once again used the show's title for an ironic twist, with an added mischievous wink to Charles Gounod's theme music. The business of introduction is again shared, and the brother begins: "I am attempting to assist my brother Alfred in introducing this evening's chilling shocker. It is called 'See the Monkey Dance.'" After the edit, Alfred, attached to strings like a marionette, continues: "There seems to be no end to the humiliations which I suffer in the name of art and profit. See the monkey dance, indeed." The epilogue is fully in the hands of the brother as he closes this episode from "brother Alfred's own theater of the absurd." Ingenuously, he pulls up an Alfred doll, puts it in a suitcase, and reflects: "He plans to present some more buffoonery when he returns next time. If he returns."

Between the two acts featuring both brothers, the duo appeared in two additional routines. In the prologue to "Most Likely to Succeed" (AHP 260) Alfred seems to be the successful one, as his brother is tied up in the trunk of a car that Alfred is washing, claiming his brother hired him. In the epilogue Alfred presumes both will appear again, as the trunk key is locked inside the trunk. A brother also returned for one of the more malleable and shape-shifting versions of Alfred. In "The Long Silence" (AHH 25) the brother introduces the episode, as Hitchcock is a bit late after, appropriately, having given "some lessons in masking one's own identity." Alfred shows up in unexpected form as a bathing beauty, then, after changing clothes behind a screen, he emerges shape-shifted from bathing beauty to dog.

What this gallery of doubles clearly suggests is that Allardice put Hitchcock in carnivalesque situations with a different type of humor from the corporeal grotesque of the pre-television ruses focused on overeating, though the brotherly feud and the exploding of the host kept the corporeal slant that defined the franchise. The doubling in these jokes clearly relates to the multiplicity posited in Mili's stroboscopic depiction of a series of fragmented positions for Hitchcock. Allardice's scripting of the host segments neatly illustrates this poetic.

Parallel to the merriments concerning the host's identity, transformations, and doubling by way of the imaginary brother, Hitchcock played recurrently with the nature of the television medium and televisuality at large.[60] Hitchcock's place or "placelessness" was constantly brought to the fore as the studio was described as physically located inside the console. In "Momentum" (AHP 39) a big, never-sleeping eye, not unlike the CBS logo, is watching the audience watch the host. If one is so inclined, the unblinking eye could be the sponsor's, the network's, or Nielsen's keeping track of the ratings and thus "watching" audiences watching. Since television is frightful from the inside, Hitchcock reads ads, hoping to find another job. One catches his eye; it is for a job as the host of a television program. The prospective candidate must be "witty, charming, handsome, and gracious, and willing to work every week." The job turns out to be as host for *Alfred Hitchcock Presents*. Fittingly, the story is called "Help Wanted" (AHP 27).

Shifting to another genre, as sitcoms gradually began to dominate the broadcasting schedule, Hitchcock illustrates how a comedy show can be concocted from readily available, distilled ingredients in "Coming, Mama" (AHP 217—a far from comedic episode). After adding water to the contents of a cereal-like box, we have a spick-and-span family as protagonists. Besides a laugh track, the ingredients are as follows: "Retorts, witty. Replies, devastating. Quips, modest. Reproofs, parental. Mots, bons, and takes, double. All that is necessary is to slice the results into thirty-nine segments." Many of these ingredients mirror Allardice's own scripting for Hitchcock. Meanwhile, the show proper had its own distilled components: happy families were substituted with dysfunctional ones; murder of course, at times food related, was always served up; and the episode was topped with the surprising twist before the host, if need be, pontificated about further developments, more often than not in witty quips and double takes.

Several strands of self-consciousness permeated the host segments, foremost in regard to his identity but also concerning the overall makeup of television, from spoofs on the nature of broadcasting and the bizarre activities inside the television world, often in a literal sense, to an indirect lampooning of it. This was a sidebar to the dominant discursive avenue: attacks on the sponsor and commercial television in general. Evidencing the critical role of the host frame and its brisk shooting tempo, Hitchcock was, according to an anonymous interviewer, "prouder of this accomplishment than he [was] of the success of the series itself."[61]

For stories in which bodies were converted to corpses more or less weekly and framed by commercials advertising deodorant, toothpaste, pills, and even laxatives, Hitchcock's own bodily imprint served as anchoring point for the television series. The introduction leading to the host segment conspicuously highlighted the permeable interplay between profile and "real" body, which inspired legions of commentaries (fig. 2.7). The trademark sketch accompanied by Gounod's "Funeral March of a Marionette," both of which opened the show, became one of the most recognizable and cherished franchise logos in media history.

Predictably, as Hitchcock entered the tube, the host and his physicality garnered as much attention as the teleplays. *Time* unabashedly set the tone for the

2.7. Shooting of the credit sequence for *Alfred Hitchcock Presents*. Photograph courtesy of Getty Images.

reception of Hitchcock television by succinctly titling its appraisal "The Fat Silhouette," holding on to the established mode of body-slanted Hitchcock raillery.[62] And the *New York Herald Tribune* offered a more protracted version of the signature-like opening sequence in similar style:

> Mr. Hitchcock, as I suppose everyone now knows, is a man of redoubtable circumference. In fact, he might be described as one of those Englishmen on whom the sun never sets. And he has a face like a slightly malevolent kewpie doll. On his program, the physiognomy and body are first outlined gently in pencil, then inked in. Finally, the man himself floats in, still in darkness. Then they turn the lights on and there he is. CBS, I guess, feels that it would be too great a shock to present the man, cold, without advance preparation, and maybe they're right.[63]

Newsweek followed suit with its unflattering quip: "One of TV's newest cynosures is a penguin-fat man with a pendulous nose, gimlet eyes, and a lower lip like a battered sugar scoop."[64] Allegedly first devised as a jigsaw puzzle and sent to friends as a Christmas greeting in the early days back in England, the Hitchcock cartoon, with minor variations, subsequently turned into a personal form of autographed calling card / artwork / marketing logo. In the 1930s, Hitchcock, in lieu of an agent, had formed a company in Great Britain to cook up this type of gimmickry in addition to advertising schemes and Hitchcock news items, The Hitchcock Baker Productions Ltd. The cartoon's self-styled body outline is extremely expansive, with the protruding nose underlined, the lips almost floating outside their bodily anchoring, and the multiple chins subsumed as one curving line topping the line indicating the spherical body. Hitchcock held on to this trademark over the years and often commemorated an encounter by presenting an impromptu drawing to his lunch or dinner "date." Larry Wolters, in an article illustrated with the autographed profile, pointedly claimed, "It's a trademark, but it doesn't tell much about him."[65] Still, the unmistakable fat silhouette marked a genre-defined realm with Hollywood prestige, much sought after by television in the 1950s.

Television both cemented and reframed Hitchcock's popularity and creative agency. Host segments rife with frivolous horseplay and repartee introduced a strand of ironic gravitas that appropriated core elements from the former grotesqueries, albeit played in a novel register. This process of separation, fissure, and split defined the host figure as standing apart from both sponsor and stories in his own abstracted performance space, a figure almost pasted into or onto it.

The Host as Dandy

In a discussion of Hitchcock's brand of humor, James Naremore detected a considerable dose of influence from Thomas De Quincey's dandyesque outlooks summed up in the title of his fictional memoir, *On Murder Considered as One of the Fine Arts* (1827).[66] The aesthetic approach to the art of murder was, however, not at the core of Hitchcock's macabre spiels. His murder advocacy was rather on the cozy side, homely acts of kindness and consideration as opposed to De Quincey's theatrical slitting of throats. Hitchcock's preferred methods for homicide were strangulation and poisoning, the latter harshly dismissed by De Quincey: "Fie on these dealers in poison, say I: can they not keep to the old honest way of cutting throats, without introducing such abominable innovations from Italy? I consider all these poisoning cases, compared with the legitimate style, as no better than wax-work by the side of sculpture, or a lithographic print by the side of a fine Volpato."[67] Aside from a macabre sensibility and an evocative title, Hitchcock operated in a register with precious few links to De Quincey. Along this line, the always-helpful Hitchcock, in an interview for Italian television in 1960, reeled off a blueprint for how Britain's then prime minister, Harold Macmillan, could politely murder his wife with a friendly cocktail, should he be so inclined.[68]

When Hitchcock talked about the somewhat whimsical English murder tradition, the sensibility of his discourse was shared with contemporaries such as George Orwell rather than De Quincey's historiography, with its penchant for philosophers as victims. And Hitchcock's interest in poisons correlated with his quest for the perfect murder—that is, homicides that could not be detected and thus were aesthetically pleasing in a very different manner than De Quincey's showy penchant for the drama of slit throats.[69] In this respect Hitchcock was eminently in step with Cary Grant's character in *Suspicion* (1941), who appears to have plans to murder his wife when he a little too eagerly picks the brain of a coroner concerning undetectable poisons. Hitchcock did, however, offhandedly and in a tongue-in-cheek way, pronounce murder a fine art in a newspaper article he authored when standing in for the columnist Dorothy Kilgallen. "The hallmark of fine murder," he writes, "is that it is practiced in moderation." Before elaborating on a crime story he would like to do, and the plot for *Dial M for Murder* (1954), then in production, Hitchcock came up with a truly signature-like sally: "An artistic murder invariably leaves one with a good appetite."[70] On the flip side, as a hypothetical victim, Hitchcock in a television interview held on to eating as the preferred method: "Q: If you were going to be murdered, how would you choose to have it done? A: Well, there are many nice ways: Eating is a good one."[71]

For several reasons, Alfred Hitchcock was positioned outside the class precinct of both the gentleman and the rebellious new dandyism cultivated by the privileged of the postwar generation he belonged to. The latter circle had reached Oxford via Eton or other institutions of learning for the upper crust, while Hitchcock was trained within a context of engineering, craft, and design, with an eye toward the utilitarian world of commerce. In contrast, as Henry Fielding epigrammatically put it, the gentleman was "bred up to do nothing."[72] With his lower-middle-class mercantile background and as a Catholic, Hitchcock stood apart from a disillusioned generation of dandies who, with prospects of ample leisure, cultivated beauty in rebellion against a parental generation that had pushed young men to be slaughtered on the battlefields as Britain's imperial era gradually petered out.

Nihilistic attitudes after the senseless deaths of a multitude of gifted young men were the driving undercurrent for the dandies' retreat to aestheticism and sophisticated pleasures outside the traditional manly world of sports, military careers, and politics. Scandalous designs pursued within the context of avant-garde art, refined collecting, disdain for physicality outside sexual play and art, and disdain for middle-class values and work ethic overall set them apart from society at large. The cockney world of the working class and small-time merchants, which the Hitchcock family belonged to, was virtually unknown for the Hitchcock-era dandies.

In contrast to the dandy's effete aestheticism, Hitchcock's artistic inclinations were not steered toward l'art pour l'art. His foray into the film industry had precious little fine art clout when he was pitching title cards and hoping to be hired as a title designer. Superficially, Hitchcock's taste for dicey pranks aligned him with the dandies' frivolous larks, but his buffoonery had a coarser edge in tune with the irreverence of the grotesque and was thus removed from the gambols orchestrated when Oxford aesthetes ventured into London nightlife in the 1920s. And in terms of class, most of the Oxford crowd ended up in the arts, letters, diplomacy, and politics—W. H. Auden, Cecil Beaton, Anthony Burgess, and Evelyn Waugh, to mention just a few. Hitchcock traveled in other circles but carved out a niche for himself, in alliance with journalists, that worked as a fusion of cinematic salon, public sphere, and master class. In such interactions he set off his own persona and filmmaking as points of reference for critical protocols of cinematic appreciation.

John Barrell has charted the conceptual transformations of the gentleman in several publications on eighteenth- and nineteenth-century English literature.[73] In the margins such shifts are also discernible in detective and crime fiction from Sherlock Holmes to Lord Peter Wimsey, as the intellectual pursuit of detection turned into a plausible activity removed from pure leisure, but one distinctly devoid of any tints from the world of trade and commerce belonging to the "gents." Sleuthing was instead an unattached, hobby-like "occupation" and primarily an engagement with entangled intellectual dilemmas. It was play, not work. Over the centuries the concept of the gentleman had turned into a free-floating signifier decoupled from the old links to landed property, ancestry, and even wealth. In the industrialized age, bred gentlemen did not have to be born gentlemen, especially when the cities and towns became the prime sites for generating money, new wealth, and the display of gentle manners. And for the upkeep of land and possession, old money desperately needed the new moneymakers with liquid resources, which led to matrimonial practices further blurring the formerly fixed boundaries of class distinctions. Simultaneously, manners and appearances, morals and codes of conduct, especially in relation to women, took on a new prominence as the idea of the gentleman trickled down to the bourgeoisie.

The dandies' contempt for the bourgeois world was monumental en route to nobler pursuits. Hitchcock, too, belittled the world of commerce from which he hailed, most famously in the ridicule of his television sponsor. Hitchcock, however, wore the bland uniform of commerce in contrast to the flamboyant dandies' sartorial style. His hamming and hogging takes a penchant for posing to its extremes without any sartorial distractions. His puffery—grotesque and otherwise—was designed to rein in a journalistic audience attracted by his eccentricities and willing to trumpet his idiosyncratic personality as the flip side to his screen excellence. When discussing Hitchcock's aesthetics, and their moral and social implications, Raymond Durgnat suggests an affinity between a mode of Hitchcock posing and dandyism: "Isn't Hitchcock's sphingine, sinister pose a spiritual successor to a dandyism, which, be it remembered, also aimed, blandly, to inculcate a certain disquiet?"[74] The key term here is "sinister pose," a self-styled mise-en-scène that Durgnat's reflective question connects to the free-floating dandy signifiers alluded to by Christopher Lee's Dracula in the gothic context of the Hammer productions. Lee had also, in fact, graced Hitchcock's screen as star in the "metafilmic" television episode "The Sign of Satan" (AHH 60). In Durgnat's reading, Hitchcock's "sinister pose" functions within an operational aesthetic struck in order to "inculcate a certain disquiet." Apart from signifiers of aloof detachment in many contexts, this posing—sinister or not—is at its most obvious in the serialized discourse concerning the coziness of domestic murders

2.8. "My Husband Hates Suspense," said Mrs. Hitchcock—while the implied Hitchcock relished it in his "other life." Alma (Mrs. Alfred) Hitchcock as told to Elizabeth Sherrill, "My Husband Hates Suspense," *Everywoman's Family Circle* 52, no. 6 (June 1958): 36–37, 69–70, 72; uncredited photograph on p. 36. Alma's psychological profiling of her husband clearly foreshadows his stance in his interview with Bob Hull ("T.V.-Talk: Hitch Hates Eggs but Loves Relish," *Los Angeles Herald and Express*, 22 September 1959, B2).

and the macabre deliberations on optimum killing techniques. In his role-play, Hitchcock often adopted conflicting stances—for example, on violence.

In a television column, Bob Hull reported on Hitchcock's take on "the utter believability of his unbelievable situations." Hull had asked Hitchcock if he could come up with plan for a "true-life" murder, one the director himself would commit. "After all, isn't he the master of the macabre?" Interestingly, Hitchcock declined, even though he had previously murdered in a photo-essay with cast members from *The Man Who Knew Too Much*. "I am," he said, "always and forevermore, a coward. I can't stand any sort of violence." Then Hitchcock took the issue to a more philosophical, meta-critical level: "I suppose you might say I live a full other life in my pictures. Have you noticed I always have some sort of a sex interest in my movies? I have been married to the same woman for 34 years and have never been with another. And since I hate violence in any form, you figure out why I have murderous action and passionate interests, albeit sometimes illicit, in my films."[75] Apart from the thematic field of gravity carved out by Hitchcock—sex and violence, to put it simply—one should bear in mind that this particular interview was motivated by a television story ("Arthur," AHP 154) involving violence done to chickens linked to a "chick," and that the food discourse was the realm that best connected the two otherwise separated Hitchcocks.[76]

While he swore off violence in the interview, yet another Hitchcock figure, à la Mili's stroboscopic identity in motion, soon emerged. The director came to the fore as an unfazed poster boy for murder, mayhem, and violence in a photo-essay published by *Esquire* in 1961, when this magazine was at its most significant and "essential to the iconography of American culture."[77] This and other carnivalizing marketing stunts reside somewhere between the version of the meek, private Hitchcock played up for Bob Hull and the more adventurous implied author, as well as the brash public performer posing in dandy style. In the *Esquire* photo-essay, plainly titled "Violence," Hitchcock presents "an ever-handy reference manual to the selection, dispatchment and disposal, with taste, of a likely victim," as a belated concession to Hull's request for a murder scenario, if you will. Standing in pointed profile, his head turned upward, in front of a home screen for slides or 8 mm home movies (fig. 2.9), he tells his implied audience that the first step is to select a suitable murder victim. This should be carried out with a mindset tuned to amusement or whimsy; one should at all costs avoid selecting a victim out of anger, emotion, or irony. The available candidates are the policeman, the girl, the rich widow, the dancing instructor, the grandmother, and the young master. The latter is singled out for an obvious reason: his violin's high C broke Hitchcock's best

2.9. Images from the photo-essay "Violence," *Esquire* 56, no. 1 (July 1961): 107–112. Photographs by Dan Wynn, courtesy of Farmani Gallery, Los Angeles.

snifter. With the victim in the symbolic crosshairs it is imperative to sport an artful disguise. Hitchcock gives us four versions of himself (in line with the stroboscopic poetics), as mortician, movie director, surgeon, and TV sponsor. As for the weapon, a tennis racket seems superior to a crossbow. From five options for getting rid of the body, Hitchcock opts for airfreight over taxidermy, the garbage disposal unit, the garbage can, or turning the boy into a dummy for keeps. Before the suited-up perpetrator reclines in a sun chair with a sizable cigar, next to a girl in bikini, the victim has been shipped by airfreight in a handful of different-sized packages, all marked "Hong Kong."[78] For Britons, this faraway Crown colony was a logical destination for dispatching unwanted bodies and troubling characters.

An odd form of triangulation emerges from the takes on violence played up for Hull and *Esquire*'s readership, respectively. In Hull's interview a private Hitchcock, subscribing to an unadventurous sex life and loathing all forms of violence, vicariously entertains a parallel "other life" on the screen, playing around with precisely such topics—and decked out as the implied author for the purpose of separation. The brash Hitchcock figure in the photo-essay, aimed at a sophisticated male readership, lays claim to full authorship of the manual on violence and, seemingly without qualms, kills off the young master before sitting down, undisguised and contentedly smoking his cigar, next to the bikini-clad girl, an adjunct with titillating implications. This nondisguise, invariably donned according to a phalanx of texts, might in fact be the most effective camouflage for the multilayered Hitchcock. And the oversized cigar was later used as phallic prop in other photo sessions as well—in particular, Philippe Halsman's work marketing The Birds and its many spin-offs. This manual version for Esquire, photographed by Dan Wynn, and the Hitchcock of the photo-essays by and large represent a seminal Hitchcock running alongside the implied author and private Hitchcock who hated suspense.

Durgnat discusses the faux dandy signifiers as performative adjuncts to Hitchcock's poetics. "To me," Hitchcock claimed, "the great art of the motion picture is by means of imagery and montage to create an emotion in the audience, and therefore, the content is a means to an end."[79] The sought-after emotions, of course, are fear and suspense, with or without humor in the mix. This affective cinema was designed to send shivers up audiences' spines. On several occasions—for example, when interviewed by Fletcher Markle for CBC's Telescope in 1964—Hitchcock pedagogically re-created the famous Kuleshov experiments, substituting differently charged image content (a dead body, a sexual situation, a table with food) placed back-to-back with an unchanging neutral image of a face to illustrate how emotional investment works in cinema as a result of juxtapositions. The same face takes on new meanings depending on the montage. This was one of Hitchcock's prime talking points in interviews, and he outlined it again the same year on the BBC program Monitor, hosted by Huw Wheldon.[80]

Thomas Elsaesser develops the concept of the dandy as foil or mask for the Hitchcock figure, proposing the character of the saltimbanque (street or carnival performer) rooted in Charles Baudelaire's prose poems as a template for Hitchcock in a form of reversed dandyism.[81] Elsaesser's line of reasoning has its background in Durgnat's observation on posing. For Elsaesser, Hitchcock's hyper-aestheticism runs in tandem with buffoonery, though in a refined and sophisticated register bracketing the grotesque. Different from the aggressive practical jokes from the early days in England, the clowning that Elsaesser alludes to is primarily associated with the English framework devised for the television show, which is the most vividly remembered public domain for the Hitchcock figure, its legend. Elsaesser's point of departure is precisely "the enigma of Hitchcock's Englishness," the affinities and rifts between the very private person and the performed public persona.

Hitchcock publicly flaunted his eccentricities and penchant for posing when he moved to Hollywood. Some of the early capers bounced back to the

London press. The *Daily Mail* columnist Paul Holt received a letter from the West Coast in 1940 reporting on Hitchcock's nightlife: "The most charming sight in this town is the bulk of our own Alfred Hitchcock at any night spot, the bigger the better. His playful habit is to choose the smallest chair, sit well out on the dance floor and spend the whole evening devouring gobs of ice cream, while the dancers alter tack to get around him."[82] Arguably, such queer poses and roguish stunts in public interlaced and cross-referenced the grotesque and dandyesque en route to the Hitchcockian.

The default observations on Hitchcock's corpulence often segued to how a gentleman's body, obese or not, should be attired—this in contrast to the dandy's sartorial flamboyance. In this respect, *Martine's Hand-Book of Etiquette* (1866) is particularly enlightening: "The dress of a gentleman should be such as not to excite any special observation, unless it be for neatness and propriety. The outmost care should be exercised to avoid even the appearance of desiring to attract attention by the peculiar formation of any article of attire, or by the display of an immoderate quantity of jewelry, both being a positive evidence of vulgarity. His dress should be studiously neat, leaving no other impression than that of a well dressed gentleman."[83] Hitchcock fully emulated the understated and unfailingly neat dress code Arthur Martine suggested for gentlemen. Sartorially discreet—he invariably donned a navy-blue suit (sometimes a shade darker), white shirt, and tie, with no jewelry—Hitchcock instead turned spectacular through his body and the repertory of stunts, spoofs, and poses, regardless of the sobriety and middle-class decorum to which his demeanor otherwise alluded. This super-formality of the Hitchcock figure was constructed for the purposes of public performance. In this respect, the choice of dress was part of a discipline in Foucault's sense, a precarious and many-layered semiosis or masking, albeit reportedly the result of practical concerns rather than display. According to Geoffrey T. Hellman, Hitchcock, having put on so much additional weight, began regularly to wear a dark suit for "cosmetic camouflage."[84] Peter Conrad, meanwhile, associates the clothing of Hitchcock's "globular body" with the corsets demonstrated by a traveling salesman in *The 39 Steps* (1935), which were designed to keep fat in check.[85] His wardrobe discipline was a rigorously observed ritual and one way that he mastered the vicissitudes of everyday life. Henceforth, Hitchcock's figure was sartorially fixed in its perennial, businesslike mold. Even on snowy slopes, the Hitchcock figure assumed his default garb, as in a photograph published in *Paramount World* in 1959 (fig. 2.10). This aesthetic was reaffirmed, reevaluated, and reframed over the years in an ongoing renegotiation of its premises—and foremost in the paratexts for the television show.

Alfred Hitchcock's
current production,
"Psycho," now in work,
is so secret a project
that nobody knows any-
thing about its theme
– not even "Hitch"
himself.

"'Snow use you ask-
ing me," says "Hitch"
as he slithers down
the Rockies.

One thing is cert-
ain, however – "Hitch"
will manage to get
himself into the pic-
ture, as usual. But
even he isn't telling
himself how.

2.10. A debonair Hitchcock on the slopes. Uncredited photograph published in *Paramount World* 5, no. 12 (December 1959): 40.

The figure and the context productively clashed when Hitchcock found himself in outlandish situations or engaged in activities associated with a more flexible dress code and expressions of involvement beyond haughty deadpan. The *Paramount World* image of the detached Hitchcock figure on a bobsled generates precisely this displaced fissure effect that borders on cartoon-like pasting, quoting an activity, as a pose, rather than performing it. In the late 1950s, when the sled ride was photographed, the register for the Hitchcock figure had been reframed, primarily via television. The capers henceforth discounted the vitality of the grotesque and the informality of being photographed in pajamas for self-conscious abstraction and uniformity. This visual quotation of the Hitchcockian dovetails with Philip Mason's formulation, "A gentleman is always a man in a mask."[86] Hitchcock, posing as Alfred Hitchcock, was seemingly always wearing a mask.

The air of formality on the sled (the original photograph seems lost, hence the dismal quality of the reproduction) contrasts starkly with the imagery from the days of full-blown grotesque. Katharine Roberts interviewed the director in 1939, and the reportage came with an illustration from Hitchcock's suite at the St. Regis (fig. 2.11). According to this home-away-from-home piece, "he said the best time to talk with him was when he was getting up, so for several days we appeared with the morning mail and the coffee. In this manner we learned that Mr. Hitchcock is spherical even when relaxed in sky-blue pajamas and blue silk dressing gown." Hitchcock was thus entertaining journalists in the same outfit as he would later in Hollywood and had before in London. The article closes with the information that he has lost thirty pounds during the last six months but is still, obviously, "spherical."[87]

In the host segments for "My Brother, Richard" (AHP 56) Hitchcock's host character mirrors the title character's dandy veneer but takes it almost beyond excess, with bowler hat, scarves, and a disdain for strenuous sports and physical activities. Posing in front of a wooden horse and looking quite bored, Hitchcock gives an extremely lethargic delivery, for the moment tinged with upper-class diction, that plays up a truly effete version of a dandy. The story features a dandy-like, cold-hearted killer out of touch with how the world works. Sharply dressed with bowler hat, tiepin, and boutonniere, Richard (Harry Townes) is a stickler for protocols of style and one of the most clear-cut dandy specimens in Hitchcock's television. Richard's obsessive neatness even forces him, after committing the murder, to pick up his victim's shirt from the floor and carefully lay it out on a table, almost as a reproach, not that wrinkles will matter much for the owner. Richard has walked into the locker room at a country club and shot his brother's gubernatorial rival point blank

2.11. Hitchcock in his suite at the St. Regis. Katharine Roberts, "Mystery Man," *Collier's*, 5 August 1939, 22. Photograph by Ifor Thomas. The negative seems to be lost; no positives have been found, only the magazine reproduction.

in the shower. His contempt for conventional codes of conduct and morals is monumental, hence the killing, a deed for which he expects to earn appreciation and gratitude and be rewarded with business favors after his brother Martin's swearing-in as governor. Suitably, in an American context the dandy has turned into a callous businessman. Mission accomplished, Richard enters Martin's home without knocking, announcing his entrance with a whistle. While mixing himself a cocktail, Richard describes the murder offhandedly between complaints about the poor quality of the vermouth and his brother's unfortunate choice of tailor, while admiring himself in the mirror in a story that does not end well for the dandy.

INTERLUDE II

DOUBLE HOSTING

The Hitchcock-directed episode "Arthur" (*Alfred Hitchcock Presents* [AHP] 154) sports a unique feature insofar as it is delivered with a double layer of first-person address in a relay, from Alfred the host in the paratext to Arthur the host "inside" the text—that is, in the story. First we encounter our customary host and his patented, stretched-out "Good evening," followed by a short lecture on the advantages of square eggs over the conventional type with their obvious shortcomings in terms of storage and transportation. As hens seem to resist the square innovation, Hitchcock explains in the prologue, an inspirational plastic model has been developed, and a slogan on the wall, "Think Square!," will hopefully egg them on in their efforts.[1]

After Alfred's prologue and the first round of commercials, suave Arthur (Laurence Harvey) addresses us directly in host fashion as he faces the camera standing inside his industrialized, medium-scale chicken coop surrounded by chickens and holding one in his arms: "Greetings! Lovely day, isn't it?" The loveliness of Arthur's day, politeness apart, presumably has, as is later confirmed, more to do with contentment concerning his carefully crafted life than anything else. The context of and rationale for Arthur's hosting and guiding us into his story remains unclear throughout, and his allusion to television and fame is mystifying, given the dark prerequisite for his particular type of feat as murderer.[2] In his own case, Arthur tells us, he is unknown—that is, not featured on television!—owing to his success. More precisely, the nature of his achievement hinges on not getting caught; such a failure would have given him deplorable notoriety in the age of television. So why spill the furtive beans on-screen by boasting about being a murderer? Furthermore, it is unclear in which form Arthur is communicating with us, since Alfred reports on

Arthur's demise in the epilogue, which adds to the mysterious spatiotemporal nature of the interior host prologue.

Arthur's polite monologue and polished informality concerning success and media matters lead up to him killing the chicken he has held and so lovingly caressed during the introduction; this in preparation for dinner—just like the proverbial eggs for omelets. Apparently, he has paused only for a moment to address us after having selected a suitable menu item. In his case, the recipe starts from scratch in do-it-yourself, hands-on food preparation, which minimizes the time span between coop, oven, and plate.

Arthur's eloquent speech, personal tone, and direct address frame an attempt at refashioning his sinister but surreptitious accomplishment. His divulging the information as a shared secret makes us complicit in his supercilious outwitting of the police. The detectives are clueless in spite of all the clues they are fed, not least the final gloating gesture underwriting Arthur's success and simultaneously writing off the murder suspicions for good. Showing his goodwill and friendship even after being suspected of having murdered his ex-girlfriend, Arthur indirectly feeds his police friend not a murder weapon but chickens that have fed on the girl's dead body. This is at least as macabre, in an oblique form of unwitting cannibalism, as the closure in "Lamb to the Slaughter" (AHP 106), the show's master recipe.

While Arthur praises the chicken he holds as dinner material in the opening scene, the camera tracks forward to close in on him and his caressing hands before he lowers them out of frame in preparation for killing the chicken. Outside the frame, he wrings its neck, which the viewer infers from his jerky movement and facial expression accompanied by a short death cackle from offscreen. As an object lesson, the abrupt brutality inflicted on the chicken supports his boasting about his success as a killer. Afterward he openly states his case: "Yes, I'm a murderer"—presumably of chickens, for starters.

Via a dissolve, the standard device for connecting scenes, the storytelling's logic follows the thrust of the disquieting host monologue by moving directly from the killing of the chicken to the oven and eliminating the messiness in between. Simultaneously, the musical dissonance drowning out the poultry farm's background cackle sonorously dissolves to merry harmony in tune with the sentiment of the approaching dinner for one. In a self-congratulatory manner, Arthur extols his conscientious method of taking care of both the farm and the cooking without helping hands. While carving, he further elaborates on the unfortunate misconception of murderers' personalities and motives. Pace popular belief, murder, at least in his case, is an act of kindness and in no sense a wanton, cold-blooded deed performed by a monster. Having established this premise, Arthur offers an illustrative demonstration of the argument after the next dissolve, at the dinner table, with regard to his killing of Helen (played by Hazel Court), a woman who took advantage of him. In this respect his former fiancée was not unique, but for Arthur a turn to chickens instead of people obviates the inconveniences of being played.

Arthur's poultry business, he claims, is scientifically run to eliminate the need for staff, as is the household, with its high-tech kitchen. Obviously he has a flair for cooking. The chicken, he lets on, is prepared to perfection in a process that matches the white, laboratory-like neatness of his business. Hitchcock, too, was a stickler for building kitchens to perfection—in his case, for Alma's culinary feats in far-off Bel Air. Arthur, of course, possesses all the right tools for carving—a chore associated with Hitchcock—and afterward the food is placed on an elegant silver tray complete with lids for carrying warm food to the table meticulously laid with a white cloth. No company is required for treating himself to a first-rate wine.

For us to better understand his case, Arthur promises a demonstration by telling what happened to Helen in more detail. This comes after his three-part introduction as internal story host, if you will (following Hitchcock's opening from outside the story): in the coop, in the kitchen, and at the table eating. After a series of flashbacks Arthur signs off in a form of interior epilogue, again returning to the direct address that precedes Hitchcock's reappearance "to tidy up afterwards for those who don't understand the endings" (as the host explains in "Revenge" [AHP 1]). And in this case, adding to it.

Arthur's prologue prompts a series of twelve flashback scenes covering the murder's impetus, execution, and aftermath, beginning with Helen breaking off their engagement for a more promising match with a certain Stanley.[3] During the establishing frame/prologue, in three interconnected scenes, the color pattern is almost clinically white: the chickens; Arthur's lab coat, which identifies him as a technician or inventor rather than a farmer-breeder; the tablecloth; and the napkin.

The flashback scenes are strung together so as to set the stage for Arthur's demonstration of his success as a murderer—and poultry farmer. These two businesses are indistinguishable, and his twofold achievements are intimately correlated. In the first flashback scene Arthur is acidly polite and eminently ironic as Helen breaks off their engagement. Her desertion seems to touch his vanity, but judging from his comments and the inflection of his voice it sounds as though he was already in the process of getting rid of her. He is, however, utterly shocked by Helen's choice of marriage candidate. Stanley is a gambler, which is forgivable, even if Helen prefers to call him a financier. But what in Arthur's estimation put Stanley beyond the pale are his appalling table manners.[4] For Arthur, how one conducts oneself at the table is the definitive test of character. Following Helen's exit a dissolve propels us to flashback scene number two, when Arthur's policeman friend, John, arrives. The visit is not official, just a casual stop to admire the farm's gizmos on the way to town. During the tour Arthur demonstrates his noisy hammer mill for grinding feed. The conversation revolves around Arthur's pleasure in perfecting his automated business and life in solitude, without having to cater to anyone else's needs or fancies. For him, all human beings are insignificant others, and the machines and automation processes obviate the need for additional hands. Furthermore, the apparatuses even provide significant help in clearing the way for and reestablishing domestic solitude when Helen intrudes on the scene after a year with Stanley, his atrocious table manners, and other undisclosed character flaws. Much could be said, of course, concerning the sexual implications of Arthur's swearing off companionship and company for a solitary life among machines and chickens.

After the police sergeant leaves and Arthur steps inside, Helen is shown sitting in an armchair and seductively declaring, "Darling, I'm back." The perturbed Arthur approaches the static camera, looking decidedly unenthusiastic in line with the conversation among the machines. His movement toward the camera dissolves to flashback scene number three, set after dinner. The escalating conflict between Arthur and his former girlfriend is obvious, given Arthur's impeccable desire for neatness and unwavering adherence to protocols of conduct, which is highlighted in the after-dinner proceedings by means of focalizing close-ups psychologically aligned with Arthur's dismay at the mess Helen causes. Her reentry into the household and chatty nervousness and anxious attempts at pleasing Arthur are left out of the soundtrack but emphasized all the more when shown as a lugubrious form of silent cinema. Meanwhile, as Helen silently but visibly blabbers, the soundtrack offers Arthur's voice-over assessment. Overlaying and literally tuning out her talking, Arthur's voice has a hollow, unheimlich quality in line with a feeling of being cornered by her invasion and occupation of his private space, praised in so many ways. Her intrusion comes with all the predictable messiness Arthur abhors, tries to control, and offsets by means of technology and otherwise. This is illustrated in quick succession when she fails to do the dishes after dinner and fills the sink with dirty tableware (close-up), then uses a china bowl as an ashtray—white, of course, with two Cupid-like figures on the rim and the surface soiled with her cigarette's ashes (close-up). Bringing her unfortunate interaction with china to a climax, she breaks the coffeepot when

Arthur tells her he doesn't want any changes in his life. From the kitchen we hear the rattling sound of the broken china as she throws away the pieces. In the meantime, Arthur has moved away from the corner, a position underlined by a low camera angle, to offer Helen a liqueur while standing behind her.

So what's to be done? He doesn't want Helen around, and she has no money and nowhere to go. As she phrases it, she'd "rather be dead" than be thrown out. Arthur eagerly supports this "wise decision," taking her platitude literally. Ergo, according to his logic outside ordinary psychology and the law, an act of kindness is required to solve the double conundrum by killing two birds with one stone, as it were. Here, in a single stroke by means of one firm grip, comes his act of kindness. As with the chicken previously, the killing is performed hands-on, now as a means to a jointly supported end, according to Arthur's twisted logic. The key scenes are eerily parallel: wringing the chicken's neck in preparation for dinner, and strangling the woman to tidy the living space of her annoying clutter and cackle. As with the chicken, he attacks Helen from behind as the camera tracks closer to her surprised face, her eyes wide and staring as she desperately gasps for air. An edit takes us back to Arthur in close-up, as he finishes the job to the accompaniment of Helen's offscreen dying "cackle" before the same dramatic music signals yet another killing job well done.

The parallel is chillingly complete in terms of the after-effects relegated offscreen. Following the killing, we assume that Arthur has given Helen to the chickens as feed. As was the plucking of the chicken in preparation for the oven, the messy business of disposing of Helen's body is left in the interstice before the next scene, which features the police sergeant's return, now in an official capacity. After the previous demonstration we know what the hammer mill can do and are very sure of what it has already accomplished.

When Arthur's friend returns in flashback scene number four, this time as police sergeant, Arthur is as always correct and forthcoming and seemingly provides all the details concerning Helen's return and subsequent disappearance, complete with left-behind luggage. Of course, he omits the little business of murder and body disposal. Time passes after the police's fruitless large-scale investigation, and in the continued absence of a body, suspicion has faded. In the final flashback, again accompanied by Arthur's voice-over, he prepares a Christmas gift basket of braised cockerels for the sergeant. In the last shot, outside the series of twelve flashbacks, Arthur is shown in front of his silos and machines. In this, his closing epilogue, he once more addresses us directly as in the opening three-pronged frame prologue, rather than in an indirect voice-over. The sergeant, once more predominantly friend

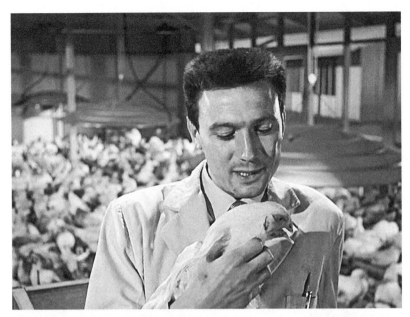

Interlude II.1 and II.2. In Arthur's grip. From "Arthur" (AHP 154).

and fellow breeder, appreciated the tasty gift and expressed a desire for the recipe of Arthur's chicken feed. Friendly Arthur listed them all apart from that special but essential ingredient—Helen, we are invited to surmise—as he starts the noisy hammer mill and the story grinds to a happy conclusion.

In Arthur's neat, orderly world nothing goes to waste owing to his effective system of recycling, not even the bones: just as in "Lamb to the Slaughter," a detective takes them home to his dog. Despite Arthur's success as a murderer, he allegedly encounters an unforeseen side effect cooked up by Jimmie Allardice and served by squeamish Alfred in the regular epilogue. As the host explains, "There was a very sad end to our story. Because of the excellent bone, meat, and blood meal Mr. Williams kept supplying them, his chickens grew to enormous size. Then it happened. One day, as he shouldered his way through the hungry flock . . . but it is too awful to describe. Please rejoin me in a minute." The break here is as neat as the story's elimination of the plucking of the dead chicken and the even messier business of processing Helen into different types of feed.

"Arthur" highlights several much discussed concerns and preoccupations within the overall Hitchcock sphere. The idea of the perfect murder; the pros and cons concerning techniques for killing, often with a predilection for strangling demonstrated both on and off the screen; the perennial problem of getting rid of dead bodies—here handled with efficient dispatch; obsessive neatness in the mechanics of work and the rituals of domestic life; the synergetic overlap between murdering and eating; symbolically edible bodies and cannibalism predominantly connected to women as a kind of foodstuff, clean or unclean (Helen is, of course, soiled after the Stanley episode).[5] Related to this are the complexities of the avian code. Here birds feast on a human body, Hitchcock tells us, well in advance of The Birds (1963). The dialogue, Arthur's mannerisms, and his overall code of style, neatness, and sadistic politeness impress us as a peculiar form of upper-class Englishness, with a high measure of decorum complete with unwavering courtesy even at its most ironic, caustic, and noncommittal. Arthur, a self-made man and working dandy, comes across as a highly intelligent protagonist with a disdainful and self-serving Nietzschean streak beneath a polite, friendly, and collaborative façade as he rationalizes his crime without even a drop of conventional morals.

3. HITCHCOCKIAN REFLECTIONS

TRACES, PROXIES, DOUBLES, AND CORPSES

The Stroboscopic Poetics

Alfred Hitchcock's high-profiled physicality was foregrounded as a shrewd marketing model twisted around in countless self-deprecating variations and perpetuated in gossip columns. Writing in this established style as *Marnie* (Universal Pictures) was opening in Tokyo in 1964, and naturally starting out with a body quip for brand identification, Marjory Adams nailed what was at stake in this corporeal strategy: "Corpulent Alfred Hitchcock is better known to world filmgoers than most of his stars. He has used his paunchy figure and his agreeable fat face to publicize his mystery films all over the five continents."[1] For the marketing of *Marnie* in Japan, he had "ordered a full-face of himself" to be put on the posters for the film, with his eyes "recast in an Oriental slant." Through the circulation of his bodily imprint and distinctive yet malleable facial features, Hitchcock and his perennially lampooned corporeality had become inextricably tied to notions of the Hitchcockian and, as David O. Selznick had observed in 1943,[2] had an application beyond Hitchcock's body of work reaching even outside cinema. In the context of his own work, this somewhat elusive adjectival category called up spine-chilling narrative plotting that connected svelte actor bodies to audience bodies, with Hitchcock's own physicality hovering as a frame for creatively grounding the experience.

In this chapter I add yet one more layer to the corporeal marketing of the franchise, as succinctly noted by Adams, by exploring how body-tinged notions inside the films and teleplays resonate with ideas about the body of work as Hitchcockian. In line with the stroboscopic multiplicity of Hitchcock, he figures in this chapter in many shapes and forms: in tones, themes, and suspense patterns read as Hitchcockian; in casting consistency further reinforcing this perception; and in Hitchcock's visible presence inside the work in cameos. This authorial presence spills over to ideas about resemblances that mark characters as Hitchcock surrogates or proxies. His producers in turn deflect attention away from themselves to safeguard a style colored and apprehended exclusively as Hitchcock's. Finally, the crass physicality in stories that deal with murder and the manhandling of corpses rubs shoulders with a variety of disembodied figures that have a life of their own. All in all, the intense focus on bodies and corporeality in the films and teleplays dovetails with the marketing models that oscillated between Hitchcock's overflowing presence in the flesh and the logotype's sparse abstraction that stamped the work as his.

By doubling the host frame, the title character in "Arthur" (AHP 154) offered a second creative guide to the teleplay's style and narrative structure, which was made up of a string of flashbacks demonstrating a murder and its motivation and aftermath. In rounding off the teleplay, Alfred, not quite himself, reported on the grisly devouring of his smug cohost and authorial proxy. Physical dissimilitude apart, Arthur fits into a roster of characters having marked affinities with Hitchcock—merely functional in this case, distinctly physical in others—while a host of disembodied doubles underscored the brand corporeality that framed the franchise and its body plotting. This surrogate function encompasses not only brothers in fat such as Charles Laughton's characters but also a multitude of roles suggesting a more comprehensive, albeit highly charged, type of surrogacy within the franchise for Hitchcock's daughter, Pat. In the larger context of family plotting, Pat Hitchcock occupies a special place as an obvious surrogate on screens big and small, and with intricate tensions. The latter dynamics took on an array of forms and practices that Paula Marantz Cohen calls "the daughter effect."[3] Pat Hitchcock was also integral to the promotion of the franchise and eventually made the Hitchcock archives available for us to study today. She is a key informant and even coauthor for the wider realm of the Hitchcock family, especially concerning the creative input from Alma Hitchcock.

Alfred Hitchcock toyed with a revised notion of creative control back in 1937 in a signed trade-press article uncannily titled "Directors Are Dead."[4] Here Hitchcock was of course flirting with Hollywood and a hoped-for future studio contract when singling out the producer as the critical figure to consider as indelibly putting his stamp on the production in the manner of a Selznick. A few gifted directors, Hitchcock argued—himself included, one presumes—could, however, excel in a new type of multitasking role as producer-director. This shifting of emphasis was thus far from a wholesale plea for dismissal of creative control; agency still mattered for Hitchcock, especially his own as a prospective producer-director, not to mention brand and franchise.[5]

The Hitchcock figure that was paraded before the press, from the Manhattan spiels onward, was a carefully crafted role. In the aptly titled essay "The Man behind the Body" (1964) John D. Weaver underwrites the multiplicity suggested by the stroboscopic line of figures I have used as an emblem for Hitchcock's strategy (fig. Intro.1). According to Weaver, "this shadowy, stylized realm [the body of works] has been ruled for forty years by a calm, ample creature of habit who has made his bundle [by] frightening film audiences while living the orderly nine-to-six life of a civil servant."[6]

The split embodied by the notion of civil servant, or, rather, the cultivated set of Hitchcock figures, was never absolutely outside the body of works. The strategy was predicated on breaking down this conventional critical divide as Hitchcock established himself as a physically overflowing force hovering over the oeuvre as an inescapable reading frame and ghost in the machine—the Hitchcockian. In addition he visibly trespassed into the work as a cameo or was incorporated indirectly via surrogate characters and practices. In this sense Hitchcock is both a recognizable marketing body or logo attached to the work and a figurative anchor for its many processes of meaning. In the meaning game he can be actually spotted; inferred; or merely posited figuratively, thematically, or narratively. This triangulation matches the film medium's diverse mode of signification, which straddles the three types of signs that make up the semiotic spectrum at large: icons (representation by way of resemblance or imitation), indexes (by way of traces or analogies), and symbols (by way of coded conventions). Hitchcock's cameos and his appearance in paratexts, trailers, and photo-essays operated predominantly in the iconic register, while the more elusive notions I have designated as Hitchcockian function as traces and conventions. Surrogate characters such as Arthur harness elements across the semiotic categories on a case-by-case basis.

Roland Barthes approaches the role and figuration of the author/director in general as a process of inscription when discussing fictional texts. For Barthes, too, as in Hitchcock's drastic essay title, authors and directors are dead in the traditional sense; criticism interprets letters or works as a function or extension of the author's biography. Weaver's conundrum concerning the mismatch between the Hitchcockian and the life of private Hitchcock is thus a holdover from a time when authors/directors were alive, so to speak.

The meaning of a text, Barthes argues, is not an extension of the author's life, nor does it have its origin there. Barthes's critical analysis of literary textuality instead matches the corporeal multiplicity for Hitchcock that I am analyzing in terms of figures and performances, as we now gradually move into the body of work. The author (director by extension), writes Barthes, "is inscribed in the novel like one of his characters, figured in the carpet; no longer privileged, paternal, aletheological, his inscription is ludic. He becomes, as it were, a paper-author: his life is no longer the origin of his fictions but a fiction contributing to his work; there is a reversion of the work on to the life (and no longer the contrary)."[7] This is particularly relevant for an understanding of the inside versions of Hitchcock. "Ludic" is a key term for how the Hitchcockian was played up, and equally productive is Barthes's notion that the work reverts back to the life and not the other way around. The corporeal strategies ingeniously put into play an oscillation or conflation between work and performance, but with no "real" Alfred Hitchcock to be singled out among the Hitchcock figures. The trappings from the work eventually became impossible to shake off from life. Hitchcock could not avoid performing the Hitchcockian.

Barthes's "figure in the carpet" is a critical concept he picked up from a famous story of this title by Henry James. In this novella from 1896 about an author and his critic, the meaning inscribed by the author in the weaving of the text is rendered as an enigma to be unraveled by the critic/reader. Once the critic has detected the figure in the carpet as a token not just for one specific text, the oeuvre at large is cracked open. Penelope Houston, invoking Henry James's story in a Hitchcock context, outlined the implication of this notion for the critical project of authorship theory as a cinematic canon around a select group of directors began to take shape in the 1960s. The authorship theory outlined by Andrew Sarris and others when this critical perspective gained foothold in the United States involved a quest for the essential thread that holds a cinematic oeuvre together as a grand, perennial set of intertwined themes.[8] From this perspective a personal film style transcends studio constraints and colors an auteur's work at large. For a small pantheon of directors, this group of critics maintained, such a personal style merited the canonical status as auteur. Hitchcock was one of the paradigmatic examples; the reevaluation of his work in the mid-1960s in such terms started in France in a critical process analyzed by Robert E. Kapsis and debunked by Hollis Alpert.[9]

I have no ambition here to unravel capital meaning for Hitchcock as a pattern of grand design, as "the figure in the carpet," or as a set of figures on different carpets. Following Barthes, instead, Hitchcock is a bulky figure that is attached to the work as logotype and also seeps into the text as a figure—sometimes one we can actually spot, not merely the hard-to-discern figure (or, better, figurative pattern) on the carpet in Henry James's sense. Arguably Hitchcock can be found not as a carefully hidden meaning cluster but as a many-sided figuration bearing on his physicality. Corporeal brand recognition overwrites, but does not exclude, meaning ciphers.

Missing the careful orchestration of this process, Charles Higham's dismissal of Hitchcock in an edgy essay is as highbrow as Alpert's from around the same time. "I believe," writes Higham, "that the understanding of Hitchcock's *oeuvre* can only be reached when it is seen in the hard, unwavering light of his commercial-minded philistinism. He remains at heart a cheerful London showman with tough contempt for the world he has made his oyster."[10] Hitchcock was indeed an exceptional showman, but he was also a master puppeteer vying for full agency and creative recognition. Every body, his own included (actors as "cattle" was not just a fun pun), performed courtesy of Hitchcock's sleight of hand; this was the full-bodied showman's message, which in turn invoked the whole battery of Hitchcockian notions, including cameos and surrogate figures and figurations. John Russell Taylor is in step with this analysis when he notes, "The stunts serve their purpose. The pictures hit the papers, they keep Hitchcock a physical presence in the minds of the public, they are all part of his extraordinary talent for selling himself and his work."[11]

In this chapter I explore Hitchcock's figurative presence in the works through a group of ersatz Hitchcock figures, or surrogates, as well as a whole series of body approximations and practices in tune with the franchise's corporeal focus. I approach the cameos in more cursory form owing to their overt alignment with Hitchcock and because they have already been discussed in depth in the critical literature, foremost by Thomas M. Leitch and David Sterritt.[12] I explore near-body agency in a seminal series of teleplays featuring influential dummies, marionettes, ghosts, and corpses bearing on the franchise's signature-like body plotting and patterns for casting. In the film context, *Vertigo* (1958) pivots on intricate doubling, both in physical and in dummy form, not to mention the exchange between Norman and Mother in *Psycho* (1960). Doubling by way of mirrors and thematic associations is also key, as is the way casted actor bodies with preset significations revert back to the shadow figure who fronts as a logo for the television franchise. This corporeal cluster serves as a legend for how body-related strategies, tropes, and themes played out the Hitchcock brand on-screen, similar to the stroboscopic lineup of Hitchcock figures.

Cameos and Surrogates

In his cameos Hitchcock never takes on character status and he never speaks; instead, his bodily presence primarily functions as difficult-to-discern (though becoming progressively easier) logotypes for the audience to detect in a game-like fashion. The audience awareness of such a Hitch spot to scout for eventually became a distraction and had to be handled with dispatch in the films' openings so as not to steal too much attention. Hitchcock's unsuccessful attempt to board a bus during the credit sequence of North by Northwest (1959) presents a successful case in point. The cameos are Leitch's point of departure for a study of Hitchcock's narratives in the light of game theory.[13] In its most simple terms, the presence of the Hitchcock figure proclaims his authorial supremacy over the narrative. As Leitch convincingly shows, the nature of the game shifted across Hitchcock's career, most conspicuously so when he signed up for television and from there took his figure's performance mode to the film trailers. A visual fixture, Hitchcock's body was universally recognized; still, he continued to jestingly negotiate his unstable identity, and always with fat in the mix. In one of the countless self-deprecating jokes, here under the rubric "On Art," Hitchcock explained the threat to his identity should he lose fat:

> Hitchcock was asked to sit for a famous English artist. . . . Hitchcock turned down every request. . . . "Well, if you do me from the front I shall appear fat. . . . If you do me from the side I shall appear fat. And of course, if you do me from the rear I shall appear fat."
>
> "But if I paint you thin it won't be you," protested the artist.
>
> "True," Hitchcock answered. "Therefore why should I waste my time sitting for someone else?"[14]

This paradox is quite logical, unless one wishes to be somebody else, as Hitchcock as television host claimed he did on multiple occasions in the paratextual games.

In another context, Hitchcock himself, whatever that means in this bewildering gallery of doubles and surrogates, outlined the rationale for the cameo appearances and body doublings. Here, too, fat is the premise for the glib ruse. In a ghost-authored (what could be more appropriate?) after-dinner speech, Jimmie Allardice had Hitchcock wax eloquent on the question "Who is the real Alfred Hitchcock?" Banter aside, it is the inveterate Hitchcock issue of corpulence that the director flagellantly toys with by way of the ironic humor and scintillating wit that Allardice invariably offered Hitchcock as if it were the master's own ad-libbing. Attesting to the importance of casting and cameos, Hitchcock reflected pensively:

> There seems to be a widespread impression that I am stout. I can see you share my amusement at this obvious distortion of the truth. . . . I am certain that you are wondering how such a story got started. It began nearly 40 years ago. As you know, I make a brief appearance in each of my pictures. One of the earliest of these was *The Lodger*, the story of Jack the Ripper. My appearance called for me to walk up the stairs of the rooming house. Since my walk-ons in subsequent films would be equally strenuous—boarding buses, playing chess, etc.—I asked for a stunt man. Casting, in an unusual lack of perception, hired this fat man! The rest is history. HE became the public image of Alfred Hitchcock. Changing the image was impossible. Therefore I had to conform to the image.

As the speech proceeds, we learn that the life of the "cherubic friend" came to a tragic end when he drowned during the shooting of *Lifeboat*. Casting was then instructed to find a leading man for the next picture who mirrored a "detailed description of [Hitchcock's] true self":

> Casting did an expert job. The result: Cary Grant in *Notorious*.
>
> As you know, I still remain a prisoner of the old image. They say that inside every fat man is a thin man trying desperately to get out. Now you know that the thin man is the real Alfred Hitchcock.[15]

Rhetorical license permits the director to conveniently skip over Gregory Peck in *Spellbound* (1945) in the leap from *Lifeboat* (1944) to *Notorious* (1946). If nothing else, the speech neatly illustrates the adroit conniving that Allardice deployed for Hitchcock. Richard Gehman phrased this doubling slightly differently: "In person, when he speaks, it is as though there is another Hitchcock inside directing him. It is a careful creation of character, fully as contrived as anything he does on the screen."[16] Robert C. Cumbow's productive idea about relaying fears from Hitchcock (or the Hitchcock figure) to his different-looking characters pushes the focus away from the cameos to the issue of surrogate characters and figurations—some of them virtually Hitchcock lookalikes, others his bodily opposites.[17]

David Sterritt's analysis of the cameos outlines a related trajectory, while in the process shifting focus from cameos to surrogates. He proposes three functions for the Hitchcock figure when it appears in a cameo: first, a limited comment on the action, often with a "sardonic" undertone; second, a "wish to approach and 'keep an eye on' his characters"; and third, a message to the audience that he is the "presiding spirit" of the films.[18] This is in keeping with the bodily focus as our analytical mainframe. Sterritt amps up the third aspect of the cameo game by identifying surrogate figures in the films as being somehow aligned with the director as an extension of the cameos. They are, by definition, merely a stroboscopic flicker of recognizable Hitchcock presence to spot. Surrogates, however, are more commanding owing to their visible longevity or poignant symbolic representation of Hitchcock in order to graft a physical or psychological Hitchcock profile onto characters or other figurations. Surrogates would therefore be more useful proxies than the cameos for keeping the proceedings in line. From a more interrelated perspective, the cameos create an unequivocal Hitchcock awareness that suggests taking the spotting game a bit farther by finding surrogates in addition to cameos. For Sterritt, surrogates can be human characters as well as human-like figures or figurations. Among his examples are the painting of the laughing jester in *Blackmail* (British International Pictures, 1929), the Statue of Liberty in *Saboteur* (1942), and the presidential faces on Mount Rushmore in *North by Northwest*. Similarly, the whole series of bird images and the avian code at large in *Sabotage* (Gaumont British Picture Corporation, 1936), "Lamb to the Slaughter" (AHP 106), and a host of other teleplays, as well as the parlor crammed with stuffed birds in *Psycho*, are of this order.

The sublime mismatch between a Falstaffian Hitchcock figure consuming and reviewing dishes and what another Hitchcock, as it were, dished up on the screen generated an endless amount of copy over the years, as the foodie and fatso became a cultural fixture overwriting the notions of an implied thin author. These two Hitchcock extremes were ingeniously doubled and placed back-to-back in the cameo for *Lifeboat*, in which Hitchcock's former bodily largesse was placed side-by-side with his new lean self in an ad for a miracle drug allegedly having produced the slimmed-down Hitchcock figure.

Not unlike the devil, and in addition to cameos and surrogate characters, the Hitchcockian, arguably, is in the details, as style, narrative plotting, patterns of prop use, and casting consistency all mobilized in suspenseful ways and in a humorous, ironic register. Across the set of vicarious Hitchcock figures and figurations, the humor, tone, and suspense—three keywords picked up from the title of a seminal study by Susan Smith[19]—are critical for identifying the brand and its doubling mechanisms and surrogacy figuration. Meanwhile, the matching of Hitchcock figures in relation to a phalanx of character bodies or near bodies gave the impression of an elusive and elastic identity, with fat as a key critical lens.

Reflecting on Hitchcock's stylistic mastery and consistency, Vincent Canby invokes the director's conspicuous voice—most frequently heard in the hosting of the television show. Regarding the scope of the film cameos in the television era, Canby notes that "his unheard voice in any movie is as unmistakable as his image that is always seen, though fleetingly."[20] This "unheard voice" is a succinct formula for the aesthetic mechanisms of Hitchcock's cinema. With not even a fleeting cameo presence in the teleplays, the Hitchcock figure still exerted a commanding presence in the host segments, voice and all, as a totalizing signature emblem for the franchise.

Susan Smith frames the surrogacy discussion in several layers in her splendid reading of *Sabotage*, a film from decades before Hitchcock's television engagement. With shared plumpness as the premise, she posits an authorial alignment in surrogate terms for the film's saboteur, Verloc (Oscar Homolka), and Hitchcock. (Oscar Homolka, however, was not quite in Hitchcock's weight class.) In Verloc's final act of sabotage he blows up his wife's kid brother, Stevie—whether by design or by accident is unclear—when, owing to distractions that delay the boy en route, the bomb that he is unwittingly carrying for Verloc goes off before he reaches his destination. When Mrs. Verloc realizes what her husband has done, she knifes him at the dinner table. "This self-destructive aspect of Hitchcock's disposal of his main authorial surrogate," Smith writes, "is further suggested by the ambiguous depiction of the murder," which she interprets as Hitchcock's "implied suicide."[21] Underpinning her reading, Smith points to the occupational affinity between the saboteur and Hitchcock, albeit in different wings of the film business, as Verloc runs a movie theater. From these observations, Smith argues for a role for Hitchcock as mischievous film saboteur and more broadly designates his cinema as an ingenious form of convention-shattering sabotage in his bending of suspense strategies into unexpected screen resolutions. In her reading, the surrogacy function is aligned with a conceptualization of filmic storytelling and play featuring a character with cinematic agency due to his occupation and coupled with a symbolic reading of what sabotage entails, in reality and symbolically.

In preparation for the bombing, Verloc meets with the Professor, the actual bomb maker. The Professor, in true Hitchcock style, hides the device in the tray of a birdcage when sending it over to the cinema. Verloc, in turn, presents the two lovebirds to Stevie. The avian symbolism here takes on pointed significance as a cockerel is heard crowing twice during Verloc's visit to discuss the bomb plans at the Professor's place. This in addition to the presence of Disney's *Who Killed Cock Robin?* on Verloc's screen. Smith harnesses the overtones of the crowing by the half-italicized form "*cock*erel," which she reads as an implication of the filmmaker "with the material source of the sabotage function itself." This "gestures towards Hitchcock's own authorial presence in the background and in a way that seems to symbolically proclaim the director's involvement with sabotage as an implied assertion of film-making potency."[22]

With this in mind, let us revisit Arthur, the internal story host in the teleplay "Arthur," and his cocky gesture of sending cockerels to his unsuccessful police friend as a Christmas present. In Arthur's case the cockerels are associated with feed containing human remains as an undisclosed seasoning. Following Smith's logic for this Hitchcock-directed teleplay, we could say Hitchcock symbolically proclaims his authorial presence in an even more pronounced form than the mere background crowing in Sabotage. In the context of surrogates, and aligned with Smith's reading, Hitchcock would be materially implicated in Arthur's murder in spite of the unwillingness even to shoulder responsibility for imaginary violence and murder scenarios that Hitchcock expressed when Bob Hull interviewed him after the press preview of "Arthur."[23] Following Smith, we can add to Hitchcock's business card not only "saboteur" but also "murderer," which is further reinforced by his multiple appearances in significant strangling situations, in step with Arthur's method for killing off his ex-fiancée. Played by Laurence Harvey, Arthur is one of the different-looking bodies onto which Hitchcock grafts his own proclivities and obsessions with cleanliness, control, and a fixation on methods for the perfect murder. In this sense, Arthur as internal story host tells Alfred's story as much as his own.

The symbolical death wish for Hitchcock that Smith suggests in relation to Verloc returns as Peter Conrad assumes a surrogacy function in The Trouble with Harry (1955). Again, shared fat is the overt common denominator. Here Conrad associates Hitchcock with the dead Harry, who is "played" or embodied by the uncredited Philip Truex—whose father, Ernest Truex, later appeared in Alfred Hitchcock Presents (AHP). "As it happens," Conrad writes, "Harry is a fat man, whose face remains concealed. This supplies Hitchcock with his slyest incognito: playing dead, he awards himself the title role."[24] Conrad's chapter on fat in Hitchcock is masterful, especially his poignant discussion of Charles Laughton's two Hitchcock roles. Concerning Harry, Conrad's observation is moot. Harry's face is clearly visible on several occasions, which carries little significance for the argument; more troublesome is the fact that Truex was not a fat man, which somewhat spoils dead Harry's role as a stand-in for Hitchcock.

Discussing surrogacy in the same film, David Sterritt instead proposes a Hitchcock affinity with Edmund Gwenn as the Captain. This carries more weight, but in a different register from Conrad's Harry suggestion. Gwenn's Captain is fat, English, and has a penchant for not entirely truthful story-telling, thus sharing obvious traits with Hitchcock, plus a first name similar to Alfred—Albert—like the two Mr. Pelhams (minus fat) in "The Case of Mr. Pelham" (AHP 10). Gwenn had already been cast in two Hitchcock roles in Britain, and prior to taking on the role as Captain he appeared in *Foreign Correspondent* (1940) as a hired assassin who clumsily falls to his own demise as he tries to push the intended victim from a tower. In a prescient media aside, the Captain, apropos the busy traffic around the dead Harry, reflects, "Next thing you know, they will be televising the whole thing." Shortly thereafter Hitchcock began hosting television, with this film as model for the tone in the paratexts, and once featuring Gwenn. The role in "Father and Son" (AHP 75), in fact, was Gwenn's very last. If Santa was sometimes a moniker for Hitchcock, Gwenn's most famous role was as Kris Kringle in *Miracle on 34th Street* (Twentieth Century Fox Film Corporation, 1937). Naturally stocky, Gwenn put on additional fat rather than being padded up for the part. That he never managed to lose this bulk made him an ideal Hitchcock surrogate as the yarn-spinning Captain in *The Trouble with Harry*.

The most elaborate reworking of the Harry template took the form of a television function hosted in Miami in 1958. Here Harry's body was substituted for the true franchise body, albeit in inanimate and diminutive form. Young & Rubicam, AHP's and the sponsor's ad agency, had concocted the goofy idea of burying a small-scale replica of Hitchcock, as yet another version of doubling, in a time capsule on a Florida beach, and the television host cheerfully participated (fig. 3.1).[25] The opening gambit was a somewhat mystifying advertisement placed in several New York papers for a gravedigger who was "close-mouthed, experienced in all soils, adept at concealment," and who "should be 6 feet deep, 60 minute man but genteel." Hitchcock's effigy was to be buried at night, and the following evening a "Find the Body Contest" was held for "Grave Robbers and Amateur Fiends."[26] Twenty-one boxes were buried, one with the Hitchcock doll. The person who found the little Hitchcock effigy was to be awarded an automobile, a tiny Fiat 600 Sedan, not unlike the old Austin that fit Hitchcock like a swimsuit according to Alva Johnston.[27] Additional prizes were offered to the best-costumed diggers. Alfred and Alma Hitchcock attended in person to congratulate the winner, who turned out to be a lifeguard! Thirty-six hundred people took part in the search.

This public function, gravitating around Hitchcock effigies, body approximations, and exhuming, neatly illustrates the multiple strands of surrogacy and body play that more than anything defined the franchise and the realm of

3.1. Hitchcock in a time capsule to be buried—and exhumed—on the beach at Florida's Cranston Park. Photograph courtesy of Photofest. The image was also published in
Bristol-Myers's in-house publication *The Beam* (23, no. 3 [March 1958]: 1).

the Hitchcockian. Thus the critical function for the patterns of surrogacy, as for the cameos, was to invoke notions about an omnipresent Hitchcock body in command of all aspects of the narrative—be it for the purpose of sabotaging narrative conventions (*Sabotage*), testing out methods for perfect murders ("Arthur") and body disposal (*The Trouble with Harry* and "Arthur," among many teleplays), or spinning yarns (*Trouble*). The surrogacy function as discussed in the critical literature is perfectly attuned with Hitchcock's stance in his interview with Bob Hull after the press screening of "Arthur": "I suppose you might say I live a full other life in my pictures."[28] This "other life" operated in forms of surrogacy and affiliations with characters, fat or thin, as well in symbolic forms associated with the franchise's prime pivot—Hitchcock's body.

Like Father, Like Daughter

For the overall figuration of gender in Hitchcock's cinema, Pat Hitchcock takes on a momentous role in Paula Marantz Cohen's probing of "the daughter effect" and its repercussions. For Cohen, Pat's influence kept Daddy Hitchcock in check as long as her putatively critical gaze could question his every move in a weighty father-daughter allegiance and power balance both on and off the set. Cohen frames Hitchcock's gendered world as highly influenced by his relation to his daughter, who was unflatteringly featured in three of his movies: as Chubby in *Stage Fright* (Warner Bros., 1950), inscribed in fat affiliation (gender apart) with her portly father; as the salty, bespectacled, and symbolically strangled Barbara in *Strangers on a Train* (1951); and as the married gossip Caroline in the real estate office in *Psycho* (1960), strategically placed in the sightline of the Hitchcock cameo figure.[29]

Twisting Cohen's analysis, one might nominate Pat Hitchcock as the most obvious and proximate surrogate crisscrossing the Hitchcock oeuvre in many dimensions on and off the screen (figs. 3.2 and 3.3). I focus mainly on two strands: the father-daughter dynamic as it played out in conjunction with *Strangers on a Train*, which revolves around one recurrent practice, strangling; and Pat Hitchcock's role as custodian for the franchise in later years. In the later role Pat also emphasizes her mother's importance for the franchise.

Analyzing the daughter effect at work during the shooting of *Strangers on a Train*, Cohen posits a power struggle that plays out on the set and in the narrative as a consequence of a shifting dynamic between father and daughter. At twenty-two, Pat was a young actress—a profession not admired by her father—and not a little girl anymore. Two years later she was married and left home. And in true postwar suburbia style, she was soon the mother of

3.2. Father and daughter on the staircase—an architectural element fraught with signifi-
cance in films and teleplays and often signaling murderous designs. According to William
Rothman, staircases and bar patterns signify "loss of control or breakdown" (*Hitchcock:
The Murderous Gaze* [Cambridge, MA: Harvard University Press, 1982], 33). Courtesy of the
British Film Institute.

3.3. In an article illustrated with a photograph from the Hitchcock domicile the stern father points a finger like a gun at his screaming daughter. As a skilled young actress, she is registering fear while her mother, Alma, smiles in the background. "Patty the Boo," *American Magazine* 134, no. 1 (July 1942): 75. Photograph by Paul Dorsey.

two, and, in 1959, of three. In addition to her three film roles in the 1950s, she appeared quite regularly on AHP, in ten episodes between 1955 and 1960.

In Cohen's reading, Pat's authority waned after she married and deserted her father. Unchecked, Cohen maintains, Hitchcock now allowed himself to take screen revenge on her and other desiring women while reserving the sharpest stings for mothers. This was in tune with a postwar debate in the United States that singled out moms as responsible for the culture's increasing loss of sense and values. The dividing line between young girls and moms was, however, quite flimsy. Perhaps this is why Pat's most negative screen appearance, now a married mother in a married role, was in *Psycho*. According to Cohen, the father/director retaliates and punishes his grown-up daughter for her three strikes: for being an actress (that is, for enrolling in the undignified cattle business); for abandoning the home; and for turning into a mature, sexually active woman, confirmed by her motherhood.[30] Cohen does not consider Pat Hitchcock's ten roles in the teleplays after she had married. Her final role in AHP was in an episode aired just a few days before *Psycho*, after which she retired from screens big and small.

Never the leading lady type, Pat Hitchcock did most of her acting for television, predominantly in her father's television series in subordinate parts, and usually as a maid.[31] In her first lead, in a costume piece, she plays a daughter whose mother vanishes, as the title of the episode states, "Into Thin Air" (AHP 5), after which all traces of her and her mother having stayed at "their" hotel are eradicated. It turns out that the hotel was covering up her mother's fatal demise so as not to scare away prospective guests coming to Paris for the World Exposition. In Pat Hitchcock's only romantic part, as a schoolteacher in "The Belfry" (AHP 33), her hopes for love are brutally annihilated the day after her engagement. A mentally challenged young man who is in love with the schoolteacher cannot accept the fact that she loves another man, and he kills the fiancé right off the bat with an axe. In one deranged blow, Pat Hitchcock's character is cut off from the double helix of desire and turned into a seemingly untouched widow before even marrying. Symbolically, Pat's sexuality is rolled back and annihilated.

In the critical literature an incident during the shooting of *Strangers on a Train* figures prominently as an indicator of Hitchcock's sadistic treatment of women, which did not spare even his own daughter. On the basis of a widely reprinted press release from Warner Bros., Donald Spoto singles out Pat's adventures on the Ferris wheel while shooting the film's final scenes at the fairground as a crucial element in his analysis of Hitchcock's dark side. The story gained traction as yet another Hitchcock joke, albeit a decidedly cruel one, and, giving it added significance, was published of his own volition through his studio. According to the press release:

> Patricia begged for a ride on the ferris wheel. When she and her escort got aboard and the wheel took them to the top, Hitchcock ordered the concession stopped and the lights turned off.
>
> Hitchcock then deserted the couple and returned to another corner of the set to guide Farley Granger and Robert Walker through a scene.
>
> The stranded couple hooted and hollered for help, but were trapped in the air for an hour until the wheel was ordered lowered by Hitchcock and the "prisoners" released.

Spoto dramatizes the story, which in the quoted news item above is conveyed verbatim from the press release, by omitting Patricia's escort from his narrative and upping the hooting and hollering to hysterical fear. Patricia, in turn, has played down the episode by relating it to a bet between father and daughter and reducing the timespan from an hour to two minutes.[32]

For Cohen, the Ferris wheel story plays into Hitchcock's sadism toward screen heroines when Pat abandoned him.[33] Using the studio to publish the joke orchestrated at his daughter's expense signals an ongoing power struggle between the father and daughter, as he publicly displayed his mastery of her through the press—and in putatively jesting terms. He showed himself as on top of the game by making her powerless (and cutting the electricity to boot) high up in the air and leaving her suspended as long as Daddy deemed appropriate, meanwhile eliminating her critical gaze from the action on the ground.[34] The episode can be read as a counterpart to the constantly recounted brief imprisonment of young Alfred orchestrated by his father.[35]

Pat Hitchcock's most famous screen scene, as a deferred victim of strangling in *Strangers on a Train*, ties in with the Ferris wheel episode. Furthermore, the scene plays into a serialized strangling practice between the father and daughter. The strangling scenes involving Pat Hitchcock's character are among the most elaborate strangling scenes in Hitchcock's cinema between *Rope* (1948) and *Frenzy* (1972). In the loaded scene in *Strangers on a Train*, Bruno—after having strangled Guy Haines's promiscuous wife and hoping Guy will fulfill his part by killing Bruno's father in a one-sided murder-swap pact—demonstrates his strangulation technique on an older woman. Caught in the crosshairs of Pat's gaze, and struck by her partial similarity to his previous strangling victim (spectacles and all), he freezes. His gaze riveted to Pat's character, Bruno almost strangles the woman in a form of abject desire, before fainting from the emotional overload (fig. 3.4).

In Sterritt's expansion of surrogacy patterns beyond characters, he considers props and elements of setting, but not practices.[36] The endless deliberations on the idea and practice of the perfect murder, the historiography of famous murder cases, and the cultural differences between English and American murders have a performance component that centers on strangling both on and off the screen. Strangling scenes were a bread-and-butter aspect of the Hitchcockian and one of its quintessential macabre strands. Spoto has culled the more or less full roster of strangulation scenes in Hitchcock's cinema, but the television series also offers a bevy of scenes featuring this practice.[37] Strangling's very prominence turns it into a feature on a par with the surrogacy figurations nominated by Sterritt—and Pat was an eminent

3.4. Pat Hitchcock in the deferred strangulation scene from *Strangers on a Train* (1951).

(and willing) sidekick within this surrogacy matrix. Here the interaction between Alfred and Pat Hitchcock takes on a slightly perverse mode of transfers
and exchanges in a whole series of situations on and off the screen, with the
Ferris-wheel episode as a sidebar adding fuel to the fire. After commissioning
a bust of Patricia by the sculptor Jacob Epstein in 1949, and as a preamble to
the scene in Strangers on a Train, Hitchcock fooled around with the sculpture
in a series of photographs. Years later Hitchcock returned to the bust, now
mock-strangling the statue of Pat (fig. 3.5).[38]

Widening the significance of the bust scene, strangling was apparently
a contact sport between father and daughter in the Hitchcock household. A
photograph featuring Hitchcock strangling his daughter was published in the
New York Herald Tribune column "New York Close-Up," mockingly captioned
"The Case of the Willing Victim" (fig. 3.6). "He strangles me every night before I go to bed," Pat explained. "It's better than a massage!"[39] The image
of Hitchcock mock-strangling his daughter circulated around the time Pat
Hitchcock played the visually locked-in victim of Bruno's strangling demonstration. (Her bedroom, if this was the scene for this ritual, was depicted in
the home reportage from 1942 in House and Garden, and was reached by climbing the staircase from which father and daughter descend in fig. 3.2.)[40]

Hitchcock apparently relished executing mock-strangling scenes, at times
castling the positions and turning himself into a victim in such posing stunts.
A self-inflicted strangulation was depicted in the same column in which he
later strangled Pat, and he had actors strangling him in conjunction with
the shooting of "The Perfect Crime" (AHP 81), a teleplay involving strangling
(fig. 3.6).[41] Also as a promotion for the television series, Hitchcock strangled
Mary Scott, who appears in "Mr. Blanchard's Secret" (AHP 52). He explained
strangulation techniques, albeit not hands-on, to Claude Rains during a photographed conversation (fig. 3.7), and he forcefully strangled a male dummy
(substituting for the Madeline dummy in the film) during the Vertigo party in
New York City (fig. 3.6). This onslaught of strangulation variations on-screen
and off attests to a signature-like obsession that merits the practice being
included within the general frame of surrogacy that signals the Hitchcockian and with Patricia Hitchcock as a prominent sidekick, willing victim, and
surrogate figure.

The overall family network of transfers, intertexts, and talking points be-
speaks a highly charged surrogacy role for Pat before she was a woman with
mature desires and out of Daddy's sometimes strangling reach. In Strangers on
a Train, reinforcing the surrogate track, Pat Hitchcock's character Barbara is
quite salty and outspoken in contrast to her very correct older sister, played

3.5. Alfred Hitchcock interacting with Jacob Epstein's bust of Pat Hitchcock.
Photograph by Philippe Halsman, courtesy of Magnum Photos.

by Ruth Roman. This, too, aligns Pat with Alfred Hitchcock. Barbara, looking more girlish than Pat's twenty-two, is quite savvy when it comes to criminal matters and savors the gory details about murders she picks up after befriending Detective Hennessey, Guy Haines's shadow. She eagerly tells Guy (Farley Granger) about Hennessey's role in cracking a recent axe-murder case: "The body was cut up and hidden in the butcher shop and he was locked in the icebox with the left leg for six hours." The enthusiasm for a grisly murder story with a built-in food component further reinforces Barbara's kinship with the director and thus her surrogate status. Subsequently, Barbara corners Hennessey when Guy is about to sneak off to the fairground to clear himself of the murder suspicions. Her method of delaying him is fresh and aimed at the detective's most vulnerable body parts, as she "accidentally" spills powder all

3.6. Strangulation scenes. *Clockwise from bottom: Vertigo* party in 1958, courtesy of Photofest; Tex McCrary and Jinx Falkenburg, "New York Close-Up," *New York Herald Tribune,* 8 July, 1951, D1; Hitchcock as the victim, author's collection; James Gregory (in profile), Vincent Price, and Hitchcock on the set of "The Perfect Crime" (AHP 81), author's collection.

3.7. According to the caption, Alfred Hitchcock is educating Claude Rains regarding strangulation techniques. Photograph by Nat Dallinger, courtesy of the Academy for Motion Picture Arts and Sciences.

over his crotch and eagerly tries to brush it off. This is quite an undignified situation for the authority figure and amusing in a carnivalizing fashion.

Parallel to her parts for AHP, Pat Hitchcock became even more integral to the franchise after she was appointed associate editor for *Alfred Hitchcock's Mystery Magazine* in 1956. Exactly how involved she was in the production of the magazine is impossible to tell; she remained on the payroll for decades. Pat's involvement, nominal or not, might have persuaded Hitchcock to be quite personal at times in his monthly editorials, especially in the early days of the magazine when he mentions his grandchildren by name—for example, when Pat's daughter Mary, together with her mother, played a part in "The Schartz-Metterklume Method" (AHP 188). On a more mundane note in the father-daughter dynamics, Pat Hitchcock was also in charge of the fan club that was repeatedly advertised in the mystery magazine. The club did not operate through the publisher's office, but out of Tarzana, California, where Pat and her family lived in suburban bliss. From her home she sent out autographed portraits of Hitchcock and a news bulletin to members in the club. Taking on these filial chores was a first step for the former actress who, under the umbrella of surrogacy, became the magazine editor then coauthor, custodian, and spokesperson for the franchise. Unwavering in her loyalty to the brand, she never steered from the course of promoting the notions of the Hitchcockian that she also embodied in chubby allegiance with the Hitchcock figures and their swath of bizarre practices. The many roles she played after abandoning her screen career associated her with the team that produced in Hitchcock's name and by casting actors who signaled franchise affiliation.

In 2003 Patricia Hitchcock O'Connell and Laurent Bouzereau authored a book devoted to Pat's mother, *Alma Hitchcock: The Woman behind the Man*. While revisiting familiar territory, it rewrites the authorship theory's sole focus on Alfred by putting Alma into the creative mix, albeit nominally behind the man. In the book's chronological story, organized according to Alfred Hitchcock's filmography, Alma's contributions are written into the oeuvre. By strategically siding with Alfred Hitchcock's downplaying of the shooting, and upgrading the homework, if you will, Pat's account magnifies Alma's role. Thus, according to Pat, "Hitch . . . was bored during filming because he had already done so much preparation that it was just a matter of getting the shots on film. Pre-production on my father's films was most crucial simply because that was when he made all the important decisions with Alma as his closest collaborator."[42]

The private photos culled from family albums for the many illustrations in the book on Alma feature an array of both domestic scenes and what could be

3.8. The woman behind the man: Alma snapping, Alfred posing in 1955.
Photograph by John Duprey, courtesy of *Daily News* (New York).

described as professional contexts. These "amateur" images form a parallel track to the professional home photographs published in conjunction with domestic photo-essays. When the narrative comes to a close and both parents have been put to rest, we are treated to bonus material and a chapter called "To Catch a Meal: Alma's Cookbook." This is fascinating stuff in relation to the marketing of Hitchcock, the makeover of the kitchen, and the malleable Hitchcock persona. The distinctions are once again blurred in the exchange between Alma and Alfred: she is a collaborator and his only true critic; he is the prime recipient of her gourmet cooking and simultaneously her appreciative food critic. In this partnership, cooking and cinema are highly intertwined and mutually reinforcing.

At the end of the book on Alma and Alfred's creative partnership, and following the food chapter, Pat offers some of "[her] mother's most treasured recipes." For fans, this set of recipes offers an opportunity to cook their way into the alimentary Hitchcock sphere and get a taste of the Hitchcock world. The opportunity for replication is of course standard for many star-authored manuals and how-to books. The ambition here, however, is also historical:

the recipes are followed by a section devoted to Alma's menus in 1963, the year when a modernist photo-essay was published in Look.[43] These menus are, however, not for us to cook up; instead we find a full set of actual menus served for the Hitchcocks' guests, some in facsimile, others printed from notes in a diary or album. These scripted dinners are meticulously annotated with dates, guest lists, and indications of helpers at bigger events. This postscript takes Hitchcock's American period full circle in its endeavor for accuracy. In a sense, the ambitions here mirror the Hitchcocks' very first visit to the United States, the gastronomic holiday in 1937, when stunned journalists chronicled down to the last dish Hitchcock's eating in public, with Alma as silent witness. Here the cooking and menus are in her hands as part of the creative culinary partnership that spilled over into cinema.

When Pat Hitchcock became the custodian of the Hitchcock franchise on Alfred's death, she elected to turn over the papers from her father's office at Universal to the Academy of Motion Picture Arts and Sciences (AMPAS), and they have been inventoried and archived in the Margaret Herrick Library as the Alfred Hitchcock Papers, the most important depository for studying Hitchcock. The family's collection of materials not handed over to AMPAS gradually seeps out to blur even further the boundaries for a brand that was hinged on an elaborate mise-en-scène of the public as private and the private as public, represented by the Hitchcock figure as a physical logo and with the family as enablers, collaborators, and surrogates.

Catering to Hitchcock: Producing as Surrogacy

While Hitchcock himself was only on the fringe of the day-to-day television operations, his body, voice, and spirit were in soaring command. In the process of crafting the show as fully Hitchcock's, the team toyed with story lines from his films and rehashed themes, visual motifs, and music (some of which was composed by Bernard Herrmann) from the Hitchcock canon. Adding to the Hitchcockian package, and shaping an inescapable frame for understanding all things Hitchcock in the process, the producers elected to cast quite a few of the films' stars and supporting actors in featured parts.

Over at the Paramount lot, Hitchcock had found a writer, John Michael Hayes, with a knack for scripting quintessential Hitchcockian movies. When the smooth collaboration ended after *The Man Who Knew Too Much* (1956), the gestation process for the screenplays became much more cumbersome and sometimes turned into a writing relay (*Vertigo* comes to mind), which was not uncommon in Hollywood. Henceforth writers barely survived beyond one film. Hayes, on the other hand, seems to have been a perfect foil for translating the Hitchcockian experience and managed to find a truly congenial writing style in this overarching mold for a quartet of screenplays.[44]

As Hitchcock turned to television, he entrusted the show to his long-time assistant, now a seasoned producer, Joan Harrison. Her command of the Hitchcock canon was formidable, and she formed a team with a keen knack for story scouting (Pat Hitchcock included), recruiting directors, and making casting choices that replicated the ludic mischief integral to the perception of the Hitchcockian. The typing of recurrent actors and picking up of players with a history in Hitchcock's cinema cleverly brought back the old character in the mind's eye of the connoisseurs and combined them with the new. In rare cases, Harrison had even been instrumental in molding the erstwhile character as co-scenarist—for example, the meek wife played by Joan Fontaine in Suspicion. Bringing back Fontaine for "The Paragon" (AHH 20) neatly illustrates this crossover casting between Hitchcock's cinema and television in the hands of Harrison and the producer Norman Lloyd. In this teleplay, Alice (Joan Fontaine) pesters her relatives by trying to micromanage their lives. Her husband (Gary Merrill) tries to talk her out of being such a meddling busybody, but she just doesn't get it and cannot stop intervening, even after disastrous results. The long now-or-never scene in which he tries to get her to understand what she is and reveal her true identity as a destructive meddler takes place in front of a mirror, a fixture in the show for the probing of character. This is the one and only casting of Joan Fontaine in the series, which is indicative of the producers' playfulness in relation to Hitchcockiana. Back in 1941, how to end Suspicion posed a veritable dilemma for Hitchcock and his film producer. The preferred solution was to have Cary Grant's roguish husband character poison his wife, played by Fontaine, in accordance with the novel's ending. After much deliberation and shooting several versions, they instead ended the film on a less bleak note. In "The Paragon," some twenty years later, Joan Fontaine's character, as an overdue postscript, if you will, is indeed poisoned by her husband, albeit not out of roguish motives but as the only way to stop her well-meaning but devastating interference in the lives of others. As in the film, the decisive scene takes place when Joan Fontaine's character is in bed. Joan Harrison was part of the writing team for Suspicion; decades later she was the producer and steward of Hitchcockiana, finally dispensing the fatal beverage to Fontaine's character.

In this playful manner, the concept of artistic agency in the television show's production process was highly elastic, because the directing was mainly delegated to others and the script work did not involve Hitchcock. Nevertheless, the show's hook was Hitchcock's name and charisma. His name, voice, and bodily imprint were the anchoring points for a franchise framed by his on-screen presence and the few episodes he personally directed for good measure. If nothing else, Hitchcock's on-screen appearance stretched the Hitchcockian creative presence and voice beyond the prologue to encompass, infiltrate, and color all aspects of the show, perhaps even shifting the distinction between paratext and text proper. This analysis would suggest that the show served as mere pretext for Hitchcock's paratextual tomfoolery.[45] Hitchcock was keen to bring over this notion of full control, and his producers efficiently used a preset domain for further invoking the host: what we vaguely have designated the Hitchcockian.

The concept of "authorship by commission" broadens the creative agency for tracing the stylistic fingerprints and identity markers for the show. Obviously, the series circulated under Hitchcock's name and under the spell of his powerful presence in each episode's prologue and epilogue, and as the focal point of the marketing as a whole. Though he never explicitly claimed full creative responsibility for the series, Hitchcock was always in the loop, as Norman Lloyd has elucidated in his writings and comments.[46] In the day-to-day making of the show it was the producers—first Harrison, then Harrison and Lloyd, then, during the final seasons, predominantly Lloyd—who carried the torch for the Hitchcock franchise. Hitchcock hired Harrison in Britain and brought her over with the Hitchcock family in 1939. An interoffice memo exchanged in the Myron Selznick agency elucidates Harrison's critical role at that early stage: "Hitchcock says it is essential for him to have his secretary and script clerk with him on both pictures. . . . Hitchcock says this girl has worked for him for years and is invaluable to him in connection with his 'peculiar system' of writing his shooting schedule, camera angles, etc."[47]

After years of high-profile Hollywood dating, Harrison married the novelist Eric Ambler in 1958 and gradually handed more and more responsibilities over to Lloyd. Harrison never wrote about her work. After her television stint with Hitchcock, she and Lloyd produced the series *Journey to the Unknown* (Twentieth Century Fox Television / Hammer Film Productions, 1968–1969), which had links back to the Hitchcock series: Robert Stevens directed a few episodes; mystery writer Robert Bloch (author of *Psycho* and several teleplays for Hitchcock) scripted some; the actors included several familiar names from the Hitchcock canon, such as Joseph Cotten, Vera Miles, and Barbara Bel Geddes; and there were many familiar themes.

Of the Hitchcock series, Joan Harrison said, "Hitch and I are in complete accord about what goes into the show each week. . . . We agree entirely on shock value with a bit of weird humor added."[48] The standard version regarding the division of labor for the series is that Harrison singled out stories she believed Hitchcock would be interested in directing and he yielded to her judgment. As for the episodes directed by others, Hitchcock watched the material before it aired and rarely needed to intervene in more than a limited fashion. The extent of Hitchcock's early involvement during the first two seasons, when he directed most frequently, is the least documented, as Lloyd was not yet on board and nobody conducted an in-depth interview with Harrison on this topic. According to the invaluable companion volume devoted to the two series, based on multiple interviews:

> Hitchcock was involved only in a supervisory capacity—but within that role, particularly at the crucial stage of story selection, his influence seems to have been significant. Hitchcock would be presented with potential stories in synopsized form, which he would then approve or disapprove. The scripts were then developed under the supervision of Harrison and as Lloyd described: "Hitchcock seldom spoke about how a script should be shot. He had nothing to do with the picture until he saw a rough-cut. Then he would look at it and say yes or no, and usually he'd say 'Well maybe you need a close-up or an insert or something.' That was the extent he played in the actual making of it."[49]

For television, Hitchcock and the team opted for an architectural approach to creative agency in the shared Hitchcockian enterprise. When attributing authorship to a building, for example, we discount the contractor and crew and focus on the architect—producer and director in one—who works at the drawing board before calling the shots. Leading architects only supervise collaborative endeavors executed by a team of architects (say, Harrison, Lloyd & Associates) in their firm, whose work is subsumed under the leading architects' name or brand. Renowned restaurant chefs or star designers in haute couture houses employ a similar approach. By way of commissioned brand agency, Hitchcock managed to make the television show fully his own, even when not directing or storyboarding, owing to his supervising capacity for the name or brand, just like a Frank Gehry, Wolfgang Puck, or Giorgio Armani. Hitchcock's hosting—his visible presence and voice—was paramount for making the show supremely his. Because of the success of the hosting and the show's cultural longevity, the television episodes are not merely minor vehicles reinforcing Hitchcock's "serious" cinematic artistry, but a much more involved enterprise with repercussions for the oeuvre at large. The television show cannot be dismissed as a lucrative artistic vacation or sideshow that had limited bearing on the cultural and artistic circulation of the brand. The show became the most prominent marquee for the franchise, and, in spite of Hitchcock's limited involvement, the authorship commission carried out by his team—Harrison, Lloyd, and not least Allardice—secured a perception of the show as fully Hitchcock's.

Jimmie Allardice offered his own version of creative agency in the paratexts for "Ambition" (AHP 229). In the prologue Hitchcock introduces an associate, Mr. Lloyd, which is a bird sitting on a perch. For those familiar with the credits for the show, Norman Lloyd comes to mind. Lloyd was a jack-of-all-trades for the franchise. He directed many episodes, played the lead in others, and had two roles in Hitchcock movies, the title role in *Saboteur* and one of the patients in *Spellbound*. According to the hopeful host in "Ambition," Mr. Lloyd "may even take over my work permanently, thus freeing me for other duties." Mr. Lloyd, however, stubbornly refuses to introduce the episode. In the first part of the epilogue Mr. Lloyd is no longer visible; instead, a dead bird is hanging on a hook. In the second part of the epilogue the empty perch has replaced the hook. "The garrulous Mr. Lloyd is no longer with us. He has answered a higher calling," Hitchcock explains as he sits down at an elegantly set table with a bird on a dinner plate—we are even offered a cut-in to the plate for added clarity. The episode comes to a close as Hitchcock prepares to eat poor Mr. Lloyd. A few years later Allardice scripted Hitchcock in the form of an avian lecture as part of a trailer for *The Birds* (1963). The second time around Hitchcock had second thoughts and refrained from eating his bird meal.[50]

Hitchcock's presence as presenter, and his critical success in this capacity, instilled an impression of full command and agency irrespective of the actual division of labor and creative agency. The television show thus invites readings regarding tone, themes, and implied authorship that speak to a larger Hitchcockian frame of reference. The cinematic universe functioned as a sounding board for Hitchcock's television as the small and big screens blended in intricate and mutually rewarding ways, with casting as a critical component. From such a perspective, the television episodes and their paratexts are at the very heart of the Hitchcockian. The cultural imprint of his television show, which he simultaneously shaped and commissioned, outlasted the series' actual tenure.

In a veritable masterpiece in the series, "Banquo's Chair" (AHP 146), the mise-en-scène presents an interior master of ceremonies. We are not, however, treated to a second layer of hosting and direct address à la Arthur, but a surrogate director played by the quintessential British actor John Williams, a frequent Hitchcock foil who was regularly cast both in the films (*Dial M for Murder* [1954] and *To Catch a Thief* [Paramount Pictures, 1955]) and in teleplays. Forcefully arranging the proceedings, the surrogate director in "Banquo's Chair," Williams's Inspector Brent, is stripped of agency and control as the proceedings comes to a close outside his script. Other forces have taken over, leaving him crestfallen in spite of his success.

Plans developing in unforeseen directions swirled around Williams's teleplay characters. As a con man, English Jim, in "The Long Shot" (AHP 9) he murders a man and steals his identity in order to collect an inheritance in San Francisco, but he ends up getting killed by his travel companion in the Nevada desert. Making a second attempt to reach California, again preceded by murder (of his horrid wife back in England), Williams's character this time succeeds. In "Back for Christmas" (AHP 23), which again played with the polarity of Hitchcock's and Williams's two countries, Williams's character buries his wife (Isobel Elsom) in the cellar and hopes to spend the rest of his life unsupervised in a relaxed Beverly Hills environment where he can award himself a beer for breakfast, should he be so inclined. As always in Hitchcock television, perfect murder plots backfire. Here the wife's corpse is discovered, cutting short the relocation to freedom out west. The irony works on multiple levels, especially for latter-day audiences, as the perennial police officer in the Hitchcock universe, John Williams, is cast as a murderer in his two first roles for AHP. Thus, after two large film roles for Hitchcock, as well as roles in additional teleplays, Williams as Inspector Brent was eminently aligned with the franchise and its many-sided Englishness and murder plots.

Directed by Hitchcock, "Banquo's Chair" demonstrates full command of television's stylistic toolbox but still pivots on one specific device: an editing pattern with fixed camera positions correlating to a suspense arc, with a gradual shift in shot scale all the way to extreme close-up as animated dinner conversation flows across the table. Shortly after finishing *The Birds*, Hitchcock was invited to give a talk at the University of California, Los Angeles, in conjunction with an award ceremony for screenwriting. In preparation for the event he sat down with Jimmie Allardice for an extensive sparring session. This taped Q&A exchange, which took place in April 1963, covered an array of topics. One question prompted Hitchcock to launch into a lengthy digression on shot scale—the critical aspect of the storytelling in "Banquo's Chair." After elaborating on the shooting of Arbogast's murder in Psycho—a scene he often revisited in interviews—Hitchcock made an observation in passing on his own television show: "That is why I see many young directors . . . and I see it in our shows, you know . . . but I'm not on the set all the time . . . using huge heads [close-ups] for a very ordinary conversation and it's nonsense, really, because you cannot use this emphasis, this pictorial emphasis, when it's not necessary. You should stay away and keep a modest size image because you may need that big head."[51] Hitchcock thereafter steered the discussion back to cinema and The Birds, his most recent directorial endeavor. This comment on television stylistics is quite a rarity, since Hitchcock hardly ever offered detailed reflections concerning particular devices of televisual storytelling. So let's ponder the observation in the context of Hitchcock's own teleplay practice.

Even in the face of Hitchcock's mild reservations regarding occasionally misdirected and overblown shot scales on his own show, the stylistic choices seem to have rested predominantly with his producing team. Insofar as it makes sense to lump the shows together in terms of a consistent, elegantly polished style supervised by the franchise team, there are, however, some distinguishing exceptions to this wider sphere of collective authorship under the Hitchcockian umbrella or surrogacy. One such teleplay is the Emmy-awarded "The Glass Eye" (AHP 79), directed by Robert Stevens; another is the Hitchcock-directed episode "Banquo's Chair," which neatly illustrates the heady critical point Hitchcock put forward in the exchange with Allardice, his ghostwriter.

On the small screen, Hitchcock's direction of "Banquo's Chair" serves as an object lesson for orchestrating shifts in shot scale in order to achieve the sought-after maximum effect and pictorial emphasis of a big head, an extreme close-up. The orchestration, marrying the team's producing dexterity with Hitchcock's touch, is nothing less than a tour de force and a formidable signature piece in terms of small-screen stylistics. Formally, this is the most consistently told story in the entire series and, overall, the finest screen meal directed by the master of exquisite screen dining. The showcasing of the surrogacy function and its narrative preeminence is simultaneously marked as provisional and beyond control from inside the story universe.

"Banquo's Chair" aired during season four of AHP. The teleplay features four main players, plus four supporting roles and a dog. In addition, a ghost, hovering in the twilight zone between played and not played, embodied and disembodied, should not be ignored. The obligatory twist ending hinges on the very uncertainty concerning the ghost's identity and whether or not it is embodied, a theme in step with the overall bodily slant of the show. The parts are elegantly intertwined and revolve around the theme of guilt, a perennial favorite of Hitchcock's. As is often the case with Hitchcock, the seemingly lighthearted meal setting provides the pretext for handling grave matters. In this case, the dinner's elaborate orchestration is scripted by one of the characters to elicit an incriminating confession from a murder suspect invited under false pretenses.

Based on Rupert Croft-Cooke's play from 1930, which was later reworked to a short story and released in film form in 1945 (*The Fatal Witness*, Republic Pictures), the treatment for the television version was prepared by Francis Cockrell.[52] Cockrell wrote nineteen teleplays for AHP, directed two (both featuring John Williams), and was one of the key contributors in the early days. He also took on two assignments for *Suspicion* (NBC, 1957–1958). Among his teleplays was "Breakdown" (AHP 7), based on his own adaptation broadcasted in *Suspense* in 1950. "Banquo's Chair" turned out to be his last assignment for the franchise.

The teleplay features a dinner party set in 1903, and the first to arrive is Inspector William Brent, played by John Williams in a commanding role. Though he is not the formal dinner host, he runs the show in a mansion with a loaded history with the intention of scaring a confession out of a murderer during the meal. The uncertainty around actual agency as the story unfolds brings to the fore the surrogacy issue in its most complex configuration in the television series. The interior directing role is thus entrusted to a key surrogate who, nevertheless, will be taken aback by the unforeseen aspects of a spectacle slipping out of control.

From the outset, Inspector Brent is very much the director of the proceedings in every aspect, from casting to mise-en-scène, lightning, and sound effects. The teleplay is also a tripping up of a surrogate director, as the authorial function seemingly highjacks the surrogate's plan. This can be read in terms of style, as Hitchcockian cunning of the highest order, most assertively marked in a high-angle shot that soars above the characters before closing in on the guilty party in alliance with the surrogate. Wrapping matters up in the closing shots, the master of ceremonies is taking away from the surrogate's command and control. In the void, this leaves Inspector Brent flustered, almost horrified, in the teleplay's final moment before we return to the host proper. Full authority thus rests outside the purview of the story universe as set up by Inspector Brent.

Meanwhile, the host frame featuring Hitchcock toys with distance in time and space as the host propels us from now in Hollywood to then in London—and back. As Hitchcock's prologue to the show aptly phrases it, we are transported from smoggy Hollywood to "foggy London"—Blackheath, to be exact—as the Victorian era was slowly turning Edwardian. The day is 23 October 1903 at 7:20 p.m. The episode is shot in two blocks without temporal gaps and with only a single interruption, the obligatory commercial break separating the presentation's segments. Thus the audience gets the same sense of real time as the ticking clock is intended to produce in 24 (Fox, 2001–2010).

The only open murder case on the retired Inspector Brent's résumé offers the premise for the staging of the dinner. Two years ago to the day of the dinner, and in the actual dining room of the house in which Brent meticulously arranges a dinner party for four by proxy, the mistress of the house was murdered. To solve the vexing case, the inspector has enlisted the help of Major Cooke-Finch (C-F, played by Reginald Gardiner), the current owner of the house and the host in name. The Shakespearean actor Robert Stone (Max Adrian) has been invited to act as an accomplice and stage-savvy sidekick under Brent's direction. Fittingly for the Banquo setup, Stone is currently playing Macbeth. Staging and acting are prime tenors for snaring the guest of honor: John Bedford (Kenneth Haigh from "Specialty of the House" [AHP 165]), the murder victim's nephew and sole heir. In spite of Bedford's ironclad alibi, supplied by a fiancée, Inspector Brent hopes to scare a confession out of him by hiring an actress to appear as the aunt's ghost during the dinner. In the pantry a detective is hiding with his dog; the latter is to wail as a reminder of the dead woman's canine shortly before the ghost appears. The trappings and the elaborate orchestration are highly theatrical and performance driven, and the dinner accomplices are instructed to neither notice the dog's wailing nor acknowledge the ghost, thus prompting Bedford to break. The setup is decidedly Shakespearean in nature and neatly modeled on the story of Banquo's ghost, which returns to haunt Macbeth during a banquet but remains invisible to the rest of the company.[53] Brent's grand plan and staging are outlined during the teleplay's first block, before the commercial break, as he efficiently directs the proceedings, ranging from the seating arrangement and lighting effects to the timing of the offscreen dog sounds and the ghost's appearance. The host, C-F, plans to serve his guests soup followed by pheasant and a good bottle of claret. According to Brent's scenario and ghost directing, the actress playing the ghost will enter during the main course.

The guests arrive one by one. First Brent walks briskly into the dining room with C-F in tow to give the major's butler, Lein, last-minute instructions. After

Robert Stone's arrival, Brent recapitulates the background. All three men step into the pantry for a chat with the detective, Sergeant Balter, before walking back to the study for a sherry, with cuts motivated by the group's movement as it passes from one room to the next. As sherry is poured, John Bedford arrives, and the block ends with Lein announcing him. With a self-assured swagger, Bedford walks straight toward the camera in shot 21, while the three other gentlemen huddle together in a tight triangular formation. The cordon formation clearly signals that we are in for a contest of wits, with three contestants ganging up on the fourth.

As Bedford briskly approaches the camera, the shot fades to black. His movement, shot in an unbroken stretch, takes him in rapid succession through a whole range of framings, from full shot to close-up, before the picture goes black. Multiple shifts in framing and shot scale are recapitulated in a different register during the dinner. Instead of swiftly moving from full shot to close-up in a single shot, Hitchcock uses carefully calculated editing and a series of fixed shot scales that gradually and almost clinically close in on Bedford as the tension mounts. When the framing reaches extreme close-up, Bedford is on the verge of losing his composure, being just moments away from breaking and lunging at the ghost. When he gets up from the table, we hear his wine glass topple over. While the camera sticks with the extremely close framing of his face, he moves toward the imaginary ghost, which he incriminatingly threatens to kill *again*.

The first shot after the commercial break, number 22, an establishing shot, is disturbingly spectacular in a manner that calls attention to the camera and the framing of the dinner party. Arguably, this detached, Godlike perspective looking down on the scene suggests that Brent's authority on the ground is provisional. Meanwhile, the teleplay offers two tracks for close-up: the most elaborate uses an extreme close-up to chart the guilty party until his break; the second is a close-up after the murderer's breakdown that features Brent as his plan turns out to have been undercut by the presence of a ghost he has not commissioned. From the high overhead angle, Hitchcock's camera hovers over the dinner party around the table, taking in the full space of the dining room. The detached architectural observance from an authorial realm, almost in the style of a blueprint, gradually takes on uncanny dimensions on the ground. Shot 22 hence functions as a spatial harbinger for the upcoming cutting up in progressively closer shots of this master space as well as a summation of the cramped movement in the first block. (High-angle shots are significant in Hitchcock's cinema, as demonstrated, for example, in Stefan Sharff's close reading of *Family Plot* [1976].)[54]

A great deal is going on as we descend on the dinner party between courses after the commercial break. Following the sherry, the soup has run its course during the break, thus preserving a sense of real time. According to Brent's master plan, Bedford sits opposite the host with an unobstructed view across the table and all the way to the curtains in the study. Stone sits to the left of the host, and Brent is thus seated to the major's right, his back toward the sideboard where Lein prepares the food for serving. The guests have just finished the soup, and the female server removes the china before laying plates for the main course. In the beginning of this block, all four men sitting around the table are visible in more or less wide shots, overhead in the distanced shot, 22, and at ground level in shots 23 to 26 (fig. 3.9). The candelabra on the table functions as a guidepost throughout this block and is part of all camera setups except for a couple of cut-away shots to other spaces (fig. 3.10). Paradoxically, even those shots toward the ghost's space that are cued as coming from Bedford's perspective are still framed by the candelabra's branches in the upper left corner of the frame (fig. 3.11). The same angle is maintained for the last shot of the ghost from Bedford's point of view, shot 110, though at this point he is standing up after he has lunged forward.

The visually conspicuous candles also tie in with the notion of vertical lines being crucial elements and key markers in Hitchcock's cinema, as explored by William Rothman. The candles provide a grid for the proceedings in almost all the shots. In addition, the staircase's bars outside the dining room offer a rhyming set of parallel vertical lines, and the editing is neatly intertwined with the mise-en-scène. Rothman claims that this visual-bar motif, a Hitchcock signature akin to his cameo, is among other things associated with "loss of control or breakdown," which is the governing principle in the teleplay's story.[55] According to this logic, Hitchcock has an invisible cameo in the dining room.

Head size, the crucial term for framing and shot scale set up by Hitchcock together with Allardice, is meticulously calculated throughout this block, which consists of twenty-six camera setups for ninety-five shots (22–116). Initially, from shots 22 to 33, the female server's movements govern the editing. In the overhead establishing shot, with its spatial framing of the room and the placement of the four main characters, Lein the butler is standing in front of a sideboard frame left, carving the pheasant. The cut to shot 23 from the overhead shot is cued by the server's movement out of frame. This edit brings the camera down to floor level with the candelabra as a spatial yardstick for the subsequent editing and as an indicator of shot scale and point of view. From shot 27 the framing is tighter, with only three of the party visible; the camera

3.9. Camera setups from "Banquo's Chair" (AHP 146), shots
22–24.

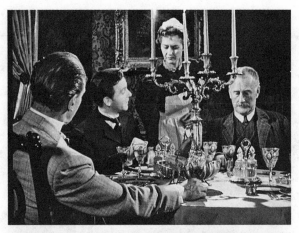

3.10. Camera setups from "Banquo's Chair" (AHP 146), shots
27–29.

3.11. The ghost from Bedford's point of view. "Banquo's Chair" (AHP 146), shot 62.

hence moves one layer closer to the participants. In shots 27 to 37 the framing consistently takes in three figures in alternating patterns, using the setups from shots 27 to 29.

The explanatory shot 39 shows the sergeant coaxing the dog in the pantry, followed by a reaction shot and Bedford looking confused. The framing in shot 40 is a little tighter than in 38, as no hands are visible, which means that Bedford is fully isolated in the frame thereafter. The pattern of alternation henceforth privileges Bedford, while Brent, off frame, continues to talk about bird watching, a hobby Stone taunts him about, most importantly in shot 44, in which Stone is alone, though in a much wider framing than for Bedford. The overall pattern here is alternation between three series: Bedford alone in the frame (38, 40, 42, 45, 47, 49, and later in progressively closer framings); two-shots featuring Brent and C-F (41, 43, 46, 48, 50, 53, 57, 68, 72, 80, 88, 90, 92, 94, 96, 98; shot 55, with its minor camera movements, is also related to this series); and Stone alone in the frame (44, 54, 58, 60, 66, and 86). These three basic setups, with the framing of Bedford progressively closing in on him, will later be intercut with a fourth shot series of the ghost in a fixed framing from Bedford's point of view in shot 62 and onward (70, 74, 76, 78, 82, 84, 89, 93, 100, 102, and 110). The editing takes us closer and closer to Bedford in shots 63, 85, 103, and finally, in shot 109, when he breaks (fig. 3.12).

3.12. The camera gradually closes in on the guilty party until he breaks. "Banquo's Chair" (AHP 146), shots 63, 85, 103, and 109.

In shot 109, which is extremely close to Bedford from the nose up, his very wide eyes stare off frame as he utters the fatal threat, "or I'll kill you again," and lunges forward toward the ghost. The camera sticks with the very close framing during his movement, which is accompanied by dramatic music. As Bedford is being placed under arrest, Brent and his cast surround him. They all enter the corridor, and Brent hands over Bedford's coat. Sergeant Balter and Bedford walk out into the rainy night. As the three men turn back, Miss Thorpe (Hilda Plowright) enters from the study, offering apologies for being late. Brent praises her ghostly performance, "Very nice, Miss Thorpe," but she informs him, "I was delayed." This totally unexpected revelation after the ghost's successful appearances motivates a cut to shot 116 for reactions. The cut-in initially privileges Miss Thorpe and the surprised Brent, who asks, "What do you mean?" Thorpe replies, "I've just this second arrived. Am I too late?" Brent swivels slightly before facing her again, then turns fully around to Stone as the camera retreats. Stone turns around toward C-F off frame, while the camera movement stops, then starts tracking forward, passing Stone to close in on Brent's alarmed face, while the music swells before a fade to black.

Using John Williams as the character to whom the direction of the proceedings, and thus the interior reading frame, is delegated is quite a significant casting choice. John Williams's domineering presence and emblematic Englishness lent him the proper authority and clout to act as master of ceremonies in "Banquo's Chair." His characters' aura of authority is, however, often circumscribed: by a bossy wife, his place within a hierarchical system, procedural matters, backfiring plans, or, as in this episode, uncontrollable uncanny circumstances. These circumstances, arguably, signal Hitchcockian style and pulling of strings, not least in the adroit manipulation of the close-up device. As it turns out in regard to agency, Brent, too, becomes a marionette through the ghostly forces we read as the director's abandoning of a surrogate character acting as director on the ground. In spite of his meticulous preparations, as scrupulous in fact as Hitchcock's preproduction efforts, Brent comes across as having been outwitted by a ghost-like force, foreshadowed in the conspicuous high-angle shot. Regardless of Brent's great execution and the desired outcome, the proceedings end in exasperation and almost horror. In the epilogue the host has no further comments on the story.

Hitchcock's comments in the epilogues, his control of the stories' further development beyond the endings and from a position outside the stories, are often utterly farfetched: he talks about a detective disguised as a dog, an unsuccessful attempt at murder with a non-frozen leg of lamb, oversized chickens feasting on the owner of a coop, and so on. Such yarns and absurdities demonstrate a relinquishing of control and privileged access to meaning; more important, they show a host presence standing apart from the stories, inviting the spectators to use their own detective skills based on familiarity with the show's universe to figure out its meaning irrespective of what Hitchcock the host might have revealed. A critical element here is distrust, as the show was predicated on an obligatory twist ending working against and partly undoing the cues—revealing but sometimes deceptive—from casting, props, mise-en-scène, and also Hitchcock's commentaries that wrap up the proceedings in a logical but somewhat unforeseen manner. Hitchcock waxing absurd engenders a general distrust of his authority as host and levels the playing field for an engagement with the audience. His having to yield to the intrusive sponsor messages between the prologue and the story further undermines Hitchcock's authority. The Hitchcockian, as a global reading frame for the show's universe, goes beyond the control of the host. The Hitchcock figure's not fully matching up with, incorporating, or controlling the Hitchcockian affords a certain interpretative freedom for the audience vis-à-vis the host when navigating the stories and their cues as well as the surrogate function posited for Inspector Brent as ghost director in "Banquo's Chair."

Simultaneously, the Hitchcockian notion tunes out the directors' importance as the producers turn into prime stewards for the show's template.

Some commentators hence consider Hitchcock's work for television to be stylistically indistinguishable from teleplays in the series that were directed by others. Whether Hitchcock or somebody else directed had little bearing on style. Such comments reflect no shortcoming on Hitchcock's part, evidencing instead the stylistic consistency that his team of producers devised and protected, irrespective of the director.

The teleplays' stylistic flourish ushered in a full-fledged embodiment of the Hitchcockian experience as promised by Hitchcock's overpowering presence in the host frame. Arguably, a formidable command of style and storytelling push the director into the frame as an emblematic form of surrogacy in tune with John Belton's characterization that the style "undermines "the invisibility of the classical paradigm," while Hitchcock's visibility in the host frame becomes a "dominant feature of the narrative experience, as that which makes it 'Hitchcockian.'"[56] On television this experience was mainly in the hands of the producers who controlled a swath of surrogate directors; the most prominent of these directors, in terms of number of credits and award recognition, was Robert Stevens.

Marionettes, Doubles, Dummies, and Stand-Ins

On one occasion, a character played by Norman Lloyd in a teleplay directed by Robert Stevens has a clever plan, which is literally put to rest by a double. As one of the lead producers for the Hitchcock television team, Lloyd was eminently responsible for producing Hitchcockian teleplays, and he also often acted in and directed them. In "Design for Loving" (AHP 123), a sci-fi story written by Ray Bradbury, Lloyd's character has procured a humanoid replica of himself to keep his wife company, since he plans to sneak away to merrier vistas. A company called Marionettes Inc. (the title of Bradbury's story) supplies the double. Lloyd's marionette turns out to be more enterprising than expected, as it overpowers the original version and puts the putative master in a coffin in the basement, henceforth taking over his life, for better or for worse, in this somewhat bleak marriage. The doubling of Lloyd in this story, in addition to him pulling strings for the franchise as producer, and Hitchcock's attempt to get a Mr. Lloyd, in the form of a bird, to take over the hosting before eating him, speaks volumes for the brand's involved playfulness and the way it toyed with identities.

The marionette theme is closely aligned with ventriloquism, a deceptive form of embodiment in partnership with a talkative dummy. The many dummies in the Hitchcock series are, however, never outside the purview of agency and virtual corporeality. For a franchise fashioned under the imprint of an inescapable body, stories featuring nonhuman agency carry a special significance. The ghost in "Banquo's Chair" in this respect has multiple siblings; even the host himself (or Alfred's "brother") once appeared as a marionette (in "See the Monkey Dance," AHH 69; fig. 2.5). Robert Stevens was also responsible for "The Glass Eye," one of the show's most memorable teleplays, which featured not a marionette but a dummy as an accessory to a ventriloquist routine. We will shortly turn to this episode, as we leave behind physical surrogates for disembodied "characters." (We should also remember that directors such as Stevens tended to be blocked out by and to vanish behind the formidable host, although Stevens was awarded the series' only directing Emmy for this particular teleplay.)

Before we delve into this dummy-related casting case, however, it bears noting that the series' inaugural dummy involved an actor who was already well known from Hitchcock's cinema. "And So Died Riabouschinska" (AHP 20), the series' first teleplay based on a story by Ray Bradbury, featured one of Claude Rains's five memorable performances for Hitchcock television. Here Rains's character, Mr. Fabian, has killed a man (by strangling—hence, perhaps, Hitchcock's instructing of Rains in fig. 3.7), a juggler who once shared vaudeville billing with him. The juggler had threatened to expose Mr. Fabian's love affair with his dummy, Riabouschinska, modeled after his lost love and former assistant. Mr. Fabian's talkative dummy cannot stop "herself" from speaking the truth, and as the detective, played by Charles Bronson, establishes the connection between Mr. Fabian and the juggler, the dummy confesses on Mr. Fabian's behalf, fittingly in front of a large mirror in the dressing room. After the deferred confession, the dummy can no longer speak for or by way of Mr. Fabian and symbolically dies. The nonorganic Riabouschinska has strange powers and virtually an identity of her own. The illusion of embodiment is naturally at the core of all ventriloquist acts, as the voice imperceptibly flows between master and dummy in an uncanny dialogue obscuring the borderline between human and dummy.

Many seasons later a ventriloquist routine closes the hour-long episode "Final Performance" (AHH 78). Here the final vaudeville turn is truly chilling and not recognized as an act, as the performer's former eminence as a ventriloquist is withheld from the internal audience of one. The teleplay features Franchot Tone as a washed-up vaudeville artist, Rudolph the Great, who dreams of making a comeback with a routine that pairs him with Rosie, a waifish girl he trains and holds captive. He plans to marry her soon, after she turns eighteen. Meanwhile, Rudolph runs a motel with cabins named after vaudeville greats. Motels off the highway are never happy settings in a Hitchcock context, and this one is no exception. A young television writer, Cliff Allen, ends up in the Al Jolson Cabin (Jolson's signature line, "You ain't heard nothin' yet," is contextually fitting) after picking up the hitchhiking Rosie as she tries to escape from being held prisoner by Rudolph. Cliff has to check in at the motel after his car breaks down, and Rosie thus returns to the place from where she wants to escape. Tone, who had been a successful theater and Hollywood film actor before taking on television, plays the pathetic Rudolph, mixing joviality with menacing threats. Realizing that Rosie plans to run away again, and that Cliff is willing to take her along to Hollywood, he dresses her up in his former wife's wedding dress and puts on his best routine for Cliff. Meanwhile, Rosie has allegedly changed her mind about leaving and wants to stay behind with Rudolph. The farewell act on his makeshift barn stage includes Rosie sitting on Rudolph's lap, but Cliff does not understand that he is witnessing a performance. The flustered Cliff insists on Rosie telling him herself that she wants to stay behind and marry Rudolph after all. Rosie's declaration convinces him, a testament to Rudolph's performance skills. Cliff walks away unaware that this was a stage routine and that Rudolph's fame rested on his ventriloquism acts. Vision, here coupled with sound and voice, is once more essential for the closure, as the camera closes in on Rudolph's trunk with a big ventriloquist label, before moving to Rosie's back and the prominent knife with which Rudolph has killed her. Rudolph's pitch-perfect voicing of Rosie thus survives the test of vision and voice accuracy as her dead body serves as his dummy.

This takes us to Jessica Tandy and Phyllis Thaxter, who were repeatedly given roles that aligned them in a form of surrogacy casting as embodiments of key features within the realm of Hitchcockiana. Many of their roles also play into the franchise's bodily confusions and perceptual insecurities. Regarding the show's production credo with respect to casting, Alfred Hitchcock nailed it in an interview for TV *Guide*: "Because there is no time to really develop character in a half hour, casting becomes the substitute for character."[57] This critical axiom guided the show in the hands of Joan Harrison and her production team. (Joan Harrison, of course, is one of the most formidable Hitchcock surrogates in charge of the day-to-day operation of the television series after her previous tenure working for the films in different capacities.) Furthermore, this portal premise for the series' mode of operation had repercussions for how audiences engaged with the teleplays. Obviously, casting in this sense was predicated on having knowing audiences who are capable of making quick translations from casting histories and actors' bodies to their hermeneutic implications for the teleplay at hand. In this spirit the clever producers took advantage of established casting signifiers associated with actors and further cemented them within the show's universe—though at times undercutting expectations by deliberate "miscasting."

On several occasions Hitchcock described the television audience as made up of smart, attentive detectives on the lookout for clues and cues while searching for the twist. Casting (whether aligned with type or working against character) provided the fuel for the interpretative game, together with significant character names and readable props within a repertoire of familiar narrative devices, among them the instant establishing of milieu, dissolves between scenes so as not to slow down the pace, mirror shots suggesting closer looks at characters, and the frequent deployment of voice-overs to bridge leaps between timeframes marked by a ripple dissolve. The overall palette of narrative and stylistic strategies worked in sync with the type of Hitchcockian humor a modernist critic such as Hollis Alpert chided. A later generation of pop critics begged to differ concerning the functions of the pivotal humor, while television-savvy audiences at the time seemed to relish their detective role in the set's casting game.

Notwithstanding Hitchcock's hosting, the show's success and longevity were predicated on the producers' knack for building a universe much as Honoré de Balzac did with his gallery of characters across novels in the anthology project La Comédie humaine. Despite the series' sprawling and open-ended roster of anthology characters, the actors' accumulated casting histories awarded them a recognizable aura across teleplays. The familiar contours of this larger universe governed the otherwise disruptive format of independent stories. The production strategy of building up multidimensional resemblances and manifold variations across stories encouraged an audience bent on detection to engage with the suspense and mystery as though being directed from a playbook. The individual teleplays were informed by genre, style conventions, setting, acting tone, and character expectations based on whether the cues provided by the casting reinforced or undercut the typing in play, and at times suggesting surrogacy, as for Claude Rains in the previously discussed dummy story. The show's decade-long survival hinged on savvy audiences capable of and enjoying playing along with the tensions between casting and the twist endings, and detecting red herrings in the process.

Joan Harrison and her producing team's master plan involved repeatedly hiring actors suited for specific plot types or familiar character traits, as well as making recurring crossover casting choices by bringing in actors from Hitchcock's cinema, such as Rains. In a wider casting sense, character expectations for actors could also be picked up from the entire domain of television and movie typing in order to set up the reading game for the audience (for example, Dennis Day in his penny-pinching role discussed in the introduction). The 1950s television audience quickly developed a keen sense of casting not only within but also across shows. This casting strategy offered viewers a pleasurable, gamelike form of character exploration based on foreknowledge in relation to the cues in a novel teleplay. The cards the producers dealt were simultaneously predictable and startling.

In this manner, the series frame ushered in a Hitchcockian human comedy even more intricate, interrelated, and involved than what Balzac offered his readers. If casting provided a template for characters at first blush, the twist ending loomed at the endgame as a potential qualifier. The show's suspense thus balanced a casting matrix, fixed yet malleable, built into an aesthetic of astonishment verging on shock, as Hitchcock phrased it in a missive to Mary Elsom.[58] The final eye-opener sometimes reconfigured character assumption based on casting, or refracted the plot in other dimensions as the suspense became disentangled—or left us flustered along with characters such as Inspector Brent, in yet another type of astonishing twist.

Jessica Tandy, one of the few actors to graduate from Hitchcock television to Hitchcock cinema, is my prime example for elucidating how Hitchcock television operated in regard to casting.[59] The choice is not self-evident, as she appeared in only three frail roles, apart from acting in a radio test for Hitchcock that was never aired. Much later she returned to the franchise for *The Birds*, and the character consistency in her three television roles had repercussions for her casting in that film. Her prominence is rivaled by the televisual ubiquity of many other actors and actresses—for example, Gary Merrill, Henry Jones, Robert Emhardt, Robert H. Harris, Robert Horton, Dick York, Mary Scott, and Barbara Baxley, to mention just a few. The actors in this latter group all have a discernible series profile, and I will look closer at Phyllis Thaxter, who also belongs to this group. The performances of those who crossed over from Hitchcock-directed films often come with lingering memories of the film roles; this is the case not only for John Williams, Joan Fontaine, Claude Rains, and Patricia Collinge but also for Peter Lorre, Barbara Bel Geddes, Vera Miles, John Gavin, Pat Hitchcock, Joseph Cotten, Hume Cronyn (Tandy's husband), John Forsythe, Mildred Natwick, Teresa Wright, Edmund Gwenn, and Tom Helmore.

"The Glass Eye" was one of the three teleplays directed by Robert Stevens that featured Jessica Tandy, and it serves as a template for Tandy's characters as directed by Stevens under the producing philosophy of Harrison, and as spelled out by Hitchcock's comment on casting praxis. This teleplay, one of eleven scripted by Stirling Silliphant, and based on a story by John Keir Cross, opened season three; Hitchcock himself directed the openers for five of AHP's seven seasons.

"The Glass Eye" is based on a narrative structure that the show employed frequently: a series of flashbacks. Thematically the story's meaning hinges on obfuscation in regard to performance and disembodiment in a routine with a dummy, a recurrent figure in other Hitchcock episodes, as we have seen. The dummy theme resonates with the prominent bodily interface for Hitchcock's cinema posited by the overall physical imprint of the franchise and its marketing. The story's cardinal prop, the titular glass eye, is critical for the teleplay's body inflection. This nonorganic prop, simulating an eye proper, travels from Alfred's palm in the prologue to the hands of William Shatner's character, Jim Whitley. Glass eye in hand, Jim begins his account, told by way of voice-over in a series of flashbacks, as he and his wife, Dorothy, are in the process of cleaning out his dead cousin Julia's cheerless apartment.

As Jim recounts the story of Julia's drab life in a small apartment in Fulham, London, the image undergoes a ripple dissolve, the show's default for signaling a time shift. Regular dissolves were the preferred device for moving between scenes, and the added ripples were its marker for moving back and forth in time. Now in the past, but at first only visually, we encounter Julia (Tandy) in her bed, sleeping. Jim's voice still guides us from the present and blends with atmospheric sounds from the past. Julia is woken by the alarm clock that Jim in the previous scene held in his hand prior to moving toward the mantelpiece and producing the glass eye from a small cabinet drawer.

In the flashback Julia draws the curtain that covers a window facing a dull brick wall, before lighting the fire in the fireplace by which her cousin stands years later. Jim tells Julia's story to his wife in a quick series of linked vignettes: Julia cooks breakfast before going to her job as a solicitor's clerk; she eats lunch by herself in a tearoom, armed with a book for company, which contrasts with a loving couple's intimacy in the background; then back in her room for dinner, she cooks on a single flame, juggling pots and pans. In true Hitchcock fashion, her dreary existence is elegantly and economically summed up in Stevens's direction across the menu from breakfast to lunch and then dinner, all framed by the voice-over spelling out Julia's loneliness and how life is passing her by. Her solitude is further marked by the absence of dialogue; she has literally no one to talk to. All the sounds from within the time slice of the first flashback are atmospheric and reflect her interaction with inanimate objects. This is, in a sense, the story of her life: a lack of physical contact, as we will learn from her misguided attempt to touch someone.

As Julia eats dinner, the voice-over guides the spectators and Dorothy back to her surprising and uncanny encounter with love. In preparation for this, the camera moves closer to her haggard face before the image dissolves to a variety theater she routinely visits on Saturday afternoons with the neighbors' boy, Allan, whom she adores. The dissolve here perfectly captures the shift from quiet despair to budding excitement, when the framing again comes closer to Julia. Stevens was a veritable master at squeezing meaning out of the dissolves he used frequently between scenes.

The upbeat music from the theater runs parallel to the voice-over narration that introduces Julia's tragic encounter with the ventriloquist Max Collodi; then the soundtrack fully shifts over to the theater and the MC's introduction of Max and his amazing dummy, George, shown from Julia's vantage point. A burst of enveloping smoke further delays the visual encounter. From Max in the flesh, the image quickly returns to a close-up of Julia's intrigued face. Mesmerized by the performance, she hushes Allan's complaining about not yet having had his customary lemonade. Returning to Max and George, the framing is now closer than the previous perspective allied with Julia's point of view from the balcony. As the frame cuts between the stage and Julia next to the nagging Allan, she positively glows and is obviously smitten with the suave Max. During intermission she buys a ticket for the evening performance, and she henceforth continues to attend all his appearances. Later she even leaves her job to follow the ventriloquist's shows on the road.

In the frame story, Jim outlines the one-sided romance from the very beginning to its devastating punctuation marked with the glass eye. A quick montage of Max's shows on the road takes Julia to a small hotel near a theater in Blackpool, where Max is currently appearing. By now Max has answered Julia's letters, expressing his gratitude for the praise but informing her that he never gives interviews. Letters continue to pass between Julia and Max, and she eventually ups the ante by sending a photograph of herself, taken ten years ago, and insisting on a meeting. When he succumbs, Julia wants to make herself over by way of a new hat, so as to better match her photo. She tries on several in a shop, naturally in front of a mirror, alluding to her innocent game of deception with a photograph slightly removed from her current self (fig. 3.13). (Pat Hitchcock, in one of her many minuscule roles in AHP, plays the saleslady.)

3.13. Jessica Tandy in "The Glass Eye" (AHP 79).

As Julia leaves the shop, she stops in front of a bigger mirror for a quick look at herself wearing the new hat. We then jump to Julia standing in front of her hotel room's mirror as she eagerly prepares for the meeting, finally deciding not to wear the hat after all, but a gauze veil instead. This preparatory sequence is as deftly compressed in Stevens's touch as the series of meals.

Reinforcing the eye/vision code set off by the title and further bolstered by Julia's desiring gaze at Max on the stage and her masquerading in front of mirrors before the meeting, the janitor at the theater winks in complicity when telling Julia where she can find the ventriloquist. Max sits behind a table in the darkened dressing room, the dummy next to him. In the alternation of shots, we see him from her point of view, while his view of her is detached and nonsubjective. Obviously, glass eyes cannot carry a point of view. As Julia touches him and kisses his hand, Max falls to the floor—he, it shockingly turns out, is actually the dummy. Julia flees in horror when she realizes that the real ventriloquist is George, a little person posing as a dummy. Abandoned and forlorn, George sits down and slowly removes his mask before reassembling Max and noticing a missing glass eye, confirmed in a close-up of the dummy's face. At this stage we return to the frame story via a rippling dissolve as Jim puts the glass eye back in its drawer. According to Jim, Julia, in her unwitting despair, instinctively picked up the glass eye. The viewer does not see this, however, in the flashback scene or the final tilted camera setup framing her flight from the dressing room. The tilting expressively confirms the suspicion that her flimsy world of hopes for love has turned topsy-turvy in an instant. Subsequently George abandons the Max routine and joins a touring circus company under his own name as a sad clown with a beautiful voice. In the final shot, with a twist underscoring an uncanny affinity between George and his old dummy, George wears a black patch over his (perhaps missing) eye.

In hindsight, the banter between the dummy George and Max onstage offers clues as to what is going on in front of Julia's eyes, though her intense and desiring gaze does not see and fully fathom. An onstage joke about love at first sight and a reevaluation after a second look speaks volumes. Vision, and its separation from touch, is critical. As we have learned, Julia's life is geared toward nonorganic objects in lieu of human beings.

In "The Glass Eye" vision is of utmost importance. Unreliable and desire-driven, vision is featured as the story's very meaning. As a corollary, we in the audience tend to see what we want from the available cues. Here we are presumably as duped as Julia before the shocking twist. The story is told by way of objects and items that in hindsight unravel a character's life and dreams. In the condensed timeframe of the teleplay, characterization is presented in pointed shorthand fashion. This neatly illustrates Hitchcock's comment on casting. In the closing shot George has seemingly lost an eye, as Max's prosthesis ends up as a tragic memento.

Hitchcock, though he seldom talked about teleplays he had not directed himself, outlined the episode's plot twist in an interview for TV Guide: "But, alas the ventriloquist is a wax dummy, and the 'dummy' an ugly dwarf. In her frustration [Julia] knocks over the sawdust-filled figure, and a glass eye rolls across the floor. It made a splendid close-up."[60] Pace Hitchcock's description, there is no close-up of a glass eye rolling across the floor. The critical weight of close-ups was key for Hitchcock's televisual poetics—here it was conspicuously absent.

In Variety's glowing review Robert Stevens's direction is bypassed. A brief mention in the review's last line illustrates how successfully Hitchcock managed to exert his influence over all aspects of the show, regardless of the actual labor involved: "To dial it was to stay with it, the arresting grip never loosening until the surprising turn of events that must have left some lookers dazed, others still groping. From Hitchcock this has come to be expected, but what a breath-taker this was, an ending to end all such endings."[61] Similarly,

CBS elected to feature Hitchcock in the combined ad for the network's awards for the 1957 season. Stevens's name is listed in the category for best direction, but the image inside the CBS eye logo shows the host, Hitchcock.

Jessica Tandy starred in two additional AHP episodes. In "Toby" (AHP 45), Tandy's first episode in the series, her character, Edwina, arrives to marry a long-lost love, Albert (Robert Harris, in one of his many roles). Albert has rented a basement apartment for her in New York City's tenement district. Having left his hometown and not managed to progress beyond working as a bookkeeper, Albert has cherished the memory of his adolescent sweetheart and is overjoyed when she tracks him down via a newspaper ad many years later. To his surprise, she arrives with a toddler wrapped in a blanket, though the baby remains hidden until the twist ending. It finally turns out that the blanket holds a cat and not the parentless baby Edwina allegedly "inherited" from her deceased sister. Edwina is high-strung and unbalanced, with mood swings triggered by the nosy neighbors. Her performance comes to a close when orderlies from the mental institution she has escaped from arrive to bring her back. Her institutionalized life, presumably a result of her lost love, foreshadows and resonates with Julia's symbolic and lovesick imprisonment, as it were, in her London apartment before and after the happy-turned-tragic Max episode. Both of these Tandy characters—in London and in New York—are frail, lonely, out of touch with reality, and formed by their lost loves in stories where critical elements are withheld and not what they seem to be. And no crimes are involved in the Tandy stories, which mainly feature psychological portraits and revealing twist endings.

Robert Stevens directed "Toby" as well as the third teleplay featuring Tandy, "The Canary Sedan" (AHP 115). This time around, the setting is exotic: Hong Kong. Tandy's character, Laura, is returning home to Hong Kong after being treated for some kind of breakdown, though not a permanent affliction as in "Toby." According to her husband, Laura had been seeing things (vision again, before the story turns to her uncanny hearing), and he blames her parents and particularly his wife's Irish childhood nurse for her frailty, or, rather, oversensitive radar. Laura's psychic skills are demonstrated during the voyage as she reads personalities on a Ouija board, which sets up the story's premise. Once she is in Hong Kong her husband seemingly avoids her, dealing with one business crisis after the other at his bank, while he insists on her having a car and a driver so she can familiarize herself with the city and make social calls. The story in an interesting way foreshadows *Driving Miss Daisy* (Zanuck Company / Majestic Films International, 1989), Tandy's last big success, but in the Hong Kong setting, interaction with her chauffeur is limited because of the language barrier.

Laura hears lingering traces in the car of a desperate voice crying over a tragic love affair. We eventually learn, via Laura's piecing together of the uncanny clues, that the car's former owner had a love affair with Laura's husband. She unravels the story by connecting the dots she "overhears" en route in a séance-like manner, so there are no flashbacks proper in this case. The story takes her to a tropical garden, once the lovers' secluded paradise. Here she discovers her husband's distinctive initials carved into the cement next to his lover's, while Laura has been more or less written off by her husband.

This threesome of stories featuring Tandy neatly illustrates the series' casting practices regarding character consistency. In all three teleplays her characters suffer tragic losses of love. She is invariably vulnerable and oversensitive, even mentally afflicted or psychic, and thus almost destined for unbearable disappointments when her dreams are shattered. As Robert Stevens was the most sought-after director for AHP, and a formidable proxy for Hitchcock on television, the fact that he directed all three stories is not in any way remarkable, though still worth noting as part of the team-forming practices in the hands of Harrison.

Tandy was also cast by the Hitchcock franchise in an episode of *Suspicion*, "Murder Me Gently" (season one, episode two), which was one of seven episodes in the series directed by Don Medford. For AHP, Tandy was recruited as an experienced television actress, but foremost as a renowned stage star, most famous for playing Blanche in the Broadway version of *A Streetcar Named Desire*, which landed her a Tony but not the part when Hollywood adapted the play (Vivien Leigh was cast instead). Tandy's stage Blanche, in a larger register, showcases the kind of character she played out in three pocket versions for AHP.

As for Tandy's profile in the late 1950s, a newspaper headline says it all: "Today It's Just One Neurotic Character after Another for Jessica Tandy—Has She Cornered the Market?" As Tandy explained in the interview: "I'm not always neurotic . . . although I must seem that way. . . . Burgess Meredith once said I had a corner on the neurotic market." The writer went on: "Miss Tandy, a successful Broadway star, has been appearing on the home screens since the early days of television. On many of these programs she has been cast as an unbalanced, neurotic woman."[62] It was this casting profile that the Hitchcock franchise picked up on and further developed in tune with its overall producing strategy.

Playing with Casting: Typing and Against Type

Phyllis Thaxter, an actress with a discernible series profile as victim in her many appearances for the franchise, was cast in an episode thinly referencing *Vertigo*; in this case, however, she plays against type. Thaxter can serve as a compressed casting case—although she appeared in much grander format, in terms of quantity, than Jessica Tandy, being cast nine times, plus twice for *Suspicion*. While not a victim here, Thaxter's character is not a poster woman for stability and sanity either. As Lucy in "Murder Me Twice" (AHP 126), Thaxter plays a woman who seemingly commits murder under hypnosis and the spell of a long-dead character, Dora Evans. Casting-wise it is quite plausible that a Thaxter character would be hyper-susceptible to hypnosis and thereby divested of her own identity and volition. As Dora, Lucy replicates the murder of Dora's husband by killing her own spouse after being hypnotized in a kind of party trick. During another session of hypnosis at the inquest, Lucy, again as Dora, and imagining herself (or performing as) a character from 1853, kills the hypnotist. Thus she is cleared of all charges but seems to have staged the whole thing by hoodwinking the hypnotist, Farnum (Tom Helmore), twice; his murder conveniently wipes out all traces of her not being outside herself in the first place, if that was the case. The motivation for her elaborate plot is never explained.

Tom Helmore, who played the mastermind in *Vertigo* who sets up Scottie (James Stewart) as a dupe, was cast in only one part in AHP. In "Murder Me Twice"—*Vertigo*-like in construction, with a character from the 1850s who seems to take possession of Lucy during hypnosis—Helmore as the hypnotist has his comeuppance, perhaps after his unpunished scheming in *Vertigo*. Because it opened not long after *Vertigo* (the franchise's most elaborate dummy and doubling story), it is tempting to see "Murder Me Twice" as the Hitchcock team fooling around with palpable Hitchcockiana.

If Lucy as Dora indeed orchestrates deferred revenge on Tom Helmore's character, her character composite here delivers the scheme to perfection. Lucy is simultaneously played alongside and against the routinely victimized Thaxter template in which, if she was introduced seemingly without complications or hang-ups, afflictions were soon ushered in. The role is thus firmly beyond the pale of the pedestrian psychology that her characters are almost invariably denied. The closure here, the twist, points to a successful coup on Lucy's part in two installments. As the DA in the final scene implores her to tell him in private whether she planned the whole thing, now that she cannot be prosecuted, she delivers her answer enigmatically, with a mischievous smile in emulation of the old English she used as Dora when presumably in a state of hypnosis. For a time it is possible to entertain the hypothesis that Lucy and Farnum are working in collusion, but this scenario is laid to rest when he visits her, hoping to blackmail his way into the cabal. He is dismissed brusquely, and we later learn that his background and credentials are somewhat tarnished. During the inquest it becomes important for him to hypnotize Lucy again precisely because of his questionable reputation. As Dora, Lucy (or Lucy playing Dora playing Lucy) again picks up the scissors and stabs the man.

In the grander scheme of things, there are quite a lot of contingencies for Lucy to master to pull off the plot successfully. Digging up the Dora story seems easy enough, but coaxing Professor Farnum into offering to hypnotize her both the first time around, when she kills her husband with a pair of scissors, and the second time, when she again uses the same murder weapon, now on Farnum, could not be fully predicted on her part. The antique scissors might have been part of the regular decorations in her home; at the inquest they were a prime exhibit and thus within convenient reach.

Typecast from the outset in Hollywood, Phyllis Thaxter was perceived as a dependable, slightly unglamorous girl-next-door type who quickly graduated to vulnerable war wife. In the critic Myrtle Gebhart's poignant characterization: "There's no glamor glitter about her, but people react impulsively to her sincerity."[63] Her very first success was on the stage in 1942, in a Chicago production of Rose Franken's play *Claudia*. The following year Thaxter took over the role on Broadway when Dorothy McGuire left for Hollywood to star in the film version. As a character Claudia grapples with coming of age and, as a young bride, overcoming her dependence on her mother, which she finally does with humor in the mix. The move toward seriously unstable characters began in 1945 with *Bewitched*, a noir-inspired B-movie for MGM. Here Thaxter plays a young woman with a split personality, which eventually lands both her and her alter ego on death row. Also in 1945 for MGM, Thaxter was cast as a high-strung and nervy bride in the star-studded *Week-End at the Waldorf*. Almost invariably, sexual uneasiness is an implied aspect of her characters.

After she started working for television in 1953, Thaxter was rarely seen on the big screen. Among her late film roles was Ma Kent, Superman's mother on planet Earth in *Superman: The Movie* (1978). Her television roles came with an assailable borderline sensibility, as did her film parts. While her character occasionally shifts from gullible victim to enterprising plotter, this is unexpected enough to constitute a twist ending in its own right. Such machinations were rare for Thaxter's harried roles, but still not outside the panorama of the disturbed personality range she portrayed virtually by default, both within and outside the Hitchcock context. Her casting profile hence served several series, and television viewers had encountered her in many similar roles—for example, in "Man out of the Rain" (*Schlitz Playhouse*, 1955), "Schedule of Defraud" (*Climax!*, 1955), "Fear Me Not" (*The Loretta Young Show*, 1955), "Obsession" (*The U.S. Steel Hour*, 1955), and "Frederick" (*Lux Playhouse*, 1959).

"Never Again" (AHP 30), the first *Alfred Hitchcock Presents* episode featuring Thaxter, uses the familiar flashback structure for memory retrieval. She plays a recently reformed alcoholic struggling with feelings of inadequacy and inferiority compared to her fiancé's smart colleagues on Madison Avenue. A party prompts her to embark on a drinking spree with a male wallflower. The narrative opens with her in bed and on the verge of waking up to an immense hangover. A series of flashbacks walks us through the story and up to the fatal moment, which is not shown, when she accidentally kills her fiancé with a broken cognac snifter. Thus, she is not at a regular hospital, but in the city jail. The episode ends with her screaming in despair as the full recognition of her predicament hits her. In the opening flashback scene, she walks around with an empty champagne glass as a token of her having overcome alcoholism, before sitting down in front of a mirror (fig. 3.14). According to the show's mirror logic, encountering her double, especially after the frame scene's hangover, signals her self-deception—and a doomed reform project.

In this inaugural role for the franchise Phyllis Thaxter is featured undiluted in emulation of her Hollywood casting history as a neurotic and insecure character in the shadow of prominent or dominating men, albeit in this case with no malicious intent. Not a glamour girl, Thaxter seldom played the romantic lead. Flashbacks and the showcasing of her mind's inner workings are integral to Thaxter's psychological characters. Her appearances, just like Jessica Tandy's, push the suspense genre toward psychological drama. Interestingly, in light of the series' regular stabs at the sponsor, the host has not a barb to offer concerning this story's world of advertising. This is in fact one of the few occasions when he dispenses with the epilogue jesting, as the gravity of the subject matter overrides the customary irony.[64] Filtered through Thaxter's character, the men and women on Madison Avenue might come across as superficial enough without additional comments to rub it in. Thaxter received rave reviews for her performance in this Robert Stevens–directed teleplay. According to *Variety*, "Thaxter scores a tour de force" and is "outstanding in creating and sustaining the mood of impending doom."[65] The *Chicago Tribune* was as appreciative, claiming that "Phyllis' splendid performance as a neurotic bottle baby who can hold neither her man nor her liquor gives this

3.14. Phyllis Thaxter doubled in "Never Again" (AHP 30).

show plenty of shock value. And even Hitchcock is subdued after the final frightening shot of Phyllis."[66] After her second role for Hitchcock, in "Fog Closing In" (AHP 41), *Variety* quickly detected a pattern in the casting: "Phyllis Thaxter, who seems to be making a career of eliminating her video mates in this series, portrays an unsavory psychotic."[67] The pattern was reversed, however, on a few occasions when husband characters eliminated Thaxter in the role as wife.

"Nothing Ever Happens in Linvale" (AHH 38) is an hour-long episode that stars Phyllis Thaxter several seasons later. Following multiple victim roles in the series, Thaxter is once more played against type, as it turns out. The story opens with a report of a missing person and suspicious behavior called in by a concerned neighbor, played by Thaxter, regarding the husband and wife next door. The neighbor's missing wife becomes a problem for the not-too-bright-but-kind-of-handsome sheriff, played by Fess Parker, and his clueless helper to figure out. The troubling neighbor in this teleplay "happens" to be yet another Harry character in the Hitchcock universe.

We eventually learn that the two neighbors are lovers and that the couple-to-be has removed Harry's wife from the equation. Their complicated cover-up comes without any narrative hints before being surprisingly revealed in a scene we're led to presume will show Harry's attack on his gossipy neighbor. Instead of whacking her, he kisses her, and we feel stupid for not having figured out the surreptitious romance. The kiss comes after the couple has led the sheriff on until he dug up Harry's backyard, only to unearth a dead dog. Simultaneously, Harry planted a story about his wife's having left him. The wife has been buried in the Thaxter character's backyard all along. The lovers then dig her up, unceremoniously throw the body over the fence between the houses, and put her into the dog's already inspected grave. Unfortunately for them, it dawns on the over-diligent sheriff that a city ordinance forbids burying animals on private lots. He thus returns to collect the dead dog, thereby ruining the clever scheme. As the sheriff begins to dig, Thaxter's character unsuspectingly communicates with Harry across the high fence believing he is alone, thus giving the game away. The teleplay's prime twist effect is that we are tricked into reading Phyllis Thaxter's character according to the conventional casting of her as a victim. For us to learn that she is actively involved in a murder plot goes decidedly against the grain of her casting—a clever calculation on the producers' part.

Harry: Identity Games and Corpses

The rollicking tossing around of a quintessential Hitchcockian name, loaded with preset significations, served as both a wink and a story clue in the hour-long Linvale episode. In the condensed half-hour format, the name Harry operated as a snappy element in the shorthand strategy for navigating time constraints—for example, when Henry Jones's Harry character lugs around a dead body in "Nightmare in 4-D" (AHP 55). The hour-long show reframed this model in regard to rhythm and story pacing while keeping the casting philosophy, though without the previous temporal straightjacket.

When Jimmie Allardice was recruited as author for Hitchcock's host segments, the *Harry* film with its irritating body was showcased as the whimsical model for tone and corporeal irreverence. Subsequently, the film and the name Harry served as entry point for a wide range of emulations concerning body disposal in the television show. The film's subversive humor and black comedy displays a lighthearted and cavalier disrespect for Harry's cadaver. Hitchcock frequently touched on the interconnected motifs of the perfect murder and body disposal—and even offered an advice manual suggesting shipping the body parts to faraway Hong Kong as the preferred method for getting rid of a chopped-up victim.[68] The carnivalesque humor and matter-of-factness concerning the Harry trouble pointedly circumvent the respect traditionally paid the dead, as the narrative reduces the corpse to a bothersome package repeatedly buried, unearthed, and lugged across autumnal Vermont.

The staple category of the macabre speaks with an upbeat inflection harking back to the practical jokes, the cockney disdain for pomposity, and a propensity for turning the high into low by making even the most somber topics into irreverent, often body-tinged jokes. The macabre hinges precisely on this type of disrespect, here turning grave matters—a corpse—into a logistical problem in a string of vignettes bordering on slapstick.[69] The name Harry is related to the verb, which early in the etymological chain meant to lay waste, while later meanings are related to harassing, assaulting, and forcing to move along. The link between the name Harry, corporeality as waste, and dead bodies in the process of being turned into waste is displayed in the television series in many forms. The idea of life as balancing on the edge of the abyss of decay is inserted into a larger chain of organic conceptualizations also bearing on food, with disgust as a critical element. For a food-obsessed oeuvre with murders as integral components, this should not come as a surprise. To be sure, cheerfulness in the face of death and murder, with nonchalance toward more or less messy disposal of bodies (not always a spirited enterprise), regularly crops up in different forms in Hitchcock's televisual world, along with characters named Harry.

Based on an original story that Boris Sobelman wrote for the show, "A Matter of Murder" (AHH 55) is perhaps the happiest emulation of *The Trouble with Harry*, played out in comedic tone. Sobelman racked up three writing credits for episodes of *Thriller* (NBC, 1960–1962), but had precious few assignments after that, mainly for *The Man from* U.N.C.L.E (NBC, 1964–1968). "A Matter of Murder" features Telly Savalas as Philadelphia Harry, a car thief with high moral principles. Harry is dismayed when it turns out that the Rolls Royce he and his crew stole at a lake while the owner, Mr. Westlake, checked the water's depth comes with a dead body in the trunk. Mr. Westlake and his wife's attractive niece, Enid, have killed off the wealthy wife/aunt whose stern portrait dominates the Westlakes' living room from above the mantelpiece.[70] Trying to capitalize on the lost automobile with the corpse, the new couple reports both the theft and the kidnapping of Mrs. Westlake, believing they have come up with the perfect murder. Soon, however, this turns into unexpected trouble, as the unwanted corpse is lugged back and forth between the parties. First, Harry and his gang sneak the car with the dead body back into Westlake's garage and pay a dependable informer to tip off the chief of police. The detectives arrive at the garage too late, however, as the couple has already repainted the Rolls and parked it at a far-off lookout spot. Coming across the repainted automobile by chance, Harry's gang members unsuspectingly steal it a second time, body and all. Harry's initial enthusiasm for the new (old) car cools considerably when he once again finds the corpse in the trunk. He sees no other solution than to pay a car smuggler to take the hot Rolls across the border to Mexico while holding on to the body. Simultaneously, the detectives decide to ransack Westlake's house and cellar, and as a last measure drag the lake. But only hours before the detectives start dragging the lake, Harry has come up with a final solution: sink the body in the water, where it was supposed to be in the first place. Both sinking and dragging take place after the end of the story. The scheming lovers are unaware of Harry's inspired idea for the body disposal, so there is no happy conclusion for the killers.

Before turning away from the Harry roster and the corpse politics, let us look at a female counterpart. "Diplomatic Corpse" (AHP 88) features Isobel Elsom billed economically as "the Aunt." This episode is the third time Elsom ends up dead in the series. Murdered and buried in the cellar in "Back for Christmas," she dies from natural causes in "The Three Dreams of Mr. Findlater" (AHP 69) just before her husband's plan to kill her is set in motion (the husband is in both cases played by John Williams). The second time around, the couple even manages to retain the same maid, played by Mollie Glessing. This is anthology casting on a minuscule level, as if the show were a continuous series and not a format fractured into standalone, unrelated episodes.[71] This casting practice is an attempt to build a recognizable franchise universe peopled by recurrent characters. Glessing's seven parts in the series were almost all as maid. Both of the Elsom-Williams-Glessing teleplays offer charmingly clichéd stories about a domesticated husband trapped in a middle-class nightmare with no room for initiative or excitement. This version of Englishness leads one to believe that nagging wives dominate and deaden British home life for their husbands.

In the third teleplay no foul play or plotting is involved, as Elsom's spinsterish aunt character dies in the backseat of a car while her niece and the niece's husband drive to Mexico. The aunt does not have the proper documentation for crossing the border, but still practically forces the concerned young couple to take her over. En route the aunt's haughtiness is especially acid when she dismissively compares American culture to British. When crossing the border the aunt is seemingly asleep, and the inspector does not bother to check her papers. At their destination it turns out that she is dead. In Mexico the car with the dead body is stolen while the young couple looks for a doctor to issue a death certificate. The youngsters hire a private detective, played memorably by Peter Lorre, to retrieve the corpse-equipped automobile. His underhanded investigation leads to multiple humorous complications—and recurrent demands for more money. The slapstick element is as pronounced as in The Trouble with Harry, mainly owing to the typing of Lorre's Mexican detective. The story thus first features a dead body, then no body in several variations, and, as a twist ending, the wrong body is shipped out of Mexico. This is discovered when the coffin is opened back in California. The template for this body play was Harry, and the name Harry in many but not all cases is a plot indicator for this register of the Hitchcockian and its corporeal politics.

Mirrors

Aligned with casting strategies, surrogacy plotting, and name play, mirror shots are of capital importance for the television show's shorthand manner of communicating information. Almost every Hitchcock teleplay I have discussed so far comes with mirror shots of crucial significance for storytelling logic and plot unraveling. According to Hitchcock's comment on casting, the compressed format of AHP necessitated critical cues in succinct form, while Joan Harrison talked about the need for an early hook.[72] The use of mirrors serves the show's singular plot principle, the twist or switch ending, and further underpins the compressed and quick-witted pattern of grafting a casting profile onto a character personality. The overflow of mirrors in cluttered interiors, especially in the half-hour format, momentarily rivets our attention, almost in freeze-frame style, to the reflected characters and suggests we scrutinize their motives, dispositions, afflictions, or plotting. While at times the teleplays' voice-overs give a crude approximation beyond the surface, with shifting degrees of sincerity, the reflected surface stands in for the easy access to a character's inner world that the narrator in a novel can offer.

Dandies, for example, are naturally vain and narcissistic enough to closely observe and admire themselves in mirrors. Unbeknownst to the character, the imminent downfall of a reformed alcoholic can be advertised to the audience in a mirror shot. An impromptu murder of a philandering husband naturally sets a wife's cover-up performance in motion in front of a mirror. A murder plot gone awry merits shattering a mirror with a fatal bottle. And the list goes on. Such doublings or splits in mirrors are harbingers for the audience, visually alerting us to the character's potentially self-involved designs and duplicity, or succinctly confirming what we have already seen or suspect. In Hitchcock's television, mirror shots impart some invisible, lurking truth beyond the reflection and what we can readily observe. Narcissism apart, the two images in the mirror-shot framing display a disconnecting mismatch, a second nature or role-playing concealed beneath the immediately visible, as if the mirror were a palimpsest in which something beyond what can be directly seen or heard is not fully concealed, in a process that simultaneously reveals and blocks until the final twist confirms or unties narrative knots. Suspense is generated in this interstice, in dialogue with our knowledge across the lexicon of casting and the larger universe of the show's plotting, network of devices, and naming and prop strategies. And if mirrors offer condensing surface clues, the show's many flashbacks connected to voice-overs invite spectators inside the characters.

Across art forms the mirror hosts a wide range of cultural and psychological meanings. In the Hitchcock context, mirror shots provide salient cues for reading characters and their psychological dispositions, and conscious or unconscious duplicity. The uncertainties and ambiguities of this suspense structure are eminently attuned to the reflective doubling that mirror shots provide in a show generally geared to identity play. The many Hitchcock figures played up in the host frame and the uncertainties swirling around dummies, marionettes, ghosts, and surrogate figures and figurations further highlight unstable identities and corporeal negotiations as key Hitchcockian strands. The philosophical implications for mirrors in the teleplays are, however, seldom more than skin deep when hinting at troubled characters or characters in trouble willing to resort to dire plotting. Some of the overall Hitchcock connotations for mirrors have been succinctly elucidated in the entry on mirrors in Thomas Leitch's Hitchcock encyclopedia.[73]

To simplify, the mirror's reflective spectrum for characters travels from innocent vanity to full-blown self-indulgence while simultaneously commenting on duplicitous role-playing, disturbed or confused patterns of identity formation, and, as the case may be, the deformation of reality writ large or small. In the Hitchcock series the characters' dispositions toward cruelty, crimes, fears, uncertainties, and especially repressed memories are associated with the mirror shots. In this sense, mirrors represent an indispensable prop for a crime series invested in suspense and twisted endings. A conspicuous mirror shot can, for example, provide a puzzling twist at the beginning of a series of psychoanalytical sessions run by, as it turns out, a nut, who is, nevertheless, still successful in retrieving a memory suppressed in the mind of the man on the couch, as in the aptly titled teleplay "The Hidden Thing" (AHP 34).

In Hitchcock's cinema the mirroring takes on a larger format and more complex connotations attuned to genre, character assumptions, and self-referentiality. An identity crisis due to misrecognition can be simultaneously frustrating and amusing when relayed by way of mirror scenes. Games of fabricated identities abound in *North by Northwest*, as Roger O. Thornhill tries to shake the identity of George Kaplan that has been pinned on him. En route from Madison Avenue to Mount Rushmore, in a string of washrooms and hotel rooms he passes in front of one mirror after another that carnivalizes the otherwise stylish and suave Thornhill. As an advertising executive he is undoubtedly the character in Hitchcock's oeuvre most attuned to consumerism, the world of sponsorship, and commercials.[74]

Psycho, produced by Hitchcock's television company and clinically free of double entendres and prospects for a happy resolution, can serve as the template for the use of mirrors. Marion (Janet Leigh) is the film's duplicitous driving force after an innocent opening scene that takes place following a sexual encounter. Not until Marion is out of character are the spectators invited to share her mirror image. Marion dresses in front of an invisible, off-frame mirror after the film's opening lovemaking scene as she talks about her desire to reframe the sordid encounters in hotel rooms, exchanging them for respectability, marriage, and family dinners. Here she is fully in tune with the mirror image we are not invited to share, hence there is no need for doubling; in other words, for such an earnest desire there is no need for us to see her reflected. The disconnection is yet to come as she leaves respectability behind. Back at the office she puts finishing touches on the post-lovemaking freshening up with the aid of her compact, still outside the scope of the audience's vision. Later at home, after deciding, seemingly on a whim, to steal the $40,000 she was supposed to deposit for her employer, we find Marion in front of yet another mirror. In step with her duplicitous, out-of-character scheme, it is now time to show two Marions as she changes clothes in preparation for driving to meet her lover in Fairvale—and in a sense to say farewell to her old self. The suitcase lies packed on the bed next to the stack of big bills in an envelope; in retrospect, this shot explains the shift in mirror coding to doubling in this scene's opening. Ominously, her slip and bra are now black, whereas before in her hotel room they were white. Abandoning her innocence, as it were, she changes to somber colors and substitutes her white handbag for a black one. Marion is then doubled again in the restroom mirror at the used-car dealership as she peels $700 from the wad of bills and sinks deeper into her "out-of-characterness." The car she buys will be her coffin, and the greenbacks will be buried with her. And this is not to mention the series of mirror shots at the Bates Motel and mansion that come later.

The complex mirror coding in Hitchcock's cinema ranges from ludic character play to the framing of highly disturbed personalities, guilty parties, and double play in multiple dimensions—both were replicated and revised for the television show, while maintaining the core meanings regarding identities, deception and self-deception, and psychological instability. This meaning cluster additionally bears on the thin distinction between casting and character that Hitchcock foregrounded for the television show. The three examples that follow demonstrate different aspects of the show's pervasive mirror coding.

"Revenge," the very first television episode aired and directed by Hitchcock, tellingly resorts to a mirror to depict the series' unfortunate inaugural murder scene. After his wife, Elsa, is raped in a trailer park, Carl (Ralph Meeker, then fresh from the violent *Kiss Me Deadly* [1955]) metes out revenge based on her on-the-fly identification of the assailant. Carl takes her cursory glance at face value, follows the man up to his hotel room, and bludgeons him with a wrench. As Carl enters the room, he and his victim are reflected in the mirror before they both move off mirror left, with the lingering reflection of Carl's shadow showing his delivery of the blows while the impact is clearly audible on the soundtrack. Apart from muting the violence visually by filtering it as a shadow play, the mirror underscores a double mis-identity: Carl in a sense loses himself by turning into a vigilante, and, ironically, he acts without hesitation according to an identification provided by a victim still in shock. This tragic fact painfully dawns on him when Elsa points out a different man as her attacker when they reach the next town.[75]

In "Jonathan" (AHP 49), Rosine (Georgann Johnson) marries her boss, Jonathan, a long-time widower. Jonathan's son Gil hates her for breaking up his extremely close relationship with his father, his only pal and partner in sports. Gil returns home for Jonathan's funeral after his father has died of heart problems. The vindictive Gil had hoped to come home for Rosine's funeral instead of Jonathan's: Gil had tried to poison Rosine by placing a spectacular cognac bottle on the mantelpiece as a wedding present before leaving home the year before, knowing that she drank and that his father did not. After Gil's departure his dad's doctor prescribed a drink now and then, and Rosine served Jonathan the cognac she knew had been tampered with.

After realizing she could never fully fit in Jonathan's life, as Gil was always the most important person for him, Rosine elected to turn Gil's plans around to her own advantage, and she confesses as much to Gil in front of a big mirror after the funeral. This is doubly fitting according to the show's logic, as the mirror here reflects two deceitful and guilty characters bent on outwitting each other. In his anger Gil smashes the mirror with the fatal bottle, and the teleplay ends on a close-up of his face reflected in the cracked mirror. Agency, loss, and guilt are thereby distributed between the parties across the broken mirror's surface (fig. 3.15). The twisted logic for the ending, as the intended

3.15. Mirror scene from "Jonathan" (AHP 49).

victim deflects the plan and in a castling move has the schemer's beloved father die instead, is decidedly ironic, as in the other teleplays featuring Johnson. Johnson acted in three roles in the series, all threesomes of sorts. One of these, "One for the Road" (AHP 62), almost replicates the story in "Jonathan," as she once again takes advantage of a murder designed for her in a story about double life marvelously directed by Robert Stevens.

"None Are So Blind" (AHP 44) addresses fundamental issues concerning vision, representation, repression, and matters of identity. The story offers nothing but mirrors for a highly self-involved character, Seymour (Hurd Hatfield), who is out of sync with everything and everyone. Even in his girlfriend's presence he obsessively admires himself in mirrors, always from his best side. Seymour is especially out of sync with his aunt, who was put in charge of the family inheritance after the death of his father, and money is the impetus for Seymour's fantasy about a life according to his own fashion and fancy. When Seymour finds a driver's license, he decides to assume the owner's identity in a plan to frame the man as his aunt's killer. There is one hitch, however, which is elucidated by the detective in charge: Seymour has mentally blocked out his not-so-good side. Even when elaborately disguising himself in front of the mirror as the man on the driver's license, Seymour is unaware of his disfiguring birthmark and fails to hide it—fatally, as it turns out, for his clever plan.

He does not even see himself as others see him; or, rather, what he sees is a phantom, an ideal self. Mirrors are clearly never very accurate; vision seems desire-driven or distorted, and too much looking spells vanity, arrogance, disconnect, deception, and blocking in the face of unseen blemishes.[76] These few examples represent a mere fraction of the encyclopedia of salient mirror shots in the Hitchcock series. Memory loss, suppression, trauma connected to mirrors, inaccurate visions, duplicity, and misrecognitions are hence too frequent in Hitchcock's television to elucidate in full.

Mirror scenes also frame the most complex figure in all of Hitchcock's television, the host. In the prologue to "None Are So Blind" we find Hitchcock masquerading in what looks like a woman's wig and wearing spectacles in front of a mirror provided by Allardice's tongue-in-cheek scripting. The host's playful identity, body image, and ego formation could serve as dramatized shorthand for the psychoanalytical literature's mirror narrative. Hitchcock claims to be trying out different wigs in line with the entertainment industry's desire for new faces. The mirror cracks when he leans forward to admire his natural self. Pensively, while trying on one more wig and pair of spectacles, he says, "I've always wanted to be someone else." This self-conscious mirror scene elucidates the identity politics, simultaneously fixed and mercurial, at the heart of the paratexts when read across seasons. The brother character is a different but related form of skewed doubling, and the photo-essays offered multiple outlets for role-playing, at times in a carnivalizing mode, while the roster of surrogacy in a multitude of dimensions reverts to Hitchcock's body, directly and indirectly, as the grounding for its significance.

In the prologue to "The Three Dreams of Mr. Findlater," we encounter the host on the couch. Hitchcock explains that he dreamed he was sitting in a huge movie theater that was showing one of his own films, but no one was in attendance. On looking into a "gigantic mirror," he recounts, "I didn't see my own face, I saw my wife's." His dream narrative motivates a sexually tinged query from the psychiatrist: "Do you and your wife sleep in a double or in twin beds?" The host answers with a characteristic self-conscious body quip: "Both. She has a twin. I sleep in a double bed." This domestic setup jestingly hints at an asexual marriage in step with the drift of many of Hitchcock's comments. The lack of differentiation between self and other/wife in the mirroring suggests a predicament with multiple possible readings for the Hitchcocks' complicated partnership and collaborative ventures inside the bedroom and, more importantly, as we know, in the kitchen.

As I have demonstrated, the franchise at large was predicated on doubling in multiple registers that bear on corporeality. "Casting" in the wider sense of ludic repetition, the recycling of names and story elements, plus build-ing a recognizable stable of characters across teleplays by appropriating and shaping the histories of actors' roles (or pulling the rug out from under the audience's expectations by counter-typecasting) shaped the construction of a show universe across seasons, formats, and genre variations. This mode of production, the stroboscopic poetics aligned with patterns of surrogacy, operated in tandem with an obsessive use of meaningful props, especially mirrors.

CONCLUSION

VIOLENT ENDINGS WITH A TWIST

Substitutions for Changing Tastes

"The Jar" (AHH 49), based on a Ray Bradbury story and directed by Norman Lloyd, is one of the best-known teleplays in the hour-long format. The story opens at a carnival sideshow and introduces a gawking, not overly smart farmer, Charlie (Pat Buttram), who stands transfixed for hours, fascinated by a magic jar. The actor who played George/Max in "The Glass Eye" (AHP 79) returns in "The Jar" as the seller of the mysterious object around which everyone congregates to speculate on the nature of its content and meaning. Charlie purchases the jar in the hopes that owning this strange item will give him respect back home. His young wife, Thedy (Collin Wilcox), however, is unimpressed, even hostile, although she appreciates Charlie's gift of a hair band with her name written in sequins. While wearing the hair band, she looks at herself in a mirror for a long time, which we should not take lightly. Patching up Charlie's confidence after Thedy's put-down, folks from all over come to the farm every night to look entranced at the jar and guess what is inside.

Speculations include an octopus, a dead relative who was lost in a swamp, and magical eyes. There are questions about whether the contents are a she, a he, or an it, and even a belief that the jar contains the heart of life and is therefore integral to the creation of the universe. Eventually, Thedy opens the jar and destroys what's inside. This takes the story to a new level, as in a graphic scene Charlie consequently strangles her, providing yet another example of this form of Hitchcockian murder method. Afterward Charlie apparently decapitates Thedy and, somehow, puts her head in the jar. Gradually, the audience notes subtle changes in the jar, and eventually a little girl notices the hair band with Thedy's name in glowing sequins.

The ending in "The Jar," with a severed head as a spectacle to speculate on, is one of the series' most macabre moments, though the gory mess is positioned off frame, as is the case with Arthur's chopping up of his fiancée for chicken feed ("Arthur," AHP 154). In an interview with Variety's Dave Kaufman, Norman Lloyd discusses how audiences reacted to the show, according to the letters they sent in response. Viewers did not mind the killing in "The Jar," Lloyd says, but they complained about Thedy's head being stuffed into the receptacle. Using Lloyd as stand-in for Hitchcock instead of the other way around, Kaufman offers further examples of the show's macabre strands, one of them by now familiar:

> Lloyd has had a story where a man fed his murdered wife's body to the chickens ["Arthur"—though it was actually his ex-fiancée], and recalls one wherein a guy lost a finger in a bet. It was chopped by the guy he bet. ["Man from the South" (AHP 168), memorably featuring Peter Lorre and Steve McQueen—though in fact the game was cut off in time by Lorre's character's wife. She, however, for the twist, was a bit short on fingers.] These stories "always brought violent letters, saying they are so macabre, why do you bring such violence to the air, we will never tune in again," remarks Lloyd. His view is that on the series now in its tenth season "we have always considered the violence of the reaction good. It means that the show is truly macabre, and has elements of suspense, clearly indicating we had created and done what we had set out to do."[1]

The prevalence of violence on television had come under attack in the late 1950s. Industry leaders met with clergymen for a comprehensive discussion on the subject in January 1959, and a month later NBC's Robert Sarnoff urged parents to take responsibility for their children's viewing habits. The western garnered the most ill repute; the number of shows in this genre had increased by 1959 to a grand total of thirty.[2] Undeterred by these discussions, Hitchcock kept up his macabre spins on television and even upped the graphic ante—for example, in "Arthur." As Leo Mishkin put it (and note the customary unflattering description of Hitchcock's physique): "In the whole continuing series of outraged cries against the practice of mystery, mayhem, and murder on television, there is one figure at least standing curiously aloof and untouched. It's a rather imposing and majestic figure, true enough, built somewhat along the lines of an up-ended blue whale, and of such massive proportions as to discourage immediately any thought of personal attack."[3]

As always, all discussions about the franchise, be they on marketing, style, or graphic scenes, were related to Hitchcock's corporeality—in Mishkin's jest too imposing to mess with. The year before, however, John Crosby had asked Hitchcock whether he felt responsible for horror pictures "getting very big even on television." Did Hitchcock feel he set this trend? Crosby reported, "He seemed—I can think of no other word—horrified." In his response, Hitchcock bypassed television and instead elected to talk about the upcoming *North by Northwest* (1959).[4]

Hitchcock was, however, messier on the big screen than in the television show, most conspicuously in *Psycho* (1960). Hitchcock's discussion of the humor in *Psycho* approached the gore from the perspective of genre and the comedic. His carnivalizing in this respect serves our "arse-about-face" function by violently reframing horrific matters in a topsy-turvy fashion, as far as genre expectations go. In this he turns around Bakhtin's dictum "Violence does not know laughter."[5] One of the marketing endeavors in the form of a photo-essay for *Psycho* perfectly captures the carnivalizing spirit by means of a menu-like organization of the story material in tune with the well-established food discourse.[6] In an interview, Hitchcock elaborated on his frame of mind for the film:

> To me, *Psycho* was a big comedy. Had to be. . . . If I were doing *Psycho* as a serious picture, it would be done in terms of a case history. It certainly wouldn't be done in terms of the haunted house and the mysterious figure. They're all comic—they're bound to be. When you design a picture of that kind, you're laughing up your sleeve when you can hear the audience screaming.
>
> It's no different from a man who designs a roller coaster. He may hammer the nails and the screws in seriously, but the total result is going to be screaming.[7]

Discussing Hitchcock's seemingly changing attitude toward violence in the early 1960s, Robert Sklar focuses on the photo-essay published in *Esquire*.[8] Here Hitchcock's consistently playful stance on violence comes to an end, according to Sklar. Henceforth, the customary ironic expounding on merry murders was replaced with new types of concerns in relation to guilt, complicity, and violence, at least on the big screen. No more packages to Hong Kong. Sklar considers *Psycho* the benchmark for this shift and connects it to graphic murder scenes in *Torn Curtain* (1966) and *Frenzy* (1972), further evidencing death's sticky physicality for perpetrators and victims, and simultaneously turning spectators into complicit voyeurs in a complex game of identification. The larger Hitchcock discourse does not, however, bear out such a clear-cut break as the isolated murder scenes in Sklar's three films might suggest. In Robert E. Kapsis's reading of *Psycho*, the shift in tone and heightened level of violence and horror are understood as concessions to a younger audience relishing the style of the low-budget horror shockers.[9] The shift to fiercer violence might therefore be ascribed to audiences' genre expectations as much as authorial rethinking in the aftermath of the studio era, which Sklar invokes as a parallel explanatory track for a shift in brand emphasis.

In a prescient observation made in passing a couple of months after the opening of *Psycho*, Murray Schumach noticed a formula shift concerning Hitchcock's work at large. In an interview with Joan Harrison he describes her as "the guardian of the pre-'Psycho' Hitchcock formula of murder with a chuckle." According to Harrison, "Our murders . . . are very polite. We try to avoid horror for horror's sake. We seldom show details of gory murder. We don't like to show people hitting other people on the head [except with a leg of lamb]. And, unless absolutely essential, we avoid screaming."[10] *Psycho* seems particularly attuned to the mindset carrying the television show, apart from the shower scene and its aftermath as Norman disposes of the dead body. This is particularly revealing in the trailer, which features a host-like Hitchcock acting as guide to the film and placed in the film's actual setting, which he returned to for Jeanloup Sieff's camera.

Hitchcock's pronouncements on violence to the media and his practices, irrespective of screen size, continued to be compounded, contradictory, and carnivalizing, and thus quintessentially Hitchcockian, as *Psycho* continued to reverberate in several teleplays. In contrast to Norman's sticky and troublesome corpse disposal in *Psycho*, Arthur's is clean, economical, almost scientific, and ultimately ironic—and just as neat and offscreen as those of the *Esquire* photo-essay and "The Jar."

If Hitchcock seems overtly serious owing to his upgrading of the physical aspect of violence on-screen, he distances himself from the work through a parallel discourse that undercuts the investment in seriousness by way of a performative or furtive chuckle, however out of place. Such double takes go to the heart of the carnivalizing spirit. This heteroglossia was neatly summed up in an NBC biography from this period, which claimed that, even to his friends, "Hitch is a kind of multiple personality . . . and defies understanding completely."[11] Should one take seriously the pronouncements on *Psycho*'s horror as a private exercise in black humor, the film might illustrate this shift in genre and a turn to gothic Americana as a counterpoint to the pastoral, dark-but-lighthearted humor played out in *The Trouble with Harry* (1955), set in a neighborhood where Hitchcock was appointed honorary mayor.[12] In this respect, *Psycho* was fully aligned with the darkness that *Shadow of a Doubt's* (1943) Uncle Charlie brought to idyllic Santa Rosa, a town where murder stories before his arrival were nothing but amusing diversions told on the porch.

If we stick to *Psycho* as a benchmark, this multiplicity of tones, stances, and poses is particularly evident from the photo-essay for this film that ran parallel to stern marketing efforts aimed at making sure the audience did not miss the beginning of the movie. The guiding exhibition principle, presented in a trailer aimed at exhibitors and in the film's press booklet, was to admit no one after the screening began. Jimmie Allardice had Hitchcock explain this by way of the characteristic food metaphors: "Surely you do not have your meat course after your dessert at dinner. You will therefore understand why we are so insistent that you enjoy PSYCHO from start to finish, exactly as we intended that it be served."[13] This regulated serving was not the first exercise in audience discipline. In the press brochure for *Vertigo* (1958), Hitchcock cautioned exhibitors not to let anybody "be seated during the last ten minutes" of the film.[14] This "rule" was upgraded when *Vertigo* was screened in France, in a campaign headlined "Catch It from the Beginning," the kick-off of which coincided with Hitchcock's visit to Paris. In the in-house magazine *Paramount World*, he poses holding an alarm clock and pointing to the hands indicating the starting time.[15] This image was later tweaked for the "See It from the Start" campaign for *Psycho*, with the director again looking stern and this time pointing at his wristwatch. Hitchcock's French campaign was not an accidental idea: his suspense rival Henri-Georges Clouzot had pioneered precisely this type of campaign for *Les diaboliques* (Filmsonor / Vera Films, 1955). The efforts to discipline the audience for *Psycho* thus came about as a spin-off and not from an inspiration that he had during editing, as Hitchcock claimed.[16]

Promotion in general overdetermines how spectators engage with a film, uniquely so in the case of *Psycho*. Seeping into and coloring the reception of a film are a whole smattering of promotional "epiphenomena," to use Barbara Klinger's productive term (in turn borrowed from Stephen Heath), in the form of exhibition materials (posters, ads, radio spots, trailers) and various intermedia featuring materials on stars, directors, and the production process published in newspapers and on radio and television.[17] This bleed is of course different in nature from the paratexts that are attached to the teleplays. And because of the almost constant presence of Hitchcock figures or surrogates in various media, the reception of any film and teleplay in his name was highly charged by his public persona, his biographical legend, and the cultural foreknowledge of the eponym "Hitchcockian."

Psycho features a slightly awkward, impromptu meal that Norman prepares for Marion before Mother shows up for the subsequent shower scene, the height of violence in the film. True to customary Hitchcock concerns, the film was marketed as a cooking class in a photo-journalistic spin allegedly authored by Hitchcock, and in the same frivolous manner as later in the *Esquire* lecture: "May I recommend a meal fit for a killer? Start with the antipasto of one passionate peccadillo and 40,000 greenbacks. The main dish: mayhem, rare. Now you know the menu of my new film-flam—'Psycho.' But as you'll see, much depends on the chef." A series of photos with captions provides further plot points: "Take two lovers . . . mix well with one odd fellow . . . blend in one rainy night . . . and a knife" (here the Hitchcock figure is threatened by a gigantic knife [fig. C.1], and in the next image outside the house, his head seems to float in the darkness); "season with a ghost house and a corpse . . . one quivering culprit . . . and a witless witness . . . add one scheming director" (Hitchcock with hat in what looks like a dark circus ring, stark lighting, his outfit taken from the cameo appearance), "and the plot boils."[18] The multiplicity of roles for Hitchcock, harking back to Gjon Mili's stroboscopic lineup, is a critical feature in the *Psycho* photo-essay: as chef/director hunkering down under the knife, he wears his cameo costume in front of a backdrop not seen in the film. The carefree mixing of thrilling ingredients in the photo-essay draws on the macabre intersection of food preparation and palatable thriller fare dished up with good cheer and calculated to offset the story's unsavory aspects. The tone is flippant in the extreme, and Hitchcock inserts himself into the proceedings, using both his cameo appearance and his pedestrian alias, the latter also used for the trailer. When discussing violence, he in passing invokes the nursery rhyme "Jack and Jill," which features a boy and girl, a head injury, and a mother hovering in the house.

This recipe for murder was not a unique marketing stunt. A couple of months earlier Hitchcock had posed for Gordon Parks's camera, which resulted in a full-page photograph in *Life* and a short, playful text bearing on the upcoming premiere of *Psycho* (fig. C.2). The caption tells us: "A blooming flower of cinematic evil, Alfred Hitchcock peers malignantly out from under the garden shrubbery and strangles a rose." The text alliteratively describes his business as "murder, mayhem and malevolence" and his look as "cheerful and cherubic." His face is "red and merry" owing to "years of devotion to the civilizing influence of good wines." The film Hitchcock hopes to be able to make someday comes with the key ingredients I have discussed from multiple perspectives—namely, "the story of the perfect murder in which the killer does away with a corpse by using it as a gourmet's savory concoction."[19] For

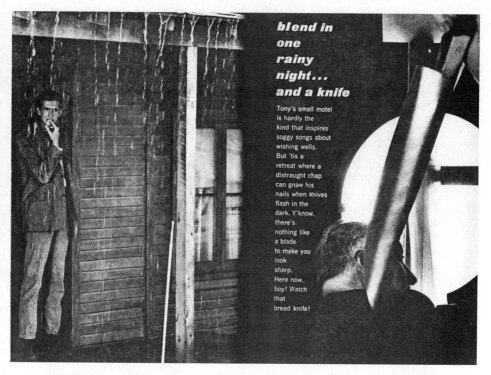

C.1. Photo-essay for marketing *Psycho* (1960). Alfred Hitchcock, "My Recipe for Murder," *Coronet* 48, no. 5 (September 1960): 49–61. Photographs by Eugene Cook, courtesy of Universal Studios Licensing LLC.

now he has to settle for the milder, more palatable *Psycho*. Still, and again with strangling in the mix and unrelated to *Psycho*, he describes his new film as a shift in genre, as "pure horror" is substituted for the customary thriller fare in line with Sklar's contention. Horror apart, Hitchcock still considered the film a comedy and did not hesitate to burlesque it in the marketing spins.

In his discussion of *Psycho*, William Rothman notes close affinities between the teleplays and the world of the films in general, and the Shamley-produced *Psycho* in particular, before positing a radical difference between them.[20] Given the prologues and Hitchcock's placement outside the stories as an ironic and detached commentator obliquely ushering in the teleplays, Rothman argues that we, as spectators, are allowed only the vision the host prescribes for us. The teleplay world is all Hitchcock's and totally overdetermined by the ironic prologue frame (although the irony is primarily directed at what immediately follows, the first commercial, which counteracts and dilutes Hitchcock's reach and authority in a form of blocking). We are thus

C.2. "Phantom Face in the Foliage," *Life*, 11 July 1960, 54. Photograph by Gordon Parks, courtesy of the Gordon Parks Foundation.

standing apart, outside, just like Hitchcock and the camera. Rothman claims this is not the case with *Psycho* since there is no ironic frame. Instead, he argues, we encounter a camera born into the world of the film, a world that therefore could be ours.

The putative differences Rothman sets up between film exhibition and the overall frame for television, ironic or not, seem pertinent only from the perspective of a reading of a film totally severed from the wider contextual sphere of marketing, which at times accompanies audiences all the way through the lobby. Presuming that film spectators come to the theater with a clean slate and start out as newborns in alliance with the camera misses the highly convoluted reading frames that audiences brought to the screenings of *Psycho* in particular. Hitchcock's performance in the film's trailer provided the same type of ushering in as in the teleplays; and, more importantly, the viewing experience itself was circumscribed by caveats and conditions imposed from outside by Hitchcock's voice via loudspeakers, and his "appearing" in the marketing essay and as a disciplining cardboard figure in the lobby while audiences lined up, as Linda Williams has demonstrated. As Williams comments: "In the discipline imposed by Hitchcock [or the Hitchcock figures], the efficiency and control demonstrated outside the theatre need to be viewed in tandem with the patterns of fear and release unleashed inside."[21]

Hence, to exclusively situate Hitchcock inside *Psycho* as cameo and surrogate structure only squanders his extreme prominence in shaping and harnessing the viewing experience and its violence, from "outside" also, for this particular film. Before the "newborns" entered the theater, they were subjected to a process of labor and delivery conditioning them for the experience inside; thus they brought along an epiphenomenal reading frame with carnivalizing elements in play to offset the shocks.

The marketing spins undercut the seriousness of *Psycho* in the manner alluded to in Hitchcock's description of its comedic nature, as a spoof whipping gothic elements into a horror soufflé. Toying with this spirit for two episodes from the final television season, Hitchcock's team headed by Norman Lloyd revisits locations from *Psycho*, as did Hitchcock previously for Jeanloup Sieff's camera, to indulge in some carnivalizing of its own. In "Off Season" (AHH 93), the last of all the television shows, the prime location is a motel—in fact, the old structure used as the Bates Motel—and John Gavin, who played Marion's lover in *Psycho*, is the leading man. Gavin's character believes his wife is unfaithful and shoots her and her lover, only to discover, in a final twist in a story with virtually no humor, that the woman in question was the sheriff's wife, not his own. This closing out of season ten and the show at large represented a mere afterthought in relation to a previous teleplay spoofing *Psycho*. "An Unlocked Window" (AHH 81), from the same season, is set in the Bates family house, using all the famous interiors—the staircase where Detective Arbogast is killed and the basement where Mother is finally tucked away—settings introduced by Hitchcock in the trailer for the film. The episode is predicated on character ambiguity, as the killing team from *Psycho*, the double Norman/Mother, is substituted for a male killer gender masquerading as a nurse, but without the psychological underpinning outlined in the film. The episode brims with gothic paraphernalia—bar patterns, shadows, noises from the basement, black cats, and telephones not working—and the events take place during a severe rainstorm. As one more nod to the larger Hitchcockian universe in this spin-off episode, Louise Latham, the mother in *Marnie* (1964), returns as a weird housekeeper who is overly fond of the bottle—which brings back the critical role of casting.

If Hitchcock remained unscathed in the debates on violence before *Psycho*, as Mishkin claimed, the criticisms eventually caught up with his television. Change was in the air a few seasons later. Larry Wolters quoted unnamed "random reflections" bearing on this issue: "We're fed up with Alfred Hitchcock's demonstrations of the techniques of horror crimes in violation of the TV code of good practices. The bosses on CBS ought to bring him into line."[22] By then Hitchcock had already had one episode canceled by his former network, NBC. "The Sorcerer's Apprentice"—like *Psycho*, based on a story by Robert Bloch—was shot in the summer of 1961 but was considered too gruesome to merit broadcasting. Here a young, not overly smart boy, Hugo, is led on by Diana Dors's alluring character, Irene, a beautiful assistant to a carnival magician whom she wants to ditch for the muscular high-wire artist. Duped by her opulent charms, Hugo kills his master, the magician. Believing that he has mastered the magician's powers, the boy sets out to prove his point after an altercation in which Irene gets knocked out. Hugo places Irene's body in the box and fatally saws her in two without any healing magic to undo the harm inflicted on her body. This was too much Hitchcockian body politics for NBC or the sponsor.

The National Association for Better Radio and Television did not mince words in its report from the 1964–1965 season when classifying *The Alfred Hitchcock Hour* (AHH) as "objectionable." A capsule comment further elaborated on the show's core elements and plot points: "Expert production and macabre satire, dealing with subjects that are sordid and terrifying. Shocking crimes, brutality, and sadism. In the Hitchcock show you are to see rats crawling on a corpse, a woman's face as she struggles with a sex maniac, or the contorted faces of teen-age criminals. Hitchcock's talent [or, rather, that of the production team led by Lloyd as executive producer during the final season of AHH] is not enough to make this acceptable for family viewing."[23]

Seconding the analysis of Hitchcock, NBC (again broadcasting the series after it bounced back to CBS for the two first seasons of AHH) canceled the show. "I really think," Hitchcock reflected, "the reason is fear of the horrific.... With all the criticism about violence and with congressional investigations in the offing . . . the networks are afraid to put on any shows with a bite. The result will be a continuing flood of situation comedies."[24] As it turned out, American television did not become fully family-oriented after Hitchcock signed off for good. The decade-long Hitchcock moment had, however, passed, as the show's format was not flexible enough to hold the fort when competing with series that seized upon a new era and palpable realities after the mid-1960s. Harrison and Lloyd updated, refashioned, and relocated the format to England for two seasons of *Journey to the Unknown* (1968–1969), a series replete with familiar elements and some familiar star faces from *Alfred Hitchcock Presents* (AHP), AHH, and Hitchcock's cinema.

Some things change, others stay the same. A decade on television did not manage to exorcise the longstanding reception mode for Hitchcock and its offhand physical indignities. In 1965, when Hitchcock's television tenure came to a close, a TV *Guide* issue ventured the following description, still treating the star as fair game regarding body talk: "At 65 he still resembles one of those bald, solemn, overfed bundles with pudgy, motionless arms that one sees in prams in the park."[25] This style of writing mirrors the dilemma on which Henry McLemore reported when he found himself at a loss for a fresh angle in conjunction with a lunch at the Paramount lot the year before the television show opened: "I was casting about for something to hang an interview on. I couldn't do a column on his weight. His loss of 150 pounds, reducing him from blimp to fighter size, has been written about a thousand times." Eventually, the conversation veered toward suspense on and off the screen as "Mr. Hitchcock ate a bit steak from which all the fat and most of the meat had been cut off" while recounting his customary anecdotes.[26] A couple of months later, Hitchcock discussed the upcoming television show and, again over a steak, presented a master recipe for the format.[27]

The Master Recipe

Should we heuristically slice up Hitchcockiana before and after *Psycho*, as Murray Schumach suggests, "Lamb to the Slaughter" (AHP 106) is indisputably the televisual master recipe for the first period. This is the most famous of all Hitchcock's teleplays, because of the unforgettable, macabre ending in which the hapless detectives feast on a leg of lamb that, when still frozen, had been the blunt murder weapon they were unable to find. Given that Hitchcock repeatedly mentioned this particular story as an ideal vehicle for the show, it is surprising that several seasons passed before it was actually produced.[28] Roald Dahl's story effectively rips asunder the notion of happy life in suburbia as the philandering husband walks in after work, callously announcing his plan to abandon his pregnant wife, Mary, for another woman. Generously, he will let Mary keep the baby. Unsuspectingly, Mary has eagerly awaited his return home from yet another day of police business. Her impromptu murder of her husband is totally aligned with the housewife's material world and her nurturing of the family. In an almost somnambulistic series of movements, her repurposing of the frozen meat to a lethal weapon comes almost naturally, as only a slight deviance from the daily forays between the freezer in the garage and the kitchen stove. The story's trajectory is perfectly attuned to this wifely domestic logic. After having bludgeoned her husband, Mary pauses briefly to ponder the situation, then telephones to cancel a dinner invitation. This is followed by a quick visit to the grocer for an alibi, before she returns home to discover her dead husband after an alleged break-in that she actually stages. Naturally, the teleplay includes a revealing mirror scene, a signature device for the series.

After being repurposed as a murder weapon in the living room, the leg of lamb ends up in the oven, the dominant kitchen appliance. The serving of the once-lethal meat to her husband's police colleagues as they search for a mysterious murder weapon is the most iconic scene from Hitchcock's entire television repertoire. Dahl's ending represents a veritable stroke of genius in its brisk twist of normality and kitchen routines. Barbara Bel Geddes's slightly regressive, uncanny giggle, half suppressed as she observes the feast from the living room, maddeningly marks and simultaneously distances the normalcy of the meal as the evidence is consumed with gusto. The dinner restores a form of order and everyday life in the face of murder, but the routine of eating is of course overdetermined by what the food once was. The end comes with a vengeance, not from inside the story, but as a jocular afterthought delivered in the epilogue. According to the host, Mary tried the same method once more, but owing to freezer malfunction the meat was soft. After airing, the episode received instant cult status.

We know precious little about the mechanics of the Hitchcock show's day-to-day operations. A surviving communication from Joan Harrison to Roald Dahl is therefore a rarity in itself and especially interesting given the emblematic status Dahl's story was awarded as a model for the show both before and after it was produced. Harrison's five-page letter merits attention since this is a canonical, much-talked-about teleplay, and Hitchcock directed it. Harrison's letter is dated 10 January 1958; the teleplay was filmed 18–19 February and aired on 13 April. Obviously, the production process was quite condensed. Examination of the surviving source material at the Roald Dahl Museum and Story Centre in Buckinghamshire, England, reveals that the initial treatment, contrary to expectations, was written on spec before being picked up by the Hitchcock team. Harrison's comments refer to the first draft after the contract was signed; this is version three in the archive catalogue. In this draft the Maloney family has a boy, Johnny, who sleeps upstairs as mom kills dad after the latter returns from work and announces that he wants a divorce in order to remarry. The son was deleted for the teleplay and substituted with Mary being pregnant because of Hitchcock's misgivings concerning the presence of a child in the house during a murder. This revision emotionally ups the ante and the husband's obduracy.

In the opening paragraph, Harrison mentions that she has discussed the script "at length" with Hitch and states: "He has asked me to pass on to you his feeling about it and also about the notes you sent us later." These notes have been lost. The producers' suggestions divide the teleplay into four parts. According to Harrison, the pregnancy, preferably at four to five months, will "keep a basic sympathy for the wife." Furthermore, "it is then more understandable that Mary would kill her husband." The fourth part of the teleplay takes place in the kitchen after "the detectives have completed their inspection of the house and premises." Here Mary gets the idea to have them "eat the leg of lamb and we follow the original story here until the end."

Concerning Dahl's lost notes, Harrison's letter offers some clarification: "You said in your notes that you felt wary of prolonging the final scene in the kitchen, and you are right that the moment the audience realize the cops are going to eat the leg of lamb, the story is over. It was the section before that, section 3, i.e. the police investigation that Hitch and I both feel could be prolonged and made most suspenseful." Thus Harrison's detailed suggestions for section three, which she outlines from A to F in the memo. Harrison here channels Hitchcock's, or rather her and Hitchcock's, suggestions for revision. Dahl apparently reworked the script in accordance with the production team's detailed suggestions. This second draft is labeled number seven of eight "bundles" found for this work at the Dahl Museum and Story Centre. Bundle eight is the shooting script.[29]

Another critical point for Harrison was that the murder should take place quite early in the show. "On TV we have to get our audiences 'hooked' at the start," she explains. Harrison then proceeds to outline the story in four sections. The first involves "establishing the relationships and ending with the murder." The second consists of Mary's preparations before calling the police: putting the lamb in the oven, establishing an alibi at the grocery store, and messing up the room to simulate a break-in. The third and longest part, per the producers' suggestions, has the police's various actions in the wake of the murder report. The suspense factor hinges on whether Mary "is going to get away with the killing or not."

The teleplay is shot in one unbroken temporal stretch from shots 1 to 47, followed by a dissolve when Mary goes shopping. Shot 48 in the grocery store, the only one outside the home, is fleetingly brief and dissolves back to the living room with the dead husband. Shots 49 to 62 cover Mary's theatrical entry and her dropping the groceries, her rearranging the room to simulate a struggle, the call to the police, and the first round of questioning parallel to the coroner's work and the technicians taking fingerprints. This string of scenes is punctuated by a fadeout and the middle commercial. In shot 63, after the break, the body is taken away, followed by further questioning and investigative work through shot 86 and a dissolve. Shot 87 is marked as taking place somewhat later. Mary now sits in an armchair, the mystified detectives chat in the background, and she listens. This leads to the eating of the lamb. Shot 111 ends with a dissolve to shot 112 and the final stage of the meal. The shot opens with a close-up on the plates, with nothing but bones left on the serving platter. The camera tracks to a wider shot as one of the detectives says he is going to take the bones home to his dog. In shot 113 Mary is sitting in the living room with her back right against the wall, where Patrick stood as he came home and silently downed his two whiskeys before delivering the crushing news of the divorce and in turn receiving Mary's quid pro quo blow. Mary overhears the dinner conversation while the camera closes in on her. The close shot is saved for added emphasis, as the teleplay ends with her giggle triggered by the discussion of the undiscovered murder weapon, which, as one of the detectives reflects, could be under their very noses. Indeed.

The episode is replete with animal references and imagery, naturally supplied by the production team. The walls in the house are littered with what look like cheap reproductions of animal art, depicting a dog and a horse, but most important is a series of bird pictures. In this particular episode a few shots are especially rich in their symmetrical patterns of signification. Standing at the foot of a staircase with vertical bars, Mary watches herself in a mirror when making a duplicitous telephone call to establish an alibi after having bludgeoned her cheating husband with the leg of lamb. A group of prominent motifs come together here: the doubling mirror in front of which she establishes her false alibi; the telephone as a means of communication, which is rich with filmic signification in horror contexts (and in Hitchcock's cinema as well); plus the Hitchcockian vertical-bar motif (figs. C.3–C.4).

C.3 (*facing, top*) and C.4 (*facing, middle and bottom*). Weaponized foodstuffs; framing a murderer. From "Lamb to the Slaughter" (AHP 106).

One of the avian pictures on the staircase wall features two lovebirds, an ironic marginal commentary on the scene's domestic horror—pregnant wife kills callous husband. The bird images are highly visible in several shots and symmetrically organized in the overall composition of pregnant shots, as the lovebirds are reflected in the mirror. The two additional avian pictures hanging along the stairs leading to the second floor feature single birds. Overall, the avian series, and especially the bird imagery, can provisionally, and in line with David Sterritt's analysis, be read as an emblem or surrogate for authorial self-inscription aligned with the film cameos—a form of indirect surveying inside the fictional world, which is delegated or transferred to an object or representation in the absence of Hitchcock's screen presence as cameo.[30]

Besides singling out the story as exemplary for the upcoming show, once it aired Hitchcock retold Dahl's story on multiple occasions; for example, in a 1961 *Argosy* article in which accounts of classical murder cases were mixed with fictional ones like Dahl's.[31] Here, he explains, the murder weapon becomes untraceable after literally being digested by the cops, which ties in with the idea about the perfect murder. In his story Dahl wittily alludes to the nursery rhyme featuring Mary and the lamb that loves her and follows her everywhere, by naming his "heroine" Mary Maloney.[32]

The use of Barbara Bel Geddes as Mary further reinforces the teleplay's place in a larger Hitchcock universe—she appears most prominently in *Vertigo*, and also in a couple of other teleplays. Her characters are unfailingly haunted by the elusiveness of love; as in *Vertigo*, she is unable to hold on to her great love in the Hitchcock episodes "The Foghorn" (AHP 102), "The Morning of the Bride" (AHP 136), and "Sybilla" (AHP 201). In Hitchcock's world, cellars and attics, nooks and crannies are integral to the poetics of murder in the home—this in addition to the most sacred space for domestic practices associated with women, the kitchen. Tellingly, though Dahl's story was shifted to America, the two-story house still has the murder geography restricted to one floor, using the garage with the freezer as an adjunct to the kitchen, which in turn opens to the drawing room, where the murder takes place. This stretched, horizontal spatiality is evident in the episode's closing shot, with Bel Geddes's Mary watching and listening to the dinner scene and its conversation from afar as the camera dollies in on her face.

c.5. Uncredited photograph published in TV *Guide* 6, no. 19 (10 May 1958): 12–13.

Moms, Daughters, and Other Hitchcock Women

Mary Maloney, soon to be a mother, was not the only female killer in the Hitchcock series, and the host was careful to keep a tab on the homicidal gender balance across seasons. Five seasons in to his television series, Alfred Hitchcock took stock of the accomplishments so far in statistical gender terms. He did so in his customary jesting manner and brought home his point by way of a photograph summing up his track record in this respect.[33] After 134 weeks, he claimed, "the gentler sex" had committed around 99 "sundry crimes," one of them, obviously, in "Lamb to the Slaughter." Posing in an uncredited photograph published in TV *Guide*, Hitchcock stands detached on a soapbox or platform as a stage master in the background, holding ribbons attached to the seven women in the foreground (fig. c.5). Though given free rein, according to the caption, they are still his marionettes, or he their puppeteer. Each unsmiling woman (or girl) holds a murder weapon: a hatchet, a bottle of acid or poison, a banana, and so on. The photograph is indicative of the type of humor and poetic license that permeated the show and Hitchcock's bizarre television persona. The whimsy he excels at on and off the tube strives for effect rather than veracity. In that spirit, only one of the young ladies in this rogues' gallery had in fact committed a serious crime in the show: Tita Purdom, as the deranged Millie in "Wet Saturday" (AHP 40). In the photograph she holds a hatchet. Smitten with her schoolmaster in the teleplay, she bludgeons him not with an axe but with a croquet mallet after he mentions he plans to marry someone else. Most of the girls in the group photograph played minuscule bit parts, except the always nice and nonviolent Mary Scott, who featured in several episodes, and the child prodigy Evelyn Rudie, in no way a juvenile delinquent, who played a key role in "A Man Greatly Beloved" (AHP 72). And as for one of the photographed girls, Theron Krender, it is debatable whether she even appeared on the show.

When Hitchcock ventured observations on famous homicides, real as well as fictional ones, the victims were by default women. In the televisual practice, money and passion offered the brunt of the murderous impetus for the killers irrespective of gender, but another impetus was peace of mind, as for John Williams's character in "Back for Christmas" (AHP 23). This character's wife, a quintessential mom figure in the sense I will discuss (but in all likelihood not a mother), is part of a roster of brand-defining character-types more at risk of being disposed of than younger demanding women. An example of the latter is the high-maintenance wife in "The Derelicts" (AHP 19), whose reckless dissipation drives her husband to murder in order to keep up with her demands. The key article for extravagant spending in the series was the fur coat, redolent with glamour and fraught with sexual significance.[34] Quite a few of the fur-clad young women reversed the pattern by outsourcing the killing of their older spouses to their young lovers—for example, in "Decoy" (AHP 37) and "Better Bargain" (AHP 50), and not least Angie Dickinson in an even more involved form in her role as playgirl in "Captive Audience" (AHH 5). For husbands past their prime, such young trophy wives were literally to die for.

Since the publication in 1975 of Laura Mulvey's classic essay on women's bodies in American narrative cinema as spectacle for the male gaze, Hitchcock's films have become the prime critical domain for analyzing gender issues, processes of desires and sexualities, identifications and identities.[35] These critical positions and stances, and the polemics around them, have productively enriched the film criticism and continue to do so. Tania Modleski carefully and convincingly dissected this rich body of scholarship in a postscript to the 2005 edition of her landmark study from 1988 of Hitchcock women and the spectatorships elicited by his cinema.[36] Visual pleasure apart, there's a flip side of abject in relation to a multitude of Hitchcock's mom figures as a key character-type across his work; to further complicate matters, the franchise also treats a select group of older women with much tenderness. The strand of disdain reaches as far back as *Downhill* (Gainsborough Pictures, 1927). Here Roddy (Ivor Novello), after many disappointments, finds himself as a professional gigolo in a Parisian music hall. Sick of hooking up with older women for money, he eventually manages to return to his old life. *Downhill* presents a benign version of the unvarnished disgust displayed by Uncle Charlie (Joseph Cotten) for the widows he kills off in *Shadow of a Doubt*.

Hitchcock's television has been accorded minimal attention in these discussions. Obviously, ten full seasons of teleplays create a too vast and diverse pool of characters to analyze other than by way of some surface observations, or in pertinent case studies. Mother-daughter relations, both real and symbolic, figure prominently in Modleski's study; I will zoom in on one teleplay featuring a prototypical example of this dynamic as an inflection of the character typing of mom figures in Hitchcock's oeuvre overall, as discussed by both Bernard F. Dick and Mike Chopra-Gant.[37]

Modleski's theoretical framework is predominantly psychoanalytic, but she also refers to the popular discussions of gender stereotypes in vogue during the 1940s and '50s that left their representational imprint in the female spectrum of AHP and AHH. In this context, there are also entangled mother-son relations adding to a roster ranging from the icy Mme. Sebastian (Leopoldine Konstantin) in *Notorious* (1946) to the capricious but controlling Clara Thornhill in *North by Northwest*.

In 1942 in *Generation of Vipers* Philip Wylie launched his discursive attack on America, which to his mind was run by "mom" and consumerism in dictatorial cahoots.[38] Hitchcock television fleshed out not only young girls, and some of them homicidal, but also mom figures in multiple incarnations, mixing whimsical vintage killers with a considerable number of seasoned women ripe for the cure suggested by Uncle Charlie. For Wylie, in his vitriolic attack on momism written before the onset of the baby boom, the girlish Cinderellas are mothers in the making who almost in a wink calcify into viper moms who poison the social body and suck vitality and enjoyment out of the very fabric of life. For Wylie, mom is a "human calamity." In his introduction to the 1955 edition he describes her in no uncertain terms: "The hen-harpy is but the Cinderella chick come to roost: the taloned, cackling residue of burnt out puberty."[39] Wylie did not mince words concerning meddling mom's plans for television: "She will not rest until every electronic moment has been bought to sell suds and every bought program censored to the last decibel and syllable according to her self-adulation—along with that (to the degree the mom-indoctrinated pops are permitted access to the dials) of her de-sexed, de-souled, de-cerebrated mate."[40]

Wylie's stab at 1950s televisual momism is symptomatic, as the medium had turned into a cultural behemoth cleverly portioned for family entertainment and served up across the schedule of the everyday rhythms of domestic life. His tract offers an extreme form of cultural negotiation written before the return to a full-throttle consumerism, which after the war allied itself with the coming baby boom, suburbanization, and television culture. Without fully siding with Wylie's controversial trajectory for women, in which they briskly leap from being young sexy things and Cinderellas to socially and culturally devastating members of the momism group, Hitchcock television still painted a pretty bleak image of women at large after their girlish charms and glamour had vanished.

This cultural backstory tied in with the mom-typing at work in Hitchcock's franchise. In one of the show's most blatant engagements with momism, in tune with Wylie's attacks, the frustrated Lucy (Eileen Heckart) in "Coming, Mama" (AHP 217) turns into a killer to escape from motherly scheming. The teleplay singles out mom twice over for added irony.

According to the doctor's diagnosis, Lucy's bedridden mother faked a heart attack while Lucy was out with her long-term boyfriend, Arthur. Mom despises Arthur and threatens to cut Lucy out of her will should she marry. As the story evolves, it turns out that Lucy is being framed from all sides, as the mise-en-scène makes obvious. Mom's deception is hinted at by her being introduced in a mirror shot as Lucy enters the bedroom. And after Mom's threats, Arthur presents her with an ultimatum: marry me now or never. Putting Lucy between a rock and a hard place, Arthur calls her on the telephone to drive his point home a second time. Lucy takes the call while standing in front of a mirror, sleeping pills for Mom in hand (fig. C.6). The visually conflicted doubling unequivocally depicts her adversarial situation. This is one of the series' signature mirror sequences and leaves no room for doubt as to Lucy's thorny predicament. After hanging up, she marches right back to her mother, seemingly giving in to her demands, though simultaneously serving her a lethal dose of the drug to break free. Lucy then arranges the room, just like Mary in "Lamb to the Slaughter," so that she can make a discovery the following morning for the benefit of the neighbor, who is more or less part of the household.

As Lucy learns during the reading of the will, her mother's money came from an annuity set up by her father, which would be terminated at the moth-

C.6. Eileen Heckart in "Coming, Mama" (AHP 217).

er's death. The threat to change the will was hence treacherous; Lucy would never get any money, married or not. As it turns out, this shocking revelation was not the major twist ending. Arthur was not on the up and up when presenting his marriage ultimatum. His treachery dawns on Lucy after the wedding, when she steps from one house to the other—and from one mom to the next. Arthur's mother has recently had a nasty fall and is now bedridden, fearing she will stay that way for the rest of her life. She is, however, grateful that Lucy, with her experience as a caregiver, is willing to postpone the honeymoon. In the face of this twist, Lucy tells Arthur that Mom needs sleeping pills as she menacingly walks toward the camera, seemingly ready to rid herself of the mother problem once and for all.

The Hitchcock series dished out a multitude of similarly pesky moms destructively clinging to their offspring. One of them, Jessie Royce Landis's character in "Mother, May I Go Out to Swim?" (AHP 179), drives her challenged son, played by William Shatner, to murder his girlfriend. In a parallel strand the series featured an array of very sweet ladies who occasionally dabbled in homicide. "Conversation over a Corpse" (AHP 47), in keeping with our body-accented focus, is a happy emulation of the arsenic-and-old-lace tradition featuring vintage ladies as killers. In this teleplay a realtor, Brenner, has an option on a house owned by two sisters, but they unexpectedly come into some insurance money. The developer is unrelenting, however, and bent on exercising his option. The sisters knock Brenner out by means of poison, but while deliberating on how to dispose of the corpse, they discover that he is not quite dead—so still not quite a Harry. This sparks a farcical parade of more or less harebrained ideas for killing him for good.

Patricia Collinge, who played the sweet but frail mom in Shadow of a Doubt, was cast quite regularly in teleplays offering tweaking variations on her nervous, whimsical, and seemingly brittle physical template from the film, albeit not without twists. As a family-oriented mom, she poisons herself and her son for a family reunion beyond the grave in "Across the Threshold" (AHP 175). In "Bonfire" (AHH 13), living alone in a big mansion and with a weak heart, she loses her life in a scheme: she is deliberately danced to death by Peter Falk's calculating character, who has an eye on her house for his revival activities. Not relishing living alone and moving from victim to perpetrator in the arsenic tradition, but with a twist, she takes in young men as lodgers in "The Landlady" (AHP 210), only to use them as objects for her taxidermy hobby following her not-so-nice cups of tea. This taxing hobby defies her frail appearance, which proves to be deceptive also on several other occasions. As the elderly Mrs. Snow she survives, albeit barely, the ordeal of being locked up in an airtight safe ("The Ordeal of Mrs. Snow," AHH 57). As the disabled Mrs. Cheney, she smartly circumvents the harassments of a man hell bent on finding a priceless vase in her collection ("The Cheney Vase," AHP 13).

In "The Rose Garden" (AHP 51), finally, Collinge's character, Julia, is living with her sister Cordelia in a stately mansion in Louisiana. Here Cordelia lives up to Wylie's entire lexicon of mom stereotypes, while Julia in contrast is kind, nervous, and as frail-looking as Collinge's character in Shadow of a Doubt. As this teleplay especially bears out, the complexity of Collinge's casting goes beyond any simplistic pigeonholing within Hitchcock's portraits of women and moms. Furthermore, "The Rose Garden" is abundantly rich in Hitchcockian ingredients, with Collinge and John Williams as links to his cinema. Collinge's Julia has lived in a mansion with not only the domineering and icy Cordelia but also the sister's husband. He, just like Julia, was under the unyielding thumb of his mean wife. Eventually, Julia and the brother-in-law planned to escape together, but he never showed up at the rendezvous place. Many years later Collinge has penned a crime novel, and now her enthusiastic publisher, played by John Williams, comes visiting only to discover that her story is not fictional. Soon he understands that the "novel" outlines Cordelia's murder of her husband and subsequent disposal of his body. When the sisters are away the publisher begins digging in the rose garden, but he doesn't find the corpse before the sisters return. As Julia now insists on going to the police to tell her story, Cordelia holds her at gunpoint until Williams's character intervenes.

In the prologue and epilogue to this murder-cum-body-disposal story, Jimmie Allardice scripted Hitchcock as a grave digger, just like Williams in the story, which again reinforces the many-sided surrogate bond between the two Englishmen. This family plot, directed by Francis M. Cockrell, leads us to a different type of cemetery milieu, where the Hitchcock world, as molded by his television series, was played out in full in its very last installment.

Leftovers

During the television show's tenure journalists invited to the Hitchcock home encountered exquisite cooking and a house rebuilt for this purpose, from kitchen and walk-in refrigerator to wine cellar. Lest, however, at least minimal catering to the grotesque be forgotten in later years, Alma's refrigerator contained a wax effigy of her husband's head as a memento from the shooting of *Frenzy*. In a memorable photograph by Philippe Halsman, she opens the refrigerator in preparation for a poultry meal without paying any attention to her husband's bust on one of the shelves.[41] The wax replica of Hitchcock's face is here severed from his arse in yet another carnivalizing variation on doubling and multiplicity. This is what he brought home from London as a self-referential prop, not to the hearth but to the freezer's shelf for leftovers.

Another Hitchcock bust was prominently displayed in a fanciful host setting a few years later. When shooting commenced for what turned out to be Hitchcock's final film, *Family Plot* (1976), the cemetery served as a gothic milieu for a press junket, hosted in the un-gothic sunshine on the Universal back lot. A horse-drawn hearse was part of the welcoming setup as the guests arrived; black-veiled waitresses served Bloody Marys before lunch; and an organist played "Funeral March of a Marionette." When strolling around, the guests discovered their names on headstones scattered about the lawn. Hitchcock's own gravestone, according to the *Los Angeles Times* film critic Gregg Kilday, "was decorated with a bust that wore his pendulous visage." When writing up the event afterward Kilday asked himself, "What becomes a legend most?" Discerningly, he concluded, "a simple and unwavering allegiance to the Hitchcock public image" defined by the trappings of his television hosting and the intertwining of the macabre and the humorous, a winning, inherently English combination, though adapted for American audiences.[42] In a parallel account Robert Kervin focused on Hitchcock's arrival on the scene, likening it to the introductory sequence for AHP, and in familiar prose: "The fat man climbed briskly from a black limousine and marched pompously towards Universal's graveyard set. . . . The organist, in mourning and elevated on a platform by the wrought-iron cemetery gate, stopped playing the funeral dirges when the noted director arrived, and segued fast into the Hitchcock signature tune from all those hundreds of TV episodes: 'Goooood eve-en-ing.'"[43]

As Richard Schickel observed on a related tenor a few years earlier, Hitchcock did not promote his films anymore, but rather promoted himself, "or, more properly, the public persona constructed as carefully as any of his movie plots. That persona—the slightly macabre, perversely jolly fat man—emerged as the host of his extremely popular television shows in the nineteen-fifties."[44] In this respect not only the old teleplays but also Hitchcock's television figure were part of the still-running syndication process—the figure here dusted off for a live appearance with the trappings intact.

Clearly Schickel's profiling of the marketing persona harked back even further, to Hitchcock's very first exuberant days in America in 1937. During the television decade, Hitchcock and his team mobilized for spectacular puffery the director's considerable bulk and penchant for macabre comedy, with the grotesque toned down, to keep him discursively au courant. The concept was winning, inescapable, and obviously the stuff legends are made of. In an essay published in 1976 when *Family Plot* opened, James Monaco expressed concerns that the projected persona and brazen body talk might undercut Hitchcock's critical standing: "Hitchcock has not been especially well-served by the public persona he himself has projected over the years. It is, maybe, too easy to take for granted that cynical, portly entertainer with the vaguely lugubrious sense of humor."[45] Here, as Hitchcock's active career drew to a close, the marketing ballyhoo, carnivalizing, and television signifiers surrounding him were still perceived as obstacles blocking critical appreciation.

When straddling two media, and fully coming into his own adjectivally, Hitchcock had a televisual appeal that even overshadowed his cinema for some. This is from 1958, shortly before the release of *Vertigo*: "Too many people think of Hitchcock as only a funny little man introducing his TV shows. What they fail to realize is that he has been responsible for some of the finest suspense movies ever made and is world-famous as a director-producer."[46] Or, in an alternative exchange recorded in *TV Guide*: "Look, Maude, there's Hitchcock of TV! Now what do you suppose he's doing on this *movie* set?"[47] Along these lines, the appendages of the television show more than anything came to define the self-styled realm of the Hitchcockian, as the staging of the lunch on the Universal back lot evidences.

Being a social gathering, the cemetery lunch in 1975 was less connected to the actual host segments than were the promotional events orchestrated for the television show by the sponsor's ad agency, Young & Rubicam, in the late 1950s. At the haunted-house party in New York in 1956, the guests similarly encountered a hearse outside the spooky abode, while the black-clad New York butlers from 1956 were replaced with waitresses in 1975. Invitations to the ghost party were sent out on headstone-shaped cards, and the apartment, found by Young & Rubicam via advertisements in New York dailies, was decked out in full-blown Charles Addams style, with an open coffin at the place of honor (Addams himself was in attendance, sipping Bloody Marys). A similar selection of macabre dishes was on the menus for the *Vertigo* party hosted in a skyscraper under construction in New York City and the back-lot party in 1975, while the party in Beverly Hills for "Arthur" in 1959 was all about chickens and eggs. What was served apart from drinks at the NBC junket for the *Suspicion* series, hosted at Arthur Cameron's mansion, is anyone's guess. The catering, according to Hitchcock's food preferences, came from Dave Chasen's restaurant.

The longevity of the marketing and performance strategy galvanized the brand consistency that Gregg Kilday deemed most suitable for a legend, biographical or otherwise. In many ways the Florida shindig featuring a miniature Hitchcock doll buried on the beach connects the impromptu grave digging in *The Trouble with Harry* and the grave digging in *Family Plot*—during which one of the shots comes complete with a headstone in the background with the name Harry. *Family Plot* also sports a cameo shadow for Hitchcock, in downsized format but otherwise akin to the shadow figure in the introduction to the television show. The film ends with a wink to the audience that serves a similar function to Phyllis Thaxter's closing tongue-in-cheek line giving away the fact she had faked being under hypnosis ("Murder Me Twice," AHP 126). And *Family Plot*'s medium, Blanche, is both sex-starved and hungry. This brings us back to fat theory.

When the American Film Institute honored Hitchcock with a lifetime achievement award in 1979, François Truffaut was among the parade of collaborators and colleagues celebrating him. In his speech Truffaut came up with his own version of the importance of being stout for success: "When I began to direct films, I thought Monsieur Hitchcock was fantastique, maybe because he weighed more than 200 lbs. Therefore I tried to eat more and more. I gained 20 lbs, but it obviously didn't work. I knew I had to find other ways to touch the proportions of his genius, so I asked Monsieur Hitchcock to

c.7. Hitchcock's creative process from folders (film on paper) to film in the cans brackets the significance of the in-between stage, the tedious shooting. Photographs by Philippe Halsman, courtesy of the Kobal Foundation.

give me an interview of 50 hours and to reveal all his secrets. The reason was a book, actually it was like a cookbook, full of recipes for making films."[48] The metaphor is inspired and in step with our collection of recipes for cooking up a media franchise around the contours of the Hitchcock persona and its corporeal figurations. Think of the classic image of Hitchcock standing next to his "films" piled up as a tower of marked folders, or film cans organized as a line of authorship achievement (fig. c.7). This is indeed the work in simulated physical form, with a folder per title underwriting the talking points' unrelenting focus on scripting and storyboarding prior to the tedious and insignificant shooting, after which editing was basically predetermined, if we accept the drift. According to this logic, the films as folders were symbolically in the cans before being physically finished. The desire for order was not only expressed by towers of folders or rows of film cans but also formulated as a filmography in a very Hitchcockian semiotic material, cake. The delicious cake memorial in figure c.8 and its tower of director credits for fifty films coincided with the upsurge in the prominence of Hitchcock's cinema among critics, which was around the time of the interview to which Truffaut refers.[49]

As I have claimed throughout this book, the cultural domain of the Hitch-

TORN CURTAIN
MARNIE
THE BIRDS
PSYCHO
NORTH BY NORTHWEST
VERTIGO
THE WRONG MAN
THE MAN WHO KNEW TOO MUCH
THE TROUBLE WITH HARRY
TO CATCH A THIEF
REAR WINDOW
DIAL M FOR MURDER
I CONFESS
STRANGERS ON A TRAIN
STAGE FRIGHT
UNDER CAPRICORN
ROPE
THE PARADINE CASE
NOTORIOUS
SPELLBOUND
LIFEBOAT
SHADOW OF A DOUBT
SABOTEUR
SUSPICION
MR. AND MRS. SMITH
FOREIGN CORRESPONDENT
REBECCA
THE LADY VANISHES
YOUNG AND INNOCENT
SABOTAGE
THE SECRET AGENT
THE THIRTY-NINE STEPS
THE MAN WHO KNEW TOO MUCH
WALTZES FROM VIENNA
NUMBER SEVENTEEN
RICH AND STRANGE
THE SKIN GAME
MURDER
JUNO AND THE PAYCOCK
BLACKMAIL
THE MANXMAN
CHAMPAGNE
THE FARMER'S WIFE
THE RING
EASY VIRTUE
DOWNHILL
THE LODGER
THE MOUNTAIN EAGLE
THE PLEASURE GARDEN
ALFRED HITCHCOCK

c.8. Uncredited photograph from the Alfred Hitchcock Collection,
courtesy of the Academy for Motion Picture Arts and Sciences.

cock brand is not just a set of films analyzed textually ad nauseam, but a suspense franchise revolving around an eponym and corporeal *doxa*. Alfred Hitchcock's art was predicated on building a factory, just like Andy Warhol's, in spite of Pat Hitchcock's description of the critical work as a mom-and-pop business and the studio work, if one stretches the line of reasoning, as a form of outsourcing.[50] In this sense the name and eponym "Hitchcock," just like "Salvador Dalí" and "Andy Warhol," represents intangibles beyond the oeuvre; it is a convoluted bricolage of art, commerce, marketing, and celebrity indicative of twentieth-century media culture at large. The lunch for *Family Plot* in this respect offered the full panorama and summation of the Hitchcockian, as Gregg Kilday perceptively noted. The critical elements of the Hitchcockian brand or legend were foremost picked up from the decade on television, from the host segments, and not least from the spin-off and tie-in functions orchestrated by Young & Rubicam. The paratexts also informed the film trailers scripted by Allardice and featuring Hitchcock. The luncheon at the back lot and its macabre milieu pointedly and unmistakably references Hitchcock's television series, in addition to resonating with his film *Rope* (1948), which features a meal served on top of a strangled corpse. At the back lot, as a finishing touch, Hitchcock mock-strangled his own bust (fig. C.9).

Between *Rope* and *Family Plot*, Hitchcock had turned into a legend with television at the center of the brand. A writer in *TV Guide* tried to come to terms with Hitchcock's personality as the television show came to a close: "This Hitchcock, in whom the fears almost obliterate the romance, is the mediocre version of the man. This is the stodgy, grisly, shallow show-off who makes himself an object of mockery, and who is not particularly original or interesting outside of his work. This is, unfortunately, the man who is probably best known to the TV audience. It knows Hitchcock as the grisly clown, and relates him to a series of plays which he didn't direct."[51]

The profile echoes Hollis Alpert's dismissive description a few years earlier and foreshadows James Monaco's critical apprehensions a decade later, as well as Thomas Elsaesser's dialectics between the dandy and the *saltimbanque*— and my stance on authorship by commission and surrogacy.[52] The *TV Guide* writer takes one more stab at Hitchcock in a more melancholy tone: "He is a strange, unique man who has tried to be true to the dreams of babyhood, and who has never recovered from his terrors. Whatever his flaws, when he is great, he is very, very great. It is TV's good fortune to have had him, if only as script editor, for 10 years. It is TV's bad fortune never to have had him at his best."[53] If nothing else, the sparkling table scene in "Banquo's Chair" (AHP 146) comes close.

c.9. Strangling a legend. Courtesy of Photofest.

In a speech delivered a few weeks before AHH was "axed," Hitchcock, among his string of jokes, claimed that he had gotten away with murder for ten years on television, but that "they seem to have caught up with [him] at last." Speculating on the possible punishment, which had been deferred when he was arraigned in the host segment for "Number Twenty-Two" (AHP 60) for having trespassed into television, he offered, "I suspect I shall be strapped to a chair and placed in front of an open television set."[54]

As commencement speaker at Santa Clara University after receiving his honorary degree in 1963, Hitchcock used a similar style in line with his paratextual discourse. This came as no surprise, as Allardice had ghost-authored the speech. After spending some time talking about gravestones and their inscriptions, the importance of humor, God, and matters bearing on life and death, and comparing his own degree to the one conferred on Dr. Jekyll (yet another double), Hitchcock expressed his gratitude for and appreciation of the honor. The wording, once again, illustrates the tenet of this study: that Hitchcock, by way of his television hosting, reclaimed the body discourse—set in motion during the 1937 gastronomic holiday in New York—for his own purposes and on his own terms. Still, he was trapped in the trappings of his own television image and persona, and consequently concluded: "So, when you next see my image flickering on your television screen, if I loom a bit larger, it will not mean I have gained weight—blame it instead on the righteous puff of pride."[55]

After setting the table in the introduction, I noted that in Hitchcock television every meal, around the clock, came fraught with deadly risks—or splendid opportunities for solving problems in the manner of Dennis Day's frugal character in "Cheap Is Cheap" (AHP 143). In the Truffaut interview Hitchcock was asked to come up with an idea for a film, as Bob Hull had asked about an outline for a murder scene earlier.[56] Off the cuff, Hitchcock's virtual film pitch charts the lifespan of food from its arrival in the city all the way to the flushing out of alimentary refuse in the ocean: "An anthology of food, showing its arrival in the city, distribution, the selling, buying by people, the cooking, the various ways in which it's consumed. What happens to it in the various hotels; how it's fixed up and absorbed. And, gradually, the end of the film would show the sewers, and the garbage being dumped out into the ocean. So there's a cycle, beginning with the gleaming fresh vegetables and ending with the mess that's poured out into the sewers."[57] This bleak sustenance trajectory caps the buoyant food optimism from the glorious days when Hitchcock played Falstaff in Manhattan by ending on a note of alimentary pessimism and the inescapable decay of everything organic.

For whatever it's worth, Hitchcock was apparently raised on potatoes as a child. The unsentimental manners in which he handles organic matter—whether Harry's dead body, surplus food items, or leftovers—together bespeak an overall preoccupation with bodies and their sustenance, bodies as sustenance, and this is played out in doubling strategies, corporeal insecurities, and pragmatics of murder. Undetectable poisons match undetectable bodies—for example, in the recycling model (foregoing poison for strangulation) perfected by Arthur. The city symphony Hitchcock outlined for Truffaut (the apt term is Richard L. Stromgren's)[58] and its closing zoom in on the leftovers of the agricultural food machine is as unsentimental as Harry's treatment in the afterlife. The leftovers from Hitchcock's television being flushed out in the ocean of syndication offered a frisson of the legendary accoutrements he himself rehashed for his marketing all the way to the back lot at Universal and his last hurrah. Here, finally, with the black-draped dining table and *Rope* in the balance, "an old dream" came true: "staging a gourmet meal in a graveyard" to the tune of the "Funeral March of a Marionette" and strangling his own bust.[59]

APPENDIX

DIRECTOR CREDITS FOR *ALFRED HITCHCOCK PRESENTS* AND *THE ALFRED HITCHCOCK HOUR*

In spite of his eighteen directing credits, Alfred Hitchcock was not the most frequent director of episodes in his own series. He was in fact only number seven on a list of directors according to frequency. Robert Stevens, who directed 49 episodes, tops the list, followed by Paul Henreid, with 29; Herschel Daugherty, 27; Norman Lloyd, 22; Alan Crosland Jr., 19; Alfred Hitchcock, 18; Arthur Hiller, 17; John Brahm, 14; James Neilson, 12; Alf Kjellin, 12; Bernard Girard, 12; Justus Addiss, 10; and Joseph Newman, 10.

Robert Stevens was by far the most trusted director, especially in the show's early years, and tellingly the only one to win an Emmy Award. Stevens had cut his teeth working for the series *Suspense* (59 episodes) and later directed a few episodes of *The Twilight Zone*, *Suspicion*, and *Playhouse 90*, as well as many other shows. Well known as an actor, Paul Henreid had a very short résumé as television director when he joined the Hitchcock team. Subsequently, he became highly versatile and directed quite a few western episodes, in addition to taking on assignments for crime series like *Johnny Staccato* and *Thriller*, as well as for live theater series. Herschel Daugherty enjoyed a long career as series director from the mid-1950s to 1975, spanning the whole gamut of genres. Norman Lloyd played small but significant roles in Hitchcock's *Saboteur* (1942) and also *Spellbound* (1945). He joined the producing team in 1957 and also directed a sizable number of episodes and acted in many. Lloyd and producer Joan Harrison pulled most of the strings for the show. Alan Crosland Jr. was a seasoned director when joining the Hitchcock show in 1960, and his distinguished television career lasted until the 1970s. Arthur Hiller directed for *Thriller* and *Perry Mason* among many other shows before his debut for Hitchcock in 1958. From the mid-1960s he mainly directed movies. John Brahm was a renowned suspense director and worked on many of the most famous shows: *Thriller*, *Johnny Staccato*, *The Twilight Zone*, and *Sus-*

picion, as well as a number of the playhouse shows. His career began on the big screen in the late 1930s and ended in the mid-1960s with the series *The Man from* U.N.C.L.E. James Neilson began directing for *Ford Television Theater* in 1953. In 1954 he directed for *Jean Dean, Registered Nurse*, which was produced by Joan Harrison. After a handful of titles for *Suspicion*, he directed his first AHP episode in 1958. His most frequent assignments were for *Disneyland*. After a distinguished acting career in Sweden, Alf Kjellin directed a handful of movies there in the mid-1950s. His first television job was for Hitchcock, and he continued to direct across genres until the mid-1980s. Bernard Girard directed four episodes for *Alfred Hitchcock Presents* (AHP), more or less in a stretch, and continued his assignment when the show expanded to *The Alfred Hitchcock Hour* (AHH). Girard came with experience from a multitude of other shows, ranging in genre from medical (*Medic*) to western drama (*Zane Grey Theater*). After AHH Girard directed both films and made-for-television movies. Justus Addiss had directed for *Schlitz Playhouse of Stars* and *General Electric Summer Originals* before AHP. Parallel to AHP, Addiss worked for *The Restless Gun*, later directing for *Rawhide* (10 episodes) and *Voyage to the Bottom of the Sea* (16 episodes) before retiring. Joseph Newman came in late and thus directed only for AHH. Newman had directed shorts and features since the late 1930s before crossing over to television and *The Twilight Zone*. He retired shortly after working for AHH. This credit list clearly evidences a burgeoning television industry tapping into a highly integrated pool of director talents.

The producers of the Hitchcock show obviously had a penchant for returning to winning concepts and a dependable stable of experienced directors. This did not, however, preclude testing new talents. Among directors who more or less started out for Hitchcock and later had distinguished careers on the big screen are Robert Altman, Sydney Pollack, and William Friedkin. At the same time, the show included Hollywood veterans such as Robert Florey, whose film career harked back to 1927. On the small screen he was primarily associated with *The Loretta Young Show* and was credited for 36 episodes with Young. Notably, there is only one woman in this group, Ida Lupino, and she directed only two Hitchcock episodes. Lupino started as an actress in the 1930s, began directing in the late 1940s, and then shifted to television after a handful of movies. She worked for a multitude of shows but primarily directed only a couple of episodes per series, except for *Have Gun—Will Travel* (8 episodes) and *Thriller* (9 episodes). Her acting roles for television were as numerous, at least, as her assignments as director. Similarly, the stable of seasoned writers were much in demand for other series. Original writing came late in the series, as the driving idea was to adapt previously published material or radio plays. Of the first season's 39 episodes, only a few were original stories.

The following list charts director credits chronologically across the entire span of the two series, AHP and AHH.

Alfred Hitchcock (18 episodes): AHP 1, 7, 10, 23, 40, 52, 67, 81, 106, 113, 118, 146, 154, 155, 192, 213, 231; AHH 1

Robert Stevens (49): AHP 2, 8, 11, 13, 16, 17, 18, 22, 24, 28, 30, 31, 32, 34, 39, 42, 44, 45, 53, 57, 60, 61, 62, 64–66, 71, 78, 79, 82, 95, 96, 102, 115, 119, 123, 124, 127, 140, 144, 145, 156, 165, 209; AHH 42, 45, 58, 75, 90

Don Medford (2): AHP 3, 5

Robert Stevenson (8): AHP 4, 9, 19, 20, 25, 36, 166; AHH 4

Justus Addiss (10): AHP 6, 14, 21, 55, 70, 73, 74, 76, 90, 91

Don Weis (5): AHP 12, 15, 220, 224, 265

Francis Cockrell (2): AHP 26, 51

James Neilson (12): AHP 27, 29, 35, 48, 72, 80, 84, 92, 97, 98, 104, 114

Herschel Daugherty (27): AHP 33, 38, 41, 43, 50, 56, 58, 63, 75, 94, 100, 117, 131, 135, 137, 150, 157, 161, 167, 169, 179, 198, 206, 244; AHH 24, 33, 38

Jules Bricken (3): AHP 46, 47, 69

Meredyth Lucas (3): AHP 49, 54, 59

Paul Henreid (29): AHP 68, 77, 83, 85, 86, 88, 99, 108, 116, 121, 132, 133, 142, 173, 187, 189, 208, 210, 216, 221, 223, 229, 233, 237, 239, 257, 259, 261; AHH 7

Robert Altman (2): AHP 87, 93

Don Taylor (7): AHP 89, 101, 107, 110, 112, 134, 153

Arthur Hiller (17): AHP 103, 105, 109, 111, 120, 128, 129, 136, 139, 171, 174, 181, 185, 193, 203, 215, 228

Norman Lloyd (22): AHP 122, 125, 130, 148, 149, 158, 159, 163, 172, 176, 191, 194, 195, 199, 214, 236, 238, 246, 248; AHH 6, 50, 68

David Swift (1): AHP 126

Paul Almond (2): AHP 138, 168

Bretaigne Windust (2): AHP 141, 143

John Brahm (14): AHP 147, 152, 160, 177, 180, 182, 183, 196, 211; AHH 2, 27, 52, 78, 82

Leonard J. Horn (3): AHP 151, 254; AHH 14

Stuart Rosenberg (5): AHP 162, 164, 170, 190, 202

Gene Reynolds (1): AHP 175

George Stevens Jr. (2): AHP 178, 217

Alan Crosland Jr. (19): AHP 184, 200, 204, 212, 218, 219, 222, 225, 230, 234, 235, 240, 245, 247, 253, 266; AHH 3, 8, 28

Hilton A. Green (1): AHP 186

Richard Dunlap (1): AHP 188

Ida Lupino (2): AHP 201, 207

Robert Florey (5): AHP 205, 241, 262, 264, 267

Alf Kjellin (12): AHP 226; AHH 5, 15, 18, 43, 46, 47, 48, 59, 64, 77, 87

Gordon Hessler (1): AHP 227

Boris Sagal (3): AHP 232, 249, 251

John Newland (4): AHP 242, 243, 250, 263

Bernard Girard (12): AHP 252, 255, 256, 258; AHH 1, 11, 12, 26, 31, 37, 41, 67

Richard Whorf (1): AHP 260

Josef Lejtes (1): AHP 268

Sydney Pollack (2): AHH 9, 22

Jerry Hopper (1): AHH 10

Joseph Pevney (5): AHH 13, 34, 39, 74, 80

Jack Smight (4): AHH 16, 20, 23, 29

Charles Haas (1): AHH 17

David Lowell Rich (2): AHH 19, 56

James Sheldon (1): AHH 21

Robert Douglas (4): AHH 25, 36, 55, 60

Joseph Newman (10): AHH 30, 32, 40, 44, 54, 57, 69, 72, 81, 91

Harvey Hart (5): AHH 35, 70, 73, 84, 88

Arnold Laven (2): AHH 37, 65

Laslo Benedek (2): AHH 49, 79

William Witney (1): AHH 51

Leo Penn (1): AHH 53
Harry Morgan (2): AHH 61, 89
Philip Leacock (1): AHH 62
Lewis Teague (1): AHH 63
David Friedkin (4): AHH 66, 71, 76, 86
James H. Brown (1): AHH 83
Alex March (1): AHH 85
Herbert Coleman (1): AHH 92
William Friedkin (1): AHH 93

NOTES

Introduction

1. Theodore Strauss, "The Fact Is Quicker Than the Lie," *New York Times*, 12 April 1942, X3.

2. Charles Mercer, "Credible—Incredible," *Baltimore Sun*, 7 October 1956, A21.

3. John D. Weaver, "The Man behind the Body," *Holiday* 36, no. 3 (September 1964): 86.

4. For an unrivaled analysis of television's domestic viewing fabric in the postwar period, see Lynn Spigel, *Make Room for TV: Television and the Family Ideal in Postwar America* (Chicago: University of Chicago Press, 1992). See also the excellent analysis of a somewhat later mediascape in David Morley, *Home Territories: Media, Mobility and Identity* (London: Routledge, 2000).

5. Leonard Lyons reported one of Hitchcock's earliest comments along this line, in an exchange with George Raft. Leonard Lyons, "The New Yorker," *Washington Post*, 26 July 1940, 7.

6. John Belton, "Hitchcock and the Classical Paradigm," in David Boyd and R. Barton Palmer, eds., *After Hitchcock: Influence, Imitation, and Intertextuality* (Austin: University of Texas Press, 2006), 237.

7. For an excellent account of Winchell's career, see Neal Gabler, *Winchell: Gossip, Power and the Culture of Celebrity* (New York: Knopf, 1994). See also Jeffrey Lyons, *Stories My Father Told Me: Notes from the "Lyons Den"* (New York: Abbeville, 2011); Jennifer Frost, *Hedda Hopper's Hollywood* (New York: New York University Press, 2011); Samantha Barbas, *The First Lady of Hollywood: A Biography of Louella Parsons* (Berkeley: University of California Press, 2006). Concerning the journalistic agenda for *Time* and *Life*, see Alan Brinkley, *The Publisher: Henry Luce and His American Century* (New York: Knopf, 2010).

8. Weaver, "The Man behind the Body," 86.

9. Memo dictated by Selznick to Mr. Rawson, 26 October 1943, Legal Series, box 901, folder 7, "Consolidated Files 1936–1954 Hitchcock, Alfred," David O. Selznick Collection, Harry Ransom Center, University of Texas at Austin.

10. Walter Winchell, "Ingrid Bergman's Romance with Italian Is Favorite Hollywood-Broadway Topic," syndicated in, for example, *St. Petersburg Times*, 30 April 1949, 12. The

term was soon established enough to be used in a non-Hitchcock context. See, for example, Basil Davenport's review of Michael Innes's novel *The Paper Thunderbolt*, which claims, "Friend may turn into foe with a Hitchcockian suddenness." Basil Davenport, "Grade-A Gooseflesh," *New York Times*, 11 November 1951, BR14. When the *Saturday Evening Post* advertised an upcoming issue featuring Pete Martin's interview with Hitchcock, readers were told, "His name is a byword for ghouls, gags and the gruesome!" "Behind the Screams with Alfred Hitchcock," *Washington Post and Times Herald*, 23 July 1957, A4. An upcoming piece in *Look* mentioned by Winchell was authored by none other than Winchell himself and titled "How These Celebrities Stay Thin" (19 July 1949, 46–49). Here Hitchcock explained his formula for dropping one hundred pounds: "Give up all forms of gastronomic pleasure, especially alcohol. I followed a high-protein diet and cut down my intake"; to reduce "requires a masochistic period of self-denial" (47).

11. Paula Marantz Cohen, *Alfred Hitchcock: The Legacy of Victorianism* (Lexington: University Press of Kentucky, 1995), 165.

12. Throughout the text I will refer to the combined stretch of the two series AHP and AHH as one show, or as Hitchcock's television franchise.

13. For a definitive analysis of paratexts, see Gérard Genette, *Paratexts: Thresholds of Interpretation*, translated by Jane E. Lewin (New York: Cambridge University Press, 1997).

14. Gjon Mili, *Photographs and Recollections* (Boston: New York Graphic Society, 1980); the stroboscope images of Hitchcock are on pp. 68–69.

15. Aside from the doubling, the condensed outline does not have much in common with the novel by Anthony Armstrong, *The Strange Case of Mr. Pelham* (1957), on which it was based. One of the preeminent dandy figures in British literature was named Pelham: the eponymous character in an Edward Bulwer-Lytton novel of 1828. Bulwer-Lytton's *Pelham* is fueled by a liberal agenda rather than putting forth the elegance of the dandaical body, the latter notion severely satirized by Thomas Carlyle in his *Sartor Resartus* (1833–1834).

16. In this scripting and its future paratextual derivations, Jimmie Allardice foreshadows, by many decades, Johan Grimonprez's scouting for Hitchcock look-alikes. See Johan Grimonprez, *Looking for Alfred* (Ostfildern, Germany: Hatje Cantz, 2007). In an independent art project, Grimonprez conducted casting sessions in several gallery and museum venues as a preamble to his book and other forms of documentation.

17. Thomas M. Leitch, "The Outer Circle: Hitchcock on Television," in Richard Allen and S. Ishii-Gonzales, eds., *Alfred Hitchcock: Centenary Essays* (London: BFI, 1999), 59–71.

18. Leitch, "The Outer Circle," 64.

19. For the best account of the Hitchcock reception over the years, see Robert E. Kapsis, *Hitchcock: The Making of a Reputation* (Chicago: University of Chicago Press, 1992). For studies of Hitchcock television, see Steve Mamber, "The Television Films of Alfred Hitchcock," *Cinema* 7, no. 1 (fall 1971): 2–7; Gene D. Phillips, "Hitchcock's Forgotten Films, the Twenty Teleplays," *Journal of Popular Film and Television* 10, no. 2 (summer 1982): 73–76; John McCarty and Brian Kelleher, *Alfred Hitchcock Presents* (New York: St. Martin's, 1985); J. Lary Kuhns, "Alfred Hitchcock Presents," in Ken Mogg, ed., *The Alfred Hitchcock Story* (London: Titan Books, 1999), 130–135; Andrew A. Erish, "Reclaiming *Alfred Hitchcock Presents*," *Quarterly Review of Film and Video* 26, no. 5 (October 2009): 385–392.

20. This episode ingeniously transferred Jack Benny's legendary persona from his television show, on which Dennis Day was a fixture, to a character portrait à la Benny, played by Day.

1. Feeding the Legend

1. "Alfred Hitchcock Here," *New York Journal American*, 23 August 1937, 4.

2. The last one, "How Movie Epics Are Born," was published on 31 July 1937, 9. The series began on July 26 and ran daily.

3. "Old Ruts Are New Ruts [1938]," reprinted in Sidney Gottlieb, ed., *Hitchcock on Hitchcock: Selected Writings and Interviews* (Berkeley: University of California Press, 1995), 202. On a similar note, a news snippet from London reported that Hitchcock was "rather disconcerted that the American press boosted him as an expert on food instead of British ace director." "London Talk," *Hollywood Reporter*, 2 October 1937, 6.

4. H. Allen Smith, "Hitchcock Likes to Smash Cups," *New York World-Telegram*, 28 August 1937, 7. According to Smith, Hitchcock refused to be interviewed unless he was "having a go at excellent foodstuffs."

5. Janet White, "Picture Parade," *Brooklyn Daily Eagle*, 30 August 1937, 9. In 1957 Hitchcock claimed, in almost identical terms: "My present interest in my body is almost altogether from the waist up." Pete Martin, "I Call on Alfred Hitchcock," *Saturday Evening Post*, 27 July 1957, 37.

6. Donald Spoto, *The Dark Side of Genius: The Life of Alfred Hitchcock* (New York: Ballantine Books, 1984), 170.

7. Spoto, *The Dark Side of Genius*, 155.

8. "Hitchcock 'Cuts' Tea for T-Bone," *New York Morning Telegraph*, 26 August 1937, 2; "Arrived," *Newsweek*, 6 September 1937, 25. Hitchcock offered an international ranking of eateries for an *American Journal* reporter (who mistakenly named the director Albert in the write-up). The top places, according to Hitchcock, were "The Walterspiel, in Munich; the Café de Paris, in Paris; the Horscher, in Berlin; the Caramello, at Cap-Ferrat, on the Riviera; the San Pietro, in Genoa—'And in New York,' he said, lapping up the pressed duck at the St. Regis, 'I nominate the Colony, 21, and Robert's. And of course this hotel.'" "Hitchcock, Film Director, Will Keep His 260 Pounds Busy Wielding Fork," *New York Journal American*, 27 August 1937, 3.

9. Archer Winsten, "Movie Talk," *New York Post*, 27 August 1937, 19.

10. Irving Hoffman, "Tales of Hoffman," *Hollywood Reporter*, 30 August 1937, 3. Hitchcock was at the time working for Gaumont-British.

11. George Ross, "So This Is Broadway," *New York World-Telegram*, 8 June 1938, 23. A few days later, Hitchcock dined again at the same restaurant with yet another journalist; see Eileen Creelman, "Picture Plays and Players," *Sun* (New York), 15 June 1938, 26.

12. William Boehnel, "Film Characters Weak, Hitchcock Declares," *New York World-Telegram*, 10 June 1938, 17. Boehnel's later writing vividly illustrates the cementing of Hitchcockian body quips after his culinary holiday. When reviewing *The Girl Was Young* (originally titled *Young and Innocent*, Gaumont-British Picture Corporation, 1937), Boehnel described Hitchcock as "rotund and gifted" ("'The Girl Was Young' a Sparkling Thriller," 11 February 1938, 29), and *The Lady Vanishes* is introduced as "portly Alfred Hitchcock's latest shocker" ("Excellent Spy Stuff at Globe," 24 December 1938, 8). When *Life* selected *Foreign Correspondent* (Walter Wanger Productions, 1940) as "Movie of the Week," the capsule introduction read, "Corpulent Mr. Hitchcock dreamed up a string of sinister but unrelated scenes" (26 August 1940, 42). B. R. Crisler, writing on *Rebecca* (Selznick International Pictures, 1940), settled for a more poetic designation, describing the director as

"that plump Poe of the cinema" ("Mr. Selznick Does an Encore," *New York Times*, 31 March 1940, 127). "Plump" was a favorite of Sheilah Graham's for Hitchcock in the *Atlanta Constitution* ("Errol Flynn's Leading Ladies for 'Don Juan' Will Number Ten," 1 April 1939; "Star Refuses All Dates Unless with a Producer," 20 October 1939; "Raft-Robinson Feud Turns Out to Be Fake," 14 May 1941).

13. Ezra Goodman, "Strange Case of a British Director Who Has Made an Art of Producing 'Penny Shockers,'" *Cinema Progress* 3, no. 2 (May–June 1938): 9. Regina Crewe had already summed up the strategy in 1937: "He'd rather talk of food—and eat it—than discuss methods or theory of film production." "New York Seen through British Eyes," *New York Journal American*, 11 September 1937, MS2. Consequently, when Hitchcock passed through New York City in 1939 en route to start working for Selznick, he was again first and foremost identified as the "rotund gourmet" and only second as "outstanding director," preceded with a qualifying "also." "News of the Studios," *Sun* (New York), 6 March 1939, 12.

14. Russell Maloney, "Profiles: 'What Happens after That,'" *New Yorker* 14, no. 30 (10 September 1938): 26.

15. Selznick memo, 23 August 1937, reprinted in Rudy Behlmer, ed., *Memo from David O. Selznick: The Creation of* Gone with the Wind *and Other Motion Picture Classics, as Revealed in the Producer's Private Letters, Telegrams, Memorandums, and Autobiographical Remarks* (New York: Modern Library, 2000), 269.

16. Undated interoffice memo to Dan Winkler at the Myron Selznick agency, folder 1, dated "to 4/30/39," "Hitchcock, Alfred" file, Myron Selznick Papers, Harry Ransom Center, University of Texas at Austin.

17. Both memos in Correspondence Series, folder 3, box 901, David O. Selznick Collection, Harry Ransom Center, University of Texas at Austin.

18. Interoffice memo dated 19 May 1938 relayed as telegram to Hitchcock from Dan Winkler at the Myron Selznick agency, folder 1, dated "to 4/30/39," "Hitchcock, Alfred" file, Myron Selznick Papers, Harry Ransom Center, University of Texas at Austin.

19. For a meticulous account of the overture phase prior to Hitchcock's relocation, see Leonard Leff, *Hitchcock and Selznick: The Rich and Strange Collaboration of Alfred Hitchcock and David O. Selznick in Hollywood* (New York: Weidenfeld and Nicolson, 1987). Thomas Schatz offers additional details in chapter 15 of his *The Genius of the System: Hollywood Filmmaking in the Studio Era* (New York: Pantheon Books, 1988).

20. Molly Castle, "I'll Make My Own Mustard Even in Hollywood," *Daily Mirror*, 10 August 1938, 17.

21. Quoted in Castle, "I'll Make My Own Mustard Even in Hollywood," 17.

22. See, for example, Simon Callow, *Charles Laughton: A Difficult Actor* (New York: Random House, 2012 [1997]), 132.

23. Peter Conrad, *The Hitchcock Murders* (London: Faber and Faber, 2000), 87.

24. White, "Picture Parade," 30 August 1937, 9.

25. Patrick McGilligan, *Alfred Hitchcock: A Life in Darkness and Light* (New York: Regan Books, 2003), 204.

26. Haphazard browsing offers ample examples of the body discourse in the London press. On dieting, Hitchcock suggested the following in 1931: "If a fat man were brought before the magistrate for dangerous driving he would be sentenced to, say, a week's dieting. In which case, I, for one, would always drive very slowly" ("Today's Gossip," *Daily*

Mirror, 4 June 1931, 11). Paul Holt found Hitchcock still "fat, genial, unruffled" three years later ("Recovery after a Hitch," Daily Express, 2 March 1934, 10). The Daily Mirror provided precise figures in 1936: "Five feet and a bit of genial shrewdness. Twenty stone of ambling good humour . . . stout genius of thirty-six" ("Hitchcock, 36. The Man Who Cannot Know Too Much," Daily Mirror, 11 June 1936, 14). Inviting critics home was part of the game, and here one finds a rare, conscious effort at exercising. The Daily Mirror's R. J. Whitley was one of the guests: "I found Hitch, as he is known to everybody in the cinema world, in his comfortable flat on the top floor of a six-story building a mile west of the Albert Hall. The portly Hitch, who admits that his chassis 'was built for comfort and not for speed,' chose this building because it had no lift and he thinks that a run up and down stairs is good for his Falstaffian figure" ("How I Began: Hitchcock's Career," Daily Mirror, 14 June 1935, 27).

27. C. A. L. (C. A. Lejeune), "A Genius of the Films: Alfred Hitchcock and His Work," Observer, 17 November 1935, 13.

28. Paul Speegle, "Hitchcock Up to His Second Chin in Art," San Francisco Chronicle, 27 August 1939, 18.

29. For earlier accounts along similar lines as Speegle's, see "City Center Built for Movie," New York Evening Journal, 23 January 1937, 112; and "This Englishman—a 'Hitch' to It," New York American, 21 February 1937, E7.

30. "Hedda Hopper's Hollywood," Los Angeles Times, 2 September, 15 October, 4 December 1940; 29 January, 20 May 1942; 13 April 1943.

31. "Hedda Hopper's Hollywood," Los Angeles Times, 26 April 1941, 9.

32. "Hedda Hopper's Hollywood," Los Angeles Times, 31 January 1942, 8.

33. Peter N. Stearns, Fat History: Bodies and Beauty in the Modern West (New York: New York University Press, 1997). For a slimmer version of the argument, see Stearns's "Fat in America," in Christopher E. Forth and Ana Carden-Coyne, eds., Cultures of the Abdomen: Diet, Digestion, and Fat in the Modern World (New York: Palgrave Macmillan, 2005), 239–257. For a comprehensive analysis of the cultural history of food during World War II—from starvation to abundance—after Hitchcock's relocation from European austerity to the land of plenty, especially in regard to beef, see Lizzie Collingham, The Taste of War: World War Two and the Battle for Food (London: Allen Lane, 2011).

34. William Banting, Letter on Corpulence, Addressed to the Public (London: Harrison and Sons, 1863), 13.

35. For a well-researched analysis of the discourse around fat actors in Hollywood, see Jerry Dean Mosher, "Weighty Ambitions: Fat Actors and Figurations in American Cinema, 1910–60" (PhD diss., University of California, Los Angeles, 2007).

36. Paul Holt, "Bricks or Bouquets—Let Me Have Them," Daily Express, 21 September 1935, 19.

37. Alva Johnston, "300-Pound Prophet Comes to Hollywood," Saturday Evening Post, 22 May 1943, 12. Maloney refers to the "steak-and-ice-cream" regime as a canard, which H. Allen Smith's eyewitness report from the 21 Club does not support. Maloney, "Profiles: 'What Happens after That,'" 26; Smith, "Hitchcock Likes to Smash Cups," 7. According to Maloney, Hitchcock was on a diet at the time and had lost 25 pounds of 290.

38. Philip K. Scheuer, "Town Called Hollywood: Director Pleads Off Poundage," Los Angeles Times, 30 May 1943, C3.

39. Alfred Hitchcock, "The Role I Liked Best . . . ," Saturday Evening Post, 2 December 1950, 138. According to a Newsweek interview from 1956, Hitch was, again, "down nearly

100 pounds from his top weight of 300—thanks to a diet of steak and no hard liquor." "Alfred Hitchcock—Director, TV or Movies, Suspense Is Golden," *Newsweek*, 11 June 1956, 105.

40. Frank S. Nugent, "Assignment in Hollywood," *Good Housekeeping* 121, no. 11 (November 1945): 290.

41. Martin, "I Call on Alfred Hitchcock," 37.

42. Peter Flint, "Alfred Hitchcock Dies; a Master of Suspense," *New York Times*, 30 April 1980, D23.

43. Leonard Lyons, "No Steak and Ice Cream," *New York Post*, 23 August 1943, 20. On numerous occasions Hitchcock wrote as a columnist, filling in for journalists on vacation. He stepped in for Dorothy Kilgallen at the *New York Journal American* at least twice ("The Hard Way," 1 September 1948, 5, mainly discussing the production of *Rope*; and "50 Murders for Sake of Art," 7 August 1953, 5, on murder as a fine art). He was substituting for Rick Du Brow when he wrote "Sixty Minutes Next Season" (*New York Morning Telegraph*, 21 August 1962), at the time his show expanded from thirty to sixty minutes, from AHP to AHH.

44. This claim is consistent with a Hitchcock aside in an interview with Hedda Hopper: "I learned this entire business from Americans, not from the British." Hedda Hopper, "Papa Hitchcock," *Chicago Tribune*, 29 April 1962, C16.

45. Paramount studio biography on Hitchcock, April 1955, Hitchcock Clippings, 1950s folder, Performing Arts Library, New York City; also in the Alfred Hitchcock Papers, Margaret Herrick Library, Academy of Motion Picture Arts and Sciences (AMPAS), Beverly Hills.

46. Don King, "Alfred Hitchcock Biography," 4, Clipping Files for Alfred Hitchcock, Museum of Modern Art, New York, NY.

47. "Alfred Hitchcock . . . Host, Executive Producer, 'The Alfred Hitchcock Hour,'" press release from CBS TV dated 31 August 1962, Hal Humphrey Collection, University of Southern California, Los Angeles.

48. "Cinema," *News Review*, 12 January 1939, 30. Hitchcock wrote "fishmonger" as his father's profession on his marriage license.

49. Victor Davis, "Now Hitchcock Goes Too Far . . . ," *Daily Express*, 6 May 1972, 12.

50. Dismissed by many critics in the first round, *Vertigo* is currently ranked as the best film of all time in the influential poll conducted by *Sight and Sound*. The poll has taken place once a decade since 1952. *Citizen Kane* topped the list from the start until 2012. *Vertigo* entered the top ten as number seven in 1982.

51. The later aspect is critical for Cohen's reading of Hitchcock's cinema. Paula Marantz Cohen, *Alfred Hitchcock: The Legacy of Victorianism* (Lexington: University Press of Kentucky, 1995).

52. The interview, with Gunnar Oldin, is available at http://www.svtplay.se/klipp /151469/haxmastaren.

53. Robert E. Kapsis, *Hitchcock: The Making of a Reputation* (Chicago: University of Chicago Press, 1992).

54. A full retrospective of Hitchcock's cinema at the Museum of Modern Art, New York, in 1963, curated by Richard Griffith, was important for a reevaluation of Hitchcock's significance. The series ended with four Hitchcock-directed teleplays: "Revenge" (AHP 1), "One More Mile to Go" (AHP 67), "Lamb to the Slaughter" (AHP 106), and "Bang! You're Dead" (AHP 231).

55. Hollis Alpert, "Hitchcock as Humorist," in *The Dreams and the Dreamers* (New York: Macmillan, 1962), 174, 168.

56. Alpert, "Hitchcock as Humorist," 168–169, 177.

57. Alpert, "Hitchcock as Humorist," 168–169, 170–172.

58. Susan Smith, *Hitchcock: Suspense, Humour and Tone* (London: BFI, 2000).

59. Dana Polan, "The Light Side of Genius," in Andrew S. Horton, ed., *Comedy/Cinema/Theory* (Berkeley: University of California Press, 1991), 134.

60. Richard H. Millington, "Hitchcock and American Character," in Jonathan Freedman and Richard Millington, eds., *Hitchcock's America* (New York: Oxford University Press, 1999), 145.

61. Millington, "Hitchcock and American Character," 145.

62. Lesley Brill, *The Hitchcock Romance: Love and Irony in Hitchcock's Films* (Princeton, NJ: Princeton University Press, 1988).

63. Richard Allen, "Hitchcock, or the Pleasures of Metaskepticism," *October*, no. 89 (summer 1999): 73. Allen has developed the argument in fuller form in his *Hitchcock's Romantic Irony* (New York: Columbia University Press, 2007).

64. William Rothman, *Hitchcock: The Murderous Gaze* (Cambridge, MA: Harvard University Press, 1982), 234–235.

65. *Dick Cavett Show* (ABC), 8 June 1972.

66. Robert C. Cumbow, "Of Staircases and Potato Trucks: Fear and Fatness and Alfred Hitchcock," *Movietone News*, no. 25 (September 1973): 10.

67. In his review of *Family Plot* (Universal Pictures, 1976), Andrew Sarris elaborates on the staircase motif without connecting it to obesity and food; *Village Voice*, 19 April 1976, 121–122. Richard Fisher takes cues from both Cumbow and Sarris for his discussion of staircases in Hitchcock's cinema; Richard Fisher, "Hitchcock's Figure on the Staircase," *Thousand Eyes* 1, no. 12 (July–August 1976): 3–4.

68. Cumbow, "Of Staircases and Potato Trucks," 12. In Michael Walker's *Hitchcock's Motifs* (Amsterdam: Amsterdam University Press, 2005), one section is devoted to food, and a subsection discusses Hitchcock's famous aversion to eggs. For an excellent analysis of the role of food in Hitchcock's cinema, see Dick Stromgren, "Now to the Banquet We Press: Hitchcock's Gourmet and Gourmand Offerings," in Paul Loukides and Linda K. Fuller, eds., *Beyond the Stars: Studies in American Popular Film*, vol. 3: *The Material World in American Popular Film* (Bowling Green, OH: Bowling Green University Popular Press, 1993), 38–50. Stromgren stresses the preponderance of avian fare in Hitchcock's many dining scenes and also remarks on the rough treatment of eggs and the unsavory aspects of food in the oeuvre.

69. Hwa Yol Jung, "Writing the Body as Social Discourse: Prolegomena to Carnal Hermeneutics," in Stephen Barker, ed., *Signs of Change: Premodern, Modern, Postmodern* (Albany: State University of New York Press, 1996), 262.

70. For a discussion of the grotesque in relation to Hitchcock's cinema, see David Sterritt, "The Diabolic Imagination: Hitchcock, Bakhtin, and the Carnivalization of Cinema," *Hitchcock Annual* 1 (1992): 39–67; as well as his *The Films of Alfred Hitchcock* (New York: Cambridge University Press, 1993). See also Mark M. Hennelly Jr., "Alfred Hitchcock's Carnival," *Hitchcock Annual* 13 (2004–2005): 154–188.

71. Jung, "Writing the Body as Social Discourse," 262.

72. Susan Stewart, *On Longing: Narratives of the Miniature, the Gigantic, the Souvenir, the Collection* (Durham, NC: Duke University Press, 1993), 71.

73. Oriana Fallaci, "Alfred Hitchcock: Mr. Chastity [1963]," in Sidney Gottlieb, ed., *Alfred Hitchcock Interviews* (Jackson: University Press of Mississippi, 2003), 60.

74. Mikhail Bakhtin, *Rabelais and His World*, translated by Hélène Iswolsky (Bloomington: Indiana University Press, 1984). The book's chapter 6 is devoted to a discussion of the concept "the bodily lower stratum," 368–436.

75. Bakhtin, *Rabelais and His World*, 309–319.

76. "No Problem for Mr. Hitchcock," *TV Guide* 5, no. 48 (30 November 1957): 18.

77. Bakhtin, *Rabelais and His World*, 315.

78. Gwen Hyman, *Making a Man: Gentlemanly Appetites in the Nineteenth-Century British Novel* (Athens: Ohio University Press, 2009).

79. The Hitchcock discourse is brimming with accounts of some of his more famous jokes, and they were sufficiently well known to be included in H. Allen Smith's encyclopedic *The Compleat Practical Joker* (Garden City, NY: Doubleday, 1953), 212–214. The first lengthy magazine article on Hitchcock in Hollywood came with an account of some of his successful practical jokes; Geoffrey T. Hellman, "Alfred Hitchcock: England's Best and Biggest Director Goes to Hollywood," *Life*, 20 November 1939, 33–43; photographs by Peter Stackpole.

80. John Russell Taylor, *Hitch: Life and Work of Alfred Hitchcock* (Boston: Faber and Faber, 1978), 184. This account of the episode was taken from Truffaut's interview with Hitchcock; François Truffaut, *Hitchcock*, rev. ed. (New York: Simon and Schuster, 1984), 262.

81. Walter Ames, "Hitchcock Tosses Luncheon Party—in Beverly Hills Jail," *Los Angeles Times*, 26 September 1956, C8. The event was orchestrated shortly before the second season of AHP began.

82. The fullest account of the party was given by H. Viggo Andersen in "Arsenic and Old Skeletons: Spooky Hitchcock Party Gives Vertigo to Many," *Hartford Courant*, 1 June 1958, A35.

83. For eating food from Ernie's during the shooting of *Vertigo*, described as "Kim Novak, Jimmy Stewart and some 100 extras stuffing themselves on the house," see Neil Rau, "With Hitchcock, Eatin's Real Eatin'," *Los Angeles Examiner*, 22 December 1957, IIII, 10. For an account of the *Vertigo* premiere in San Francisco and the location tour the following day, see Philip K. Scheuer, "Musicians to Honor Selves," *Los Angeles Times*, 13 May 1958, 21. For even more details, see Dan Auiler, *Vertigo: The Making of a Hitchcock Classic* (New York: St. Martin's Griffin, 2000), chapter 5.

84. Spoto, *The Dark Side of Genius*, 145.

85. McGilligan, *Alfred Hitchcock*, 372.

86. Mary Morris, "Shadow of a Doubter," *PM's Sunday Picture News*, 27 October 1946, MS13–15; photograph also on p. 1.

87. "Alfred Hitchcock England's Best Director Starts Work in Hollywood," *Life*, 19 June 1939, 66–70.

88. Hellman, "Alfred Hitchcock."

89. "Tattletale," *Los Angeles Times*, 17 September 1939, D9; Walter Winchell, "On Broadway," *St. Petersburg Times*, 2 May 1940, 13.

90. "Hitchcock Brews Thrillers Here," *House and Garden* 82, no. 2 (August 1942): 34–35; photographs by Eaton-Pix.

91. A collection of Ripley's mysteries was published in 1949 as *Minute Mysteries*, and the first collection was published as *How Good a Detective Are You?* (New York: Blue Ribbon, 1934). Ripley's work expanded to radio, and in 1949 there was even a short-lived television series featuring Santos Ortega as Ripley's hero, Hannibal Cobb.

92. "Ingrid Bergman—as played by Alfred Hitchcock," *Pageant* 2, no. 2 (March 1946): 38–41; photographs by Philippe Halsman.

93. "Movie of the Week: Rope," *Life*, 26 July 1948, 57–58, 60; photographs by Bob Landry.

94. "Dial Ham for Murder," *Life*, 24 May 1954, 126, 129; photographs by Sanford Roth.

95. "Photocrime," *Look*, 20 September 1955, 104–105, 114; photographs by Robert Vose. Vose also took the photographs for the essay "Hitchcock's World," *Look*, 26 November 1957, 51–54.

96. "Alfred Hitchcock Presents: The Great Hitchcock Murder Mystery," *Los Angeles Times* (*This Week Magazine*), 4 August 1957, L8, 11; photographs by Maxwell Coplan.

97. Hedda Hopper, "Films Projected for Noted Stars," *Los Angeles Times*, 6 November 1957, B8; Bill Fiset, "Hitchcock Hosts 'Mystery' Party," *Oakland Tribune*, 4 November 1957, E21; Army Archerd, "Just for Variety," *Variety* (daily), 4 November 1957, 2.

98. Victor Canning, "The Mystery of Kela Ouai," in Stewart Beach, ed., *This Week's Stories of Mystery and Suspense* (New York: Random House, 1948), 68–73.

99. Stanley Handman, "Alfred Hitchcock Murders a Blonde," *Ottawa Citizen* (*Weekend Magazine*), 30 May 1958, 6–7, 33, 44.

100. "Hollywood Is . . . ," *Harper's Bazaar* 96, no. 3014 (January 1963): 82–97; the photograph of Hitchcock is on p. 86. Another photograph from this session was published in Sieff's book *40 Years of Photography* (Cologne: Taschen, 2005), 82. This latter photograph is from the motel. Hitchcock, inside a room, is staring at Ina, who is standing outside. As a playful reference to work in progress, a model of a bird is placed in the image's corner foreground right.

101. See Janet Maslin, "Alfred Hitchcock," *Boston after Dark* 3, no. 24 (12–20 June 1972): 12. Reprinted in Sidney Gottlieb, ed., *Alfred Hitchcock Interviews* (Jackson: University Press of Mississippi, 2003), 107.

102. Memo dictated by Selznick to Mr. Rawson, 26 October 1943, Legal Series, box 901, folder 7, "Consolidated Files 1936–1954 Hitchcock, Alfred," David O. Selznick Collection, Harry Ransom Center, University of Texas at Austin.

103. Selma Robinson, "Alfred Hitchcock in the Hundred-Pound Mystery," *McCall's* 85, no. 7 (April 1958): 58, 150, 152–153.

104. At the *Vertigo* party in New York Paramount treated the guests to a "7 Corpse Dinner," starting with "Horror D'Oeuvres" and "Strangled Eggs." Among the entrées were "Scare Ribs" and "Ghoulash"; "Killiflowers" were one of the vegetables, and for dessert, "Ice Scream" was available. Everyone was wished a "Lethal Evening" on the menu card. For an account, see Doc Quigg, "Hitchcock Said Tops as Host," *Times-News* (Hendersonville, NC), 28 May 1958, 11.

105. Lydia Lane, "It's Time Now to Start Taking Off That Turkey and Eggnog Waistline," *Los Angeles Times*, 18 January 1955, B2.

106. Louella O. Parsons, "Kitchen No Mystery to the Master of Mystery," *Los Angeles Examiner*, 24 June 1956, Magazine Section, n.p. For yet another discussion of weight loss and diets, see Paul Foster, "Alfred Hitchcock—an Expert in Tension," *Sketch*, 2 November 1955, 451. Hitchcock, without Alma present, demonstrated how to cook beef and kidney pie in the Mary Meade Kitchen in Chicago in 1960. In one of the photos of this, Hitchcock stands in profile next to his shadow on the wall holding a frying pan. "Hitchcock Presents: Beef and Kidney Pie," *Chicago Tribune*, 24 June 1960, B6.

107. Wade H. Mosby, "Dinner with Alfred Hitchcock," *Milwaukee Journal*, 15 September

1962, 1, 3. Mosby had had one of his crime stories published in *Alfred Hitchcock's Mystery Magazine*, "Let Me Read Your Tea-Leaves," 7, no. 4 (April 1962): 56–61.

108. Quoted in Bill Davidson, "Alfred Hitchcock Resents," *Saturday Evening Post*, 15 December 1962, 62–64.

109. "The Alfred Hitchcock Dinner Hour," *Look*, 27 August 1963, 42–44; produced by Marilyn Kaytor, photographed by Cal Bernstein.

110. "The Alfred Hitchcock Dinner Hour."

111. "The Alfred Hitchcock Dinner Hour."

112. Alfred Hitchcock, "Alfred Hitchcock Cooks His Own Goose," *Harper's Bazaar* 109, no. 3169 (December 1975): 132–133.

113. Sylvie Drake, "If It's Thursday, It Must Be Hitchcock," *Holiday* 57, no. 4 (summer 1976): 32–33, 50, plus cover photo.

114. For an appraisal of Alma Hitchcock's creative role for the franchise, see Charles Champlin, "Alma Reville Hitchcock—the Unsung Partner: Alma Hitchcock," *Los Angeles Times*, 29 July 1982, 11.

Interlude I

1. In addition to having a prominent acting career, Morley was a playwright, and some of his dramas were turned into movies; he also published in many other genres. A formidable raconteur, Morley, like Hitchcock, spoke and wrote on food topics and his travel experiences. His daughter-in-law penned a biography of Morley titled *Larger Than Life*. Terence Pettigrew described him in a style that mirrors many of the stabs at Hitchcock's bulk: "Morley, who has more wobbly chins than a Shanghai drinking club, enjoys poking fun at life's absurdities, among whom [sic] he generously includes himself." Terence Pettigrew, *British Film Character Actors* (Newton Abbot, UK: David and Charles, 1982), 145.

2. According to Larry Wolters, "Hitchcock said that he had proposed a TV version of Lord Dunsany's 'Two Bottles of Relish,' in which a wife is done away with and presumably becomes the chief ingredient of a meal. He said that NBC has not yet approved the script and probably will not do so." Larry Wolters, "Hitchcock to Scare Up More TV Shows," *Chicago Tribune*, 1 July 1964, C16.

3. Alfred Hitchcock, ed., *Alfred Hitchcock Presents: Stories They Wouldn't Let Me Do on TV* (New York: Simon and Schuster, 1957). This collection was later split in two and reprinted by Dell. "My Recipe for Murder," *Coronet* 48, no. 5 (September 1960): 49–61. On a related note, dog apparently ate dog in Hitchcock's abode according to an answer to a question addressed to "Dear Alfred Hitchcock," a column that appeared periodically in his mystery magazine: "What do you feed those two dogs of yours?" "Other dogs, of course." *Alfred Hitchcock's Mystery Magazine* 3, no. 4 (April 1958): inside back cover.

4. Fred Danzig, "Nawthen-Style Race Prejudices Outlined," *Brownsville Herald*, 28 September 1960, B6.

5. For an account of Spivy's colorful career, see James Gain, *Intimate Nights: The Golden Age of New York Cabaret* (New York: Back Stage Books, 2006), 29–37.

6. Tania Modleski, *The Women Who Knew Too Much: Hitchcock and Feminist Theory*, 2nd ed. (New York: Routledge, 2005), chapter 7, "Rituals of Defilement," 103–115.

7. When AHP moved from CBS to NBC in 1960, Cecil Smith was disappointed about the selection of closing show for the summer reruns. He had hoped for an exceptional show,

namely, "one of those brilliant little shockers, such as the Robert Morley play with its overtones of cannibalism, [this] might have been in keeping with the final appearance." Cecil Smith, "Hitch Pulls the Switch, Fizzles," *Los Angeles Times*, 27 September 1960, A10.

2. Smaller Screen, Bigger Brand

1. Memo dictated by Selznick to Mr. Rawson, 26 October 1943, Legal Series, box 901, folder 7, "Consolidated Files 1936–1954 Hitchcock, Alfred," David O. Selznick Collection, Harry Ransom Center, University of Texas at Austin.

2. Dennis McDougal, *The Last Mogul: Lew Wasserman, MCA, and the Hidden History of Hollywood* (New York: Crown, 1998).

3. Val Adams, "Hitchcock Signs for Video Series," *New York Times*, 25 January 1955, 32.

4. Thomas M. Pryor, "Hollywood Notes," *New York Times*, 24 July 1955, X9.

5. Emily Belser, "Hitchcock Plots Thrills, Suspense for TV," *Los Angeles Herald and Express*, 27 July 1955, C12.

6. *TV Guide* 3, no. 40 (1 October 1955): A31.

7. Patrick McGilligan, *Alfred Hitchcock: A Life in Darkness and Light* (New York: Regan Books, 2003), 514–515.

8. Raines and Harrison co-owned a company controlling the series, which was sponsored by the Emerson Drug Company.

9. On Harrison's career, see, for example, Barbara Berch, "A Hitchcock Alumna," *New York Times*, 27 June 1943, X3; Gilbert Millstein, "Harrison Horror Story," *New York Times*, 21 July 1957, SM23; "Specialty: Murder. Alfred Hitchcock's Protégée Works at Crime 15 Hours a Day," *TV Guide* 6, no. 10 (8 March 1958): 17–19; Murray Schumach, "Woman Produces a Mystery Series," *New York Times*, 1 November 1960, 48; Christina Lane, "Stepping Out from Behind the Grand Silhouette: Joan Harrison's Films of the 1940s," in David A. Gerstner and Janet Staiger, eds., *Authorship and Film* (New York: Routledge, 2003), 97–118.

10. Alfred Hitchcock to Mary Elsom, 24 February 1955, folder 1274, Alfred Hitchcock Papers, Margaret Herrick Library, Academy of Motion Picture Arts and Sciences (AMPAS), Beverly Hills. She had previously submitted several reports from London on theatrical and literary matters and acted as a liaison; folders 1285, 1314, and 1410.

Hitchcock also approached Elsom and asked her to prod Cedric Hardwicke to secure the rights to a Bernard Shaw play. At the same time he asked her for advice in relation to a minor part in *Notorious* (1946). The letter, dated 14 May 1945 and signed "Love, Hitch," is in Legal Series, box 901, folder 6, "Consolidated Files 1936–1954 Hitchcock, Alfred," David O. Selznick Collection, Harry Ransom Center, University of Texas at Austin. For a fuller account of story scouting and the implication of "twists," see Joan Harrison's comment on what she called "switches." These are not plot-related à la O. Henry, but "twists in character." Bob Chandler, "Sound and Pictures," *Variety* (daily), 1 April 1960, 10.

11. Harold Bender, "Profile of a TV Murderer," *New York Journal American*, 6 April 1958, Pictorial Magazine and TView section, 14. Hitchcock once again recounted the plot for "Lamb to the Slaughter," which was aired a week later.

12. Ford allegedly moved money from its unsuccessful variety show, *Ford Startime*, to the Hitchcock series, broadcasted Tuesdays at 8:30 p.m., in order to market brands from the Lincoln-Mercury division; for example, the Mercury Comet.

13. Christopher Anderson, *Hollywood TV: The Studio System in the Fifties* (Austin: Univer-

sity of Texas Press, 1994). See also William Boddy, *Fifties Television: The Industry and Its Crisis* (Urbana: University of Illinois Press, 1993).

14. Jack Gould, "TV: 'Heidi' Dragged Down from Alps," *New York Times*, 3 October 1955, 53.

15. Don Page, "Hitchcock Presents Hitchcock," *Los Angeles Times*, 18 June 1961, D6–8.

16. Hal Humphrey, "Hitchcock's Writer Calls Him a Comic," *Los Angeles Mirror News*, 25 January 1960, 18.

17. Hollis Alpert, "Hitchcock as Humorist," in *The Dreams and the Dreamers* (New York: Macmillan, 1962), 168–177.

18. Jack Gould, "Glance at a New Season," *New York Times*, 6 November 1955, XII. Gould's unappreciative review was echoed a few months later in TV *Guide*, which again heaped praise on the host segments. "Reviews," TV *Guide* 3, no. 49 (3 December 1955): 18. The most glowing comments on the show in both formats, but with a special fondness for the hour format and one half-hour show in particular, "Specialty of the House" (AHP 165), came from Gilbert Seldes in "The Alfred Hitchcock Hour," TV *Guide* 15, no. 4 (26 January 1963): 14.

19. For a complete list of nominations, see Martin Grams Jr. and Patrik Wikstrom, *The Alfred Hitchcock Presents Companion* (Churchville, MD: OTR, 2001), 95–96.

20. In a rare review Gould praised "See the Monkey Dance" (AHH 69); "TV Review: Hitchcock Presents a Suspenseful Hour," *New York Times*, 10 November 1964, 95.

21. Jack Gould, "Television Today—a Critic's Appraisal: Mr. Gould Sees TV: Thumbs Up . . . and Thumbs Down," *New York Times*, 8 April 1956, SM17. Gould published yet another call for live TV after the broadcast of *The Wizard of Oz*; "Program Crisis: Television Tomorrow—'Jack and the Beanstalk,'" *New York Times*, 11 November 1956, 151. As the year closed, RKO Pictures sold its film library to a television network, thereby breaking a united Hollywood front vis-à-vis video. Already, British producers had furnished American television channels with reasonably new films. Paramount had sold shorts, and Selznick nine features. In March 1956 Laurence Olivier's *Richard III* opened on the same day on both the big and small screens—and in color—with the television version only slightly edited. Alistair Cooke of *Omnibus* was another prominent English voice on American television.

22. Bosley Crowther, "Screen: 'The Trouble with Harry': Whimsical Film from Hitchcock at Paris," *New York Times*, 18 October 1955, 46.

23. Penelope Houston, "The Figure in the Carpet," *Sight and Sound* 32, no. 4 (autumn 1963): 162. Lesley Brill argues against the perception of this film as an anomaly within the oeuvre. For him the film is eminently in tune with the romantic vision he finds central to Hitchcock's world. Lesley Brill, "'Love's Not Time's Fool': *The Trouble with Harry* (1955)," in Walter Raubicheck and Walter Srebnick, eds., *Hitchcock's Rereleased Films: From Rope to Vertigo* (Detroit: Wayne State University Press, 1991), 271–281.

24. Marie Torre, "Hitchcock the Actor," *New York Herald Tribune*, 26 February 1956, F8.

25. CBS Television, Press Information, Hollywood, transcript from *Eye on CBS*, aired 18 September 1962, Hal Humphrey Collection, Library of Cinematic Arts, University of Southern California, Los Angeles. Among praise-filled pieces on Allardice's contributions to the show, see Hal Humphrey, "A New Comedy Find," *Los Angeles Mirror-News*, 17 October 1955, 116; Sid Shalit, "Ghost Writer's Boredom Rubs Off on Hitchcock," *Daily News*, 29 November 1956, n.p.; Murray Schumach, "Hitchcock's Ghost Has Haunting Wit," *New York Times*, 13 November 1959, 23; "The Face, Hitchcock—the Words, Allerdyce [sic]," *News*

Herald (Panama City, FL), 10 January 1960, n.p; Hal Humphrey, "As Hitch Goes—So Does a Ghost," *Los Angeles Times*, 4 May 1965, D18.

26. *News Herald* (Panama City, FL), 10 January 1960.

27. According to Hazel Court, a leading lady in several teleplays, "on top of being a terrible tease, he told funny jokes and dirty jokes—Hitchcock was, of course, a true genius." Hazel Court, *Horror Queen—an Autobiography* (Sheffield: Tomahawk, 2008), 95.

28. Hitchcock endorsed Lux soap in an ad in the *Daily Mail*, 9 April 1929, 23. Already in 1925 Hitchcock's *The Pleasure Garden* (Gainsborough Pictures, et al.) had a prominent product placement for Lux detergent.

29. Mikhail Bakhtin, *Rabelais and His World*, translated by Hélène Iswolsky (Bloomington: Indiana University Press, 1984), especially chapter 5, "The Grotesque Image of the Body and Its Sources," 303–367.

30. "Integrating Programs and Sell," *Printers' Ink*, 1 April 1960, 54. A similar analysis was given by Hal Humphrey in "Selling It with Laughs," *Los Angeles Mirror-News*, 12 March 1956, 113.

31. Cecil Smith, "Hitchcock, Master of Suspense, Turns to TV," *Los Angeles Times*, 11 September 1955, D1.

32. Gwen Hyman, *Making a Man: Gentlemanly Appetites in the Nineteenth-Century British Novel* (Athens: Ohio University Press, 2009).

33. Hedda Hopper, "Hitchcock: He Runs on Fear," *Los Angeles Times*, 17 August 1958, E1.

34. Donald Spoto, *The Dark Side of Genius: The Life of Alfred Hitchcock* (New York: Ballantine Books, 1984); Charles Barr, *English Hitchcock* (Moffat: Cameron and Hollis, 1999).

35. Spoto, *The Dark Side of Genius*, 535. See also Barr, *English Hitchcock*, 14.

36. Spoto, *The Dark Side of Genius*, 536.

37. John Crosby, "Hitchcock on Horror," *New York Herald Tribune*, 8 September 1958, A1.

38. Alfred Hitchcock, "Murder—with English on It," *New York Times*, 3 March 1957, 199.

39. "Murders in U.S. Lack Charm, Says Expert," *New York Sunday News*, 26 October 1958, 74. In an interview in *Oui* (Arthur Knight, "Conversation with Alfred Hitchcock," February 1973, 82–83) Hitchcock observed that crime fiction attracts first-class writers in England but not in the United States, and that the current affluence and more generous divorce laws changed the makeup of murder in England.

40. In this liberally illustrated interview for a leading fashion magazine, *Women's Wear Daily* (Richard Natale, "There's Just One Hitch," June 1972, 32), Hitchcock displayed unusual informality in his St. Regis suite by relinquishing his jacket.

41. Larry Wolters, "A Glimpse beyond the Hitchcock Profile," *Chicago Tribune*, 23 September 1962, A14.

42. George Orwell, "The Decline of the English Murders," *Tribune* (London), 15 February 1946, 108–110.

43. For a critique of the compartmentalizing dichotomy English vs. American, see Peter Wollen, "Hitch: A Tale of Two Cities (London and Los Angeles)," in Richard Allen and Sam Ishii-Gonzales, eds., *Hitchcock: Past and Future* (London: Routledge, 2004), 13–21.

44. Allardice scripted Hitchcock's most elaborate discussion of commercials for an after-dinner speech in 1965, "After-Dinner Speech at the Screen Producers Guild Dinner," reprinted in Sidney Gottlieb, ed., *Hitchcock on Hitchcock: Selected Writings and Interviews* (Berkeley: University of California Press, 1995), 54–58. It starts off with a list of epithets partly overlapping the one in AHH 90.

45. "Integrating Program and Sell," *Printers' Ink*, 1 April 1960, 54.

46. "The Fat Silhouette," *Time*, 26 December 1955, 46.

47. Bob Thomas, "Alfred Hitchcock Appears to Be Enjoying His Success," *Dispatch* (Lexington, NC), 14 December 1957, 2.

48. Gérard Genette, *Paratexts: Thresholds of Interpretation*, translated by Jane E. Lewin (New York: Cambridge University Press, 1997), 2.

49. Michel Foucault, "Of Other Spaces," translated by Jay Miskowiec, *Diacritics* 16, no. 1 (spring 1986): 22–27.

50. Helm, "The Perfect Murder," *Variety* (daily), 23 October 1957, 14.

51. For a discussion of the Fairfax series, see Jan Olsson, *Los Angeles before Hollywood: Journalism and American Film Culture, 1905–1915* (Stockholm: National Library of Sweden, 2008), 297–308.

52. Rick Du Brow, "Hitchcock—the Master—Gets Away with Murder Every Week," *St. Petersburg Times*, 19 May 1962, B14.

53. Toward the end of season four, D. S. Frost at Bristol-Myers very politely cautioned Hitchcock and his crew to give the show their very best: "When a show has been on the air for some time, it can't help but lose a certain amount of viewer interest and enthusiasm unless a very high quality is maintained in story selection, casting, and production. Therefore an even greater effort has to be made than in the initial stages when a show is new and fresh." Praising the latest installment, "The Last Dark Step" (AHP 135), he still wants "to make sure that . . . we strive for this kind of show week in and week out." D. S. Frost to Alfred Hitchcock, 10 February 1959, folder 1274, Alfred Hitchcock Papers, Margaret Herrick Library, AMPAS. It was thus no big surprise that the show was shifted to NBC for season six and acquired new sponsors. When Cecil Smith asked Hitchcock about the move from CBS to NBC, the host shrugged and said, "Who cares? They're just sets of initials to me." Cecil Smith, "Hitch Pulls the Switch, Fizzles," *Los Angeles Times*, 27 September 1960, A10.

54. Alfred Hitchcock, "Sixty Minutes Next Season," *New York Morning Telegraph*, 21 August 1962, Hitchcock Clippings file, Performing Arts Library, New York City. This edition of the paper is not available on microfilm at the New York Public Library. Hitchcock was apparently sitting in for Rick Du Brow, according to a UPI telegram dated 20 August 1962 in the Hal Humphrey Collection, Cinematic Arts Library, University of Southern California, Los Angeles. Hitchcock offered a similar joke, though reversed, when his mystery magazine was downsized to pocket format: "All my life, I have been an impressive individual, physically. Even as an infant, I was—shall we say—a sweet bundle of avoirdupois. . . . And so it seems to me that my magazine should be ample in proportions. . . . With this issue, the unimpaired Alfred Hitchcock gives you his new, overcoat pocket-sized AHMM. The TV screen on the cover, you will note, is now of necessity the screen of a portable set." *Alfred Hitchcock's Mystery Magazine* 3, no. 2 (February 1958): inside cover.

55. Wolters, "A Glimpse beyond the Hitchcock Profile," A14.

56. Hal Humphrey, "Suspense Is Killing the Hitchcock Hour," *Los Angeles Times*, 25 November 1962, A18. After the opening episode, "A Piece of the Action," the critic in *Variety* reported that he was hard pressed to find any action and considered the story better suited to the previous half-hour format. Daku, "Alfred Hitchcock Hour," *Variety* (daily), 24 September 1962, 12.

57. *Alfred Hitchcock Mystery Magazine* folder, Alfred Hitchcock Papers, Margaret Herrick Library, AMPAS.

58. *Alfred Hitchcock's Mystery Magazine* 7, no. 4 (April 1962): cover and editorial on inside cover.

59. For the role of "vaudeo"—vaudeville and variety shows as backbone for programming—in the context of early American television, see Susan Murray, *Hitch Your Antenna to the Stars* (New York: Routledge, 2005).

60. For a fuller discussion of media jokes, see Jan Olsson, "Alfred Hitchcock, théoricien de la télevision," in Gilles Delavaud and Denis Maréchal, eds., *Télévision: Le moment experimental* (Rennes: Éditions Apogée, 2011), 546–558.

61. "No Problem for Mr. Hitchcock," *TV Guide* 5, no. 48 (30 November 1957): 19.

62. "The Fat Silhouette," *Time*, 26 December 1955, 46. Hitchcock presented a novel version on the cover of his mystery magazine. After having tried "the Piltdown Man, The Thin Man and others," the magazine proclaimed, "evolution has finally decided on the Hitchcock Man," which was characterized by a "casual, back-on-the-heels stance," "figurine delicacy of outline," and "rippling muscles in the right trouser leg and the adjacent coat sleeve." Hitchcock concludes, "There will be no further progress on the male form, definitely none. This is it." *Alfred Hitchcock's Mystery Magazine* 6, no. 8 (August 1961): cover and editorial on inside cover.

63. John Crosby, "Macabre Merriment," *New York Herald Tribune*, 16 November 1955, 27; reprinted in Albert J. LaValley, ed., *Focus on Hitchcock* (Englewood Cliffs, NJ: Prentice-Hall, 1972), 138.

64. "Alfred Hitchcock—Director, TV or Movies, Suspense Is Golden," *Newsweek*, 11 June 1956, 105.

65. Wolters, "A Glimpse beyond the Hitchcock Profile," A14.

66. James Naremore, "Hitchcock and Humor," *Strategies* 14, no. 1 (2001): 13–25.

67. Thomas De Quincey, *Miscellaneous Essays*, http://www.gutenberg.org/ebooks/10708, accessed 1 February 2013.

68. Interview by Carlo Mazzarella for the RAI program *Arti e scienze dello spettacolo*, May 1960.

69. Consequently, when Hitchcock once quoted De Quincey in an after-dinner speech, the passage did not pick up on the dramatic side of the essay: "If once a man indulges himself in murder, very soon he comes to think little of robbing, and from robbing he comes next to drinking and Sabbath-breaking, and from that incivility and procrastination. Once begun on this downward path you never know where you are to stop. Many a man dates his ruin from some murder or other that perhaps he thought little of at the time." Hitchcock scripted by Jimmie Allardice, "After-Dinner Speech at the Screen Producers Guild Dinner" (1965), reprinted in Gottlieb, *Hitchcock on Hitchcock*, 54–58.

70. Alfred Hitchcock, "50 Murders for Sake of Art," *New York Journal-American*, 7 August 1953, 5. In a later column Hitchcock describes how he was once forced by a pestering heckler at a cocktail party to spin an impromptu situation for a "great suspense classic." The opening neatly illustrates the cozy home philosophy: "Let us imagine a house, a rather small, cozy house. Let us eliminate the obvious, too easy, really pedestrian fripperies of dark wood and ghostly presences. This is a normal house, a small, cozy house." The mysterious activities going on in the house turn out to be preparations

for Christmas. Alfred Hitchcock, "World's Greatest Story of Suspense," *Chicago Tribune*, 29 November 1959, D32.

71. Budge Crawley, Fletcher Markle, and Gerald Pratley, "I Wish I Didn't Have to Shoot the Picture: An Interview with Alfred Hitchcock," *Take One* 1, no. 1 (1966); reprinted in LaValley, *Focus on Hitchcock*, 27.

72. Henry Fielding, *The History of Tom Jones, a Foundling* (London: Penguin Books, 2005 [1749]), 377.

73. Most prominently, John Barrell, *English Literature in History 1730–1780: An Equal, Wide Survey* (New York: St. Martin's, 1983), and *The Infection of Thomas De Quincey: A Psychopathology of Imperialism* (New Haven, CT: Yale University Press, 1991).

74. Raymond Durgnat, *The Strange Case of Alfred Hitchcock; or, the Plain Man's Hitchcock* (Cambridge, MA: MIT Press, 1974), 61.

75. Bob Hull, "T.V.-Talk: Hitch Hates Eggs but Loves Relish," *Los Angeles Herald and Express*, 22 September 1959, B2.

76. Among the numerous discussions of the role of food in Hitchcock's cinema, see, for example, Pierre Gras, "Hitchcock: Eating and Destruction," in Dominique Païni and Guy Cogeval, eds., *Hitchcock and Art: Fatal Coincidences* (Montreal: Montreal Museum of Fine Arts, 2000), 131–136; and David Greven, "Engorged with Desire: The Films of Alfred Hitchcock and the Gendered Politics of Eating," in Anne L. Bower, ed., *Reel Food: Essays on Food and Film* (New York: Routledge, 2004), 297–310.

77. Promotional description for an exhibition of covers from *Esquire's* golden era held at the Museum of Modern Art, New York, in 2008. Tim Arango, "News Flash from the Cover of Esquire: Paper Magazines Can Be High Tech, Too," *New York Times*, 21 July 2008, C5.

78. Alfred Hitchcock, "Violence," *Esquire* 56, no. 1 (July 1961): 107–112; photographs by Dan Wynn.

79. Quoted in Durgnat, *The Strange Case of Alfred Hitchcock*, 60.

80. Fletcher Markle, *Telescope: A Talk with Hitchcock* (Canadian Broadcasting Corporation, 1964); Huw Wheldon, *Monitor* (BBC, 5 July 1964).

81. Thomas Elsaesser, "The Dandy in Hitchcock," in Richard Allen and S. Ishii-Gonzales, eds., *Alfred Hitchcock: Centenary Essays* (London: BFI, 1999), 3–13.

82. Paul Holt, "Letters to Paul Holt," *Daily Mail*, 24 April 1940, 11. Apropos ice cream, Hitchcock as host served up the real bomb, six thousand calories, and as an additional self-conscious wink marketed it as Dieters' Delight, at his own ice-cream parlor in a television episode about teenagers attending Shamley High School: "The Gloating Place" (AHP 222).

83. Arthur Martine, *Martine's Hand-Book of Etiquette, and True Guide to Politeness* (New York: Dick and Fitzgerald, 1866), 48.

84. Geoffrey T. Hellman, "Alfred Hitchcock: England's Best and Biggest Director Goes to Hollywood," *Life*, 20 November 1939, 39. For a full-fledged psychoanalytical explication of the dress code of the period, see J. C. Flügel, *The Psychology of Clothes* (London: Hogarth Press / Institute of Psychoanalysis, 1930). Chapter 4, "Modesty," and chapter 5, "Protection," are especially relevant in regard to the idea of camouflage.

85. Peter Conrad, *The Hitchcock Murders* (London: Faber and Faber, 2000), 83.

86. Philip Mason, *The English Gentleman: The Rise and Fall of an Ideal* (London: Deutsch, 1982), 8. See also Christine Berberich, *The Image of the English Gentleman in Twentieth-Century*

Literature: Englishness and Nostalgia (Hampshire: Ashgate, 2007), 3–13, a chapter aptly called "The Gentleman—an Elusive Term."

87. Katharine Roberts, "Mystery Man," *Collier's*, 5 August 1939, 22.

Interlude II

1. Around the same time, Cary Grant's character in *North by Northwest* (1959) cautioned himself to "think thin."

2. In the story "Being a Murderer Myself," reprinted in the 1957 anthology Hitchcock edited, *Alfred Hitchcock Presents: Stories They Wouldn't Let Me Do on TV* (New York: Simon and Schuster, 1957), Arthur discloses his case to a crime-fiction editor in order to set the record straight concerning the murderer's misunderstood personality type. The story is set in South Africa and is less Nietzschean in tone than the television version.

3. Flashbacks, with or without voice-over, are a key device in the series, as in "The Glass Eye" (AHP 79). They sharpen questions about trust, truthfulness, and ability to accurately relate a series of events or account for a situation. In addition, a voice helps speed up the proceedings and gets the story going. Flashbacks abound in AHP; for example, in episodes 30, 34, 48, 79, 94, 101, 102, 103, 117, 151, 158, 166, 172, 179, 201, 216, and 259. The longer format of *The Alfred Hitchcock Hour* (AHH) also employed flashbacks as a storytelling device, albeit less consistently; for example, in episodes 12, 16, 34, 40, 43, and 47.

4. For the importance of table manners, see John Russell Taylor's succinct account of Paul Newman's visit at the Hitchcocks' Bellagio Road residence, in *Hitch: Life and Work of Alfred Hitchcock* (Boston: Faber and Faber, 1978), 256–257. Allegedly, Alfred was as upset with Newman as Arthur was with Stanley.

5. In the print edition of the story, Arthur would have been quite willing to marry the girl if she hadn't ditched him. He is also less monomaniacal in his pursuit of solitude and in fact hires a girl to help out in the house. As the story ends he is somewhat annoyed by her, and it seems that he is on his way to repeating the elimination process.

3. Hitchcockian Reflections

1. Marjory Adams, "Alfred Hitchcock Gets Proper Face in Orient," *Boston Globe*, 20 March 1964, 46.

2. Memo dictated by Selznick to Mr. Rawson, 26 October 1943, Legal Series, box 901, folder 7, "Consolidated Files 1936–1954 Hitchcock, Alfred," David O. Selznick Collection, Harry Ransom Center, University of Texas at Austin.

3. Paula Marantz Cohen, *Alfred Hitchcock: The Legacy of Victorianism* (Lexington: University Press of Kentucky, 1995), especially chapter 4, pp. 67–85.

4. Alfred Hitchcock, "Directors Are Dead," *Film Weekly*, 20 November 1937, 14; reprinted in Sidney Gottlieb, ed., *Hitchcock on Hitchcock: Selected Writings and Interviews* (Berkeley: University of California Press, 1995), 183–185.

5. For a full-fledged version of this observation, see Thomas Schatz, *The Genius of the System: Hollywood Filmmaking in the Studio Era* (New York: Pantheon Books, 1988).

6. John D. Weaver, "The Man behind the Body," *Holiday* 36, no. 3 (September 1964): 85.

7. Roland Barthes, "From Work to Text," translated by Stephen Heath, in Philip Rice and Patricia Waugh, eds., *Modern Literary Theory: A Reader* (New York: Arnold, 1996), 191–197.

8. Penelope Houston, "The Figure in the Carpet," *Sight and Sound* 32, no. 4 (autumn 1963): 159–164; Andrew Sarris, "Notes on the Auteur Theory in 1962," *Film Culture*, no. 27 (winter 1962–1963): 1–8.

9. Robert E. Kapsis, *Hitchcock: The Making of a Reputation* (Chicago: University of Chicago Press, 1992); Hollis Alpert, "Hitchcock as Humorist," in *The Dreams and the Dreamers* (New York: Macmillan, 1962), 168–177.

10. Charles Higham, "Hitchcock's World," *Film Quarterly* 16, no. 2 (winter 1962–1963): 4.

11. John Russell Taylor, *Hitch: Life and Work of Alfred Hitchcock* (Boston: Faber and Faber, 1978), 289.

12. Thomas M. Leitch, *Find the Director and Other Hitchcock Games* (Athens: University of Georgia Press, 2008); David Sterritt, *The Films of Alfred Hitchcock* (New York: Cambridge University Press, 1993).

13. Leitch, *Find the Director and Other Hitchcock Games*.

14. Alfred Hitchcock, "On Art," *Alfred Hitchcock's Mystery Magazine* 2, no. 10 (October 1957): 65.

15. Hitchcock scripted by Jimmie Allardice, "After-Dinner Speech at the Screen Producers Guild Dinner" (1965), reprinted in Sidney Gottlieb, ed., *Hitchcock on Hitchcock: Selected Writings and Interviews* (Berkeley: University of California Press, 1995), 54–58. For yet another discussion of the Grant ideal, see Charlotte Chandler, *It's Only a Movie. Alfred Hitchcock: A Personal Biography* (New York: Simon and Schuster, 2005), 1. The erudite team of Allardice and Hitchcock delivered the duality joke of the thin man inside the fat one as a familiar split, as something "they say." However, it brings to mind George Orwell—or, rather, the obese George Bowling, the protagonist of Orwell's novel *Coming Up for Air* (1939). For the forlorn Bowling, the smell of horse dung serves as counterpart to Proust's madeleine—if poetic license is accepted for the pungent, almost Hitchcockian, synesthetic cross-wiring of senses. This smell, together with the uneasy feeling incurred by Bowling's new set of false teeth, inspires a nostalgic revisiting of better days. The dichotomy between his overweight body and the svelte inner subject forms part of Bowling's depressed first-person reflections and foreshadows Hitchcock's analysis: "I'm fat, but I'm thin inside. Has it ever struck you that there's a thin man inside every fat man, just as they say there's a statue inside every block of stone?" Orwell's trope is far from unique, however, and can, for example, also be discovered in Cyril Connolly's *The Unquiet Grave* (1944), which is a notebook of sorts. Among Connolly's aphorisms one finds this claim: "Imprisoned in every fat man a thin one is wildly signaling to be let out." In general the preoccupation with obesity has a secure place in English letters, ranging from Shakespeare's Sir John Falstaff and his predecessors to Dickens (especially *The Posthumous Papers of the Pickwick Club*) to G. K. Chesterton to Kingsley Amis's *One Fat Englishman* (1963).

16. Richard Gehman, "The Chairman of the Board," *TV Guide* 12, no. 20 (16 May 1964): 11.

17. Robert C. Cumbow, "Of Staircases and Potato Trucks: Fear and Fatness and Alfred Hitchcock," *Movietone News*, no. 25 (September 1973): 6–12.

18. Sterritt, *The Films of Alfred Hitchcock*. For analysis of individual cameos, see James M. Vest, "The Controller Controlled: Hitchcock's Cameo in *Torn Curtain*," *Hitchcock Annual* 7 (1998–1999): 3–19; and Vest, "Alfred Hitchcock's Cameo in *Vertigo*," *Hitchcock Annual* 8 (1999–2000): 84–92.

19. Susan Smith, *Hitchcock: Suspense, Humour and Tone* (London: BFI, 2000).

20. Vincent Canby, "Film Maker Transformed Commonplace into Exotic," *New York Times*, 30 April 1980, D23.

21. Smith, *Hitchcock*, 12.

22. Smith, *Hitchcock*, 6.

23. Bob Hull, "T.V.-Talk: Hitch Hates Eggs but Loves Relish," *Los Angeles Herald and Express*, 22 September 1959, B2.

24. Peter Conrad, *The Hitchcock Murders* (London: Faber and Faber, 2000), 87.

25. Charles Mercer, "Job Open: You Must Dig In," *Milwaukee Sentinel*, 24 January 1958, 112; "Lifeguard Wins Car, Finds Buried 'Body,'" *Miami News*, 2 February 1958, A14.

26. Ad in *New York Herald Tribune*, 20 January 1958, 2.

27. Alva Johnston, "300-Pound Prophet Comes to Hollywood," *Saturday Evening Post*, 22 May 1943, 12.

28. Hull, "T.V.-Talk: Hitch Hates Eggs but Loves Relish," B2.

29. Cohen, *Alfred Hitchcock*, especially 67–85.

30. Cohen, *Alfred Hitchcock*, 145–146.

31. Though he tried to "further his daughter's career in the field of acting," it didn't take off outside her father's creative world. Hitchcock concluded, "I guess I'll just have to create more roles in my show for her." Marie Torre, "Hitchcock the Actor," *New York Herald Tribune*, 26 February 1956, F9.

32. "Daughter Trapped by Father's Joke," *Pittsburgh Press*, 2 January 1951, 14; Donald Spoto, *The Dark Side of Genius: The Life of Alfred Hitchcock* (New York: Ballantine Books, 1984), 346–347; Pat Hitchcock O'Connell and Laurent Bouzereau, *Alma Hitchcock: The Woman behind the Man* (New York: Berkley Books, 2003), 153.

33. Cohen, *Alfred Hitchcock*, 82–85.

34. When recounting her Dad's penchant for practical jokes in an article headlined "My Dad, the Jokester," *Citizen-News* (Hollywood), 7 July 1963, n.p., Patricia omitted the Ferris wheel joke. Taking parenting to a symbolical level, Hitchcock explained that he took "a fatherly interest" in his actors, and that his treatment of them was "warm but firm." "'They're nice children,' he says. 'They need to be petted and guided and should be patted on the head. Occasionally, they need a good spanking, too.'" Hedda Hopper, "Papa Hitchcock," *Chicago Tribune*, 29 April 1962, C16. For a comment by the joker himself from the very year he stranded his daughter up high, see Alfred Hitchcock, "Can You Take a Joke?," *Los Angeles Times*, 2 December 1951, H21. Here, deliberating on the question "Is it good manners to indulge in practical joking?," Hitchcock explains some of the rules involved: "The victim must be one that can retaliate," and must not be exposed to "physical danger" or "undue ridicule." Embarrassing the victim is fine, but exposing them to ridicule is not. As for his own practice, he says: "Except in extreme cases of self-defense or retaliation, I have given up practical joking altogether." The Ferris wheel episode wasn't mentioned. Hitchcock had, in fact, come clean already back in 1943 when describing himself as a repentant prankster. This confession came after his latest stunt: he had promised a camera-eager bartender a role in *Shadow of a Doubt* (1943), only to place him out of sight in Uncle Charlie's casket in the final scene's short glimpse of a funeral procession. Hitchcock promised to seek out his former prank victims and ask for forgiveness. "Oddities from Strange World of Make-Believe," *Hartford Courant*, 18 April 1943, 118.

35. For example, this story was one of the talking points when Hitchcock was a guest on the *Dick Cavett Show* (ABC), 8 June 1972.

36. Sterritt, *The Films of Alfred Hitchcock*, 11–14.

37. Spoto, *The Dark Side of Genius*, 353.

38. Spoto, *The Dark Side of Genius*, 353.

39. Tex McCrary and Jinx Falkenburg, "New York Close-Up," *New York Herald Tribune*, 8 July 1951, D1. The self-strangulation was illustrated in the same column on 27 February 1950 (13), and in a text full of anecdotes.

40. "Hitchcock Brews Thrillers Here," *House and Garden* 82, no. 2 (August 1942): 34–35.

41. Tex McCrary and Jinx Falkenburg, "New York Close-Up," *New York Herald Tribune*, 27 February 1950, 13.

42. O'Connell and Bouzereau, *Alma Hitchcock*, 2. For a detailed account of Alma Reville's British career and influence on her husband's touches, see Nathalie Morris, "The Early Career of Alma Reville," *Hitchcock Annual* 15 (2006–2007): 1–31. Interestingly, in another attempt at upgrading female agency, in this case Joan Harrison's role as producer, Christina Lane also used "behind" in her title. Christina Lane, "Stepping Out from Behind the Grand Silhouette: Joan Harrison's Films of the 1940's," in David A. Gerstner and Janet Staiger, eds., *Authorship and Film* (New York: Routledge, 2003), 97–118.

43. "The Alfred Hitchcock Dinner Hour," *Look*, 27 August 1963, 42–44; produced by Marilyn Kaytor, photographed by Cal Bernstein.

44. For a discussion of the films based on Hayes's screenplays, see Thomas M. Leitch, "Self and World at Paramount," in Walter Raubicheck and Walter Srebnick, eds., *Hitchcock's Rereleased Films: From Rope to Vertigo* (Detroit: Wayne State University Press, 1991), 36–51.

45. On a related note bearing on how the hosting role in general was understood by television audiences, Otto Kruger, the host of *Lux Video Theater* (NBC, 1950–1959; Kruger hosted 1955–1956), described the reception of his creative role: "All I do is come up and tell the people who I am and what we're up to. I don't have a single thing to do with the producing, directing or casting of the show. Yet I get letters every week complimenting me on my production, my directing, my casting, even my script adaptations." "Be My Guest," *TV Guide* 4, no. 5 (4–10 February 1956): 15.

46. Norman Lloyd, *Stages of a Life in Theatre, Film and Television* (New York: Limelight, 1993), 171–183.

47. Interoffice memo from Noll Gurney to Al Kaufman, 23 June 1938, folder 1, dated "to 4/30/39," "Hitchcock, Alfred" file, Myron Selznick Papers, Harry Ransom Center, University of Texas at Austin.

48. "Hitchcock & Harrison: TV's Shock Troops," *New York Tribune / Herald Tribune*, 10 July 1960, G8.

49. Martin Grams Jr. and Patrik Wikstrom, *The Alfred Hitchcock Presents Companion* (Churchville, MD: OTR, 2001), 27.

50. For a photo-montage of Hitchcock at the table apparently eating chicken while Tippi Hedren's character screams, see "Fine Feathered Friends on a Rampage," *Life*, 1 February 1963, 68–69.

51. Transcript of conversation dated 15 April 1963, pp. 13–14, folder 1546, Alfred Hitchcock Papers, Margaret Herrick Library, Academy of Motion Picture Arts and Sciences (AMPAS), Beverly Hills. The sparring session might also have been a dress rehearsal for the marketing tour for *The Birds*, which opened late April that year; an interview with Oriana Fallaci a month later in Cannes ("Alfred Hitchcock: Mr. Chastity," in Oriana Fallaci,

The Egotists: Sixteen Surprising Interviews, translated by Pamela Swinglehurst [Chicago: Henry Regnery, 1963], 239–256); and the two lengthy television interviews Hitchcock sat down for in 1964, for the Canadian CBC and the BBC, respectively (Fletcher Markle, *Telescope: A Talk with Hitchcock* [Canadian Broadcasting Corporation, 1964]; Huw Wheldon, *Monitor* [BBC, 5 July 1964]).

52. The play was published as *Banquo's Chair: A Play in One Act* (London: H. F. W. Deane and Sons, 1930); the short story is included in Croft-Cooke's *Pharaoh with His Waggons, and Other Stories* (London: Jarrolds, 1937).

53. Hitchcock was not unfamiliar with the motif of ghosts haunting the conscience of a murderer. The final scenes in *The Pleasure Garden* (1925) hinge on precisely this idea in compressed format as the girl Miles Mander's character has murdered returns to haunt him.

54. Stefan Sharff, *Alfred Hitchcock's High Vernacular* (New York: Columbia University Press, 1991).

55. William Rothman, *Hitchcock: The Murderous Gaze* (Cambridge, MA: Harvard University Press, 1982), 33.

56. John Belton, "Hitchcock and the Classical Paradigm," in David Boyd and R. Barton Palmer, eds., *After Hitchcock: Influence, Imitation, and Intertextuality* (Austin: University of Texas Press, 2006), 237.

57. "Alfred: The Great Shocker," TV Guide 9, no. 12 (25 March 1961): 18.

58. Alfred Hitchcock to Mary Elsom, 24 February 1955, folder 1274, Alfred Hitchcock Papers, Margaret Herrick Library, AMPAS.

59. Rod Taylor was cast as a lead player for *The Birds* after appearing years earlier in the Shamley-produced series of episodes *Suspicion*. He came predominantly from television to *The Birds*, and the role gave him a decade-long foothold in the movies. Henry Jones, meanwhile, in between his roles for AHP, played a small but memorable part in *Vertigo* as the icy coroner.

60. "An Old Master Opposes Sink-to-Sink TV," TV Guide 7, no. 7 (14 February 1959): 18.

61. Helm, "The Glass Eye," *Variety* (daily), 8 October 1957, 8.

62. Jim Morse, "Today It's Just One Neurotic Character after Another for Jessica Tandy—Has She Cornered the Market?," *Toledo Blade*, 11 October 1959, IV:6.

63. Myrtle Gebhart, "Got Start to Stage and Film Fame in Home State, Maine," *Boston Sunday Post*, 10 November 1946, 4.

64. On the rare occasions when the franchise offered a story dealing with a social problem, Hitchcock abandoned the jocular hosting in the epilogues: alcoholism in "Never Again," juvenile delinquency in "Number Twenty-Two" (AHP 60), disability caused by war in "The Return of the Hero" (AHP 100), gun control in "Bang! You're Dead" (AHP 231), alcoholism once again in "Hangover" (AHH 12), and juvenile gangs in "Memo from Purgatory" (AHH 74).

65. Kove, "Never Again," *Variety* (daily), 24 April 1956, 12.

66. "Previews of Today's TV," *Chicago Tribune*, 16 September 1956, 45.

67. Kove, "Fog Closing In," *Variety* (daily), 9 October 1956, 11.

68. Alfred Hitchcock, "Violence," *Esquire* 56, no. 1 (July 1961): 107–112.

69. Hitchcock's expertise concerning what to do with a corpse in the living room was so well regarded that he was consulted over the phone in the film *The Gazebo* (MGM, 1959), when Glenn Ford's character, a teleplay writer, is faced with a blackmailer-turned-dead-

body to dispose of, just like in *The Trouble with Harry*. And there is a happy conclusion after lots of slapstick—as in Harry's case, the blackmailer died of natural causes. The story was based on a play by Alex Coppel, whose material was used in the Hitchcock series four times: in "I Killed the Count" (AHP 64–66), "The Diplomatic Corpse" (AHP 88), "Together" (AHP 93), and "The Dark Pool" (AHH 29).

70. The producers' playful attention extended even to micro details, which at times work as in-jokes. When prominently placing a painting representing the wife killed off by Mr. Westlake and Enid in "A Matter of Murder," the producers had—as the detectives in the audience in command of the series global universe might notice—dusted off a previously used portrait. The very same painting had occupied a critical role in a teleplay in which the portrait of a murdered wife was narratively prominent seasons back, "Portrait of Jocelyn" (AHP 28). Jocelyn, too, was killed by her husband, but she was more successfully disposed of. To find the buried body, the police, years later, resort to setting up the killer in a plan as involved as the arrangement for "Banquo's Chair." In accordance with the show's playfulness, the portrait as a prop, second time around, functions simultaneously as in-joke and production economy.

71. A counterpart to Glessing as maid is Ray Teal's playing Police Lieutenant on the West Coast and Police Detective on the East Coast during the opening season of the series, in addition to a role as prison warden. In later seasons he acted as Sheriff, Chief of Detectives, and Fire Chief in addition to two other roles.

72. For example, Joan Harrison, letter to Roald Dahl, 10 January 1958, p. 1, RD 1/1/4/4/1, Roald Dahl Museum and Story Centre, Great Missenden, Buckinghamshire, England.

73. Thomas Leitch, *The Encyclopedia of Alfred Hitchcock: From Alfred Hitchcock Presents to Vertigo* (New York: Checkmark Books, 2002).

74. In a film often seen as an American remake of *The 39 Steps* (1935), it may be only coincidental that Eve Kendall is sitting in train car number 3901.

75. For a detailed analysis of this teleplay, see Neill Potts, "'Revenge': Alfred Hitchcock's 'Sweet Little Story,'" *Hitchcock Annual* 9 (2000–2001): 146–162.

76. Killing aunts simply did not pay off for Hatfield's characters. In his first role for the franchise, in a different sort of twosome, he played one of the brothers trying to kill their aunt with ground glass in "The Perfect Murder" (AHP 24). Ironically, the glass ends up in his own morning omelet.

Conclusion

1. Dave Kaufman, "Hitch Stitches TV Viewers' Reaction," *Variety* (daily), 6 January 1965, 8.

2. "TV Violence Discussed," *New York Times*, 21 January 1959, 63; Cecil Smith, "Parents Urged to Limit TV Crime for Children," *Los Angeles Times*, 12 February 1959, B32; Larry Wolters, "Two More Westerns Ride TV," *Chicago Tribune*, 21 January 1959, A2.

3. Undated clipping from a 1959 *New York Morning Telegraph* article, Alfred Hitchcock clippings folder, Billy Rose Collection, Performing Arts Library, New York. Upset with the overly graphic violence, the sponsor in 1961 managed to persuade the network to cancel one of Hitchcock's teleplays, "The Sorcerer's Apprentice" (AHP 268, the last one in the series, never aired).

4. John Crosby, "Hitchcock on Horror," *New York Herald Tribune*, 8 September 1958, A1.

5. Mikhail Bakhtin, "Freudianism: A Critical Sketch," in Katerina Clark and Michael Holquist, eds., *Mikhail Bakhtin* (Cambridge, MA: Belknap Press of Harvard University Press, 1986), 134–135.

6. Alfred Hitchcock, "My Recipe for Murder," *Coronet* 48, no. 5 (September 1960): 49–61.

7. Janet Maslin, "Alfred Hitchcock," *Boston after Dark* 3, no. 24 (12–20 June 1972): 12; reprinted in Sidney Gottlieb, ed., *Alfred Hitchcock Interviews* (Jackson: University Press of Mississippi, 2003), 107. The key gothic element is the Bates mansion, modeled on Edward Hopper's painting *House by the Railroad*, in turn a reconfiguration of a house in Haverstraw, New York. Charles Addams's haunted house was another offshoot from Hopper's painting, while the *Psycho* house in turn has enjoyed an afterlife in many films. For this genealogy, see Paul Bochner, "Someplace Like Home," *Atlantic Monthly* 277, no. 5 (May 1996): 40–41.

8. Robert Sklar, "Death at Work: Hitchcock's Violence and Spectator Identification," in David Boyd and R. Barton Palmer, eds., *After Hitchcock: Influence, Imitation, and Intertextuality* (Austin: University of Texas Press, 2006), 216–234; Alfred Hitchcock, "Violence," *Esquire* 56, no. 1 (July 1961): 107–112.

9. Robert E. Kapsis, *Hitchcock: The Making of a Reputation* (Chicago: University of Chicago Press, 1992), 58–60.

10. Murray Schumach, "Woman Produces a Mystery Series," *New York Times*, 1 November 1960, 48.

11. NBC biography, 19 September 1961, Los Angeles Examiner Collection, Special Collections, Doheny Memorial Library, University of Southern California, Los Angeles.

12. The certificate from Barre, Vermont, can be found in folder 947, Alfred Hitchcock Papers, Margaret Herrick Library, Academy of Motion Picture Arts and Sciences (AMPAS), Beverly Hills.

13. Alfred Hitchcock, "The Care and Handling of Psycho," brochure, Alfred Hitchcock Papers, Margaret Herrick Library, AMPAS.

14. "Paramount Pictures press sheets, 1920–1965," Margaret Herrick Library, AMPAS.

15. "Catch It from the Beginning . . . ," *Paramount World* 5, no. 1 (1959): 14.

16. Alfred Hitchcock, "A Lesson in PSYCHO-ology," *Motion Picture Herald*, 6 August 1960, 17–18. For an account of the relationship to the other disciplining initiatives, see Joan Hawkins, "'See It from the Beginning': Hitchcock's Reconstruction of Film History," *Hitchcock Annual* 8 (1999–2000): 13–29. Hitchcock privately screened *Les diaboliques* twice in September 1959, the second time on the day he met with Janet Leigh and Vera Miles, separately, according to his "Appointment Book" for 1959 (folder 1345, Alfred Hitchcock Papers, Margaret Herrick Library, AMPAS).

17. Barbara Klinger, "Digressions at the Cinema: Reception and Mass Culture," *Cinema Journal* 28, no. 4 (summer 1989): 3–19.

18. Alfred Hitchcock, "My Recipe for Murder," *Coronet* 48, no. 5 (September 1960): 49–61.

19. "Phantom Face in the Foliage," *Life*, 11 July 1960, 54.

20. William Rothman, *Hitchcock: The Murderous Gaze* (Cambridge, MA: Harvard University Press, 1982).

21. Linda Williams, "Learning to Scream," *Sight and Sound, New Series* 4, no. 12 (December 1994): 16.

22. Larry Wolters, "Hitchcock Horrors Stir Critic's Protest," *Chicago Tribune*, 18 October 1963, B23.

23. "Evaluations of the Shows," *Sun* (New York), 18 July 1965, TV section, 16.

24. "Networks Are 'Chicken'—Hitchcock," *Los Angeles Times*, 3 May 1965, 27.

25. "The Elderly Cherub That Is Hitchcock," *TV Guide* 13, no. 22 (29 May 1965): 15.

26. Henry McLemore, "The Lighter Side . . . ," *Los Angeles Times*, 19 August 1954, 14.

27. Thomas M. Pryor, "Hollywood Notes," *New York Times*, 24 July 1955, X9.

28. When shooting commenced, several newspapers reported that Hitchcock had "expressed his desire to film a murder story he considers a top-flight example of plotting." Oscar Godbout, "Burns and Allen Will Lose Gracie," *New York Times*, 19 February 1958, 54.

29. Harrison's missive, on Shamley Productions Inc. letterhead, is labeled RD 1/1/4/4/1. The first draft after the story was accepted and the one Harrison comments on is labeled RD/8/2/3. The revised version, the second draft, is labeled RD/8/2/7. Roald Dahl Museum and Story Centre, Great Missenden, Buckinghamshire, England.

30. David Sterritt, *The Films of Alfred Hitchcock* (New York: Cambridge University Press, 1993), 12–14.

31. Alfred Hitchcock, "Murder Begins at Home," *Argosy* 351, no. 3 (September 1960): 50–51, 80–81.

32. The rhyme goes as follows:

> Mary had a little lamb,
> Its fleece was white as snow;
> And everywhere that Mary went,
> The lamb was sure to go.
>
> It followed her to school one day;
> That was against the rule;
> It made the children laugh and play
> To see a lamb at school.
>
> And so the teacher turned it out,
> But still it lingered near,
> And waited patiently about
> Till Mary did appear.
>
> "Why does the lamb love Mary so?"
> The eager children cry;
> "Why, Mary loves the lamb, you know,"
> The teacher did reply.

Interestingly, Edison recited the first stanza of this nursery rhyme to test his invention of the phonograph in 1877, making this the first audio recording to be successfully made and played back.

33. "Hitchcock Gives Free Rein to THE GENTLE SEX," *TV Guide* 6, no. 19 (10 May 1958): 12–13.

34. For an overview of the cultural meanings and shifting significance of fur coats, see Carol Dyhouse, "Skin Deep: The Fall of Fur," *History Today* 61, no. 11 (1 November 2011): 26–29.

35. Laura Mulvey, "Visual Pleasure and Narrative Cinema," *Screen* 16, no. 3 (autumn 1975): 6–18.

36. Tania Modleski, "Resurrection of a Hitchcock Daughter (2005)," in *The Women Who Knew Too Much: Hitchcock and Feminist Theory*, 2nd ed. (New York: Routledge, 2005).

37. Bernard F. Dick, "Hitchcock's Terrible Mothers," *Literature and Film Quarterly* 38, no. 4 (summer 1978): 238–249; Mike Chopra-Gant, "Absent Fathers and 'Moms,' Delinquent Daughters and Mummy's Moms: Envisioning the Postwar American Family in Hitchcock's *Notorious*," *Comparative American Studies* 3, no. 3 (2005): 361–375.

38. Philip Wylie, *Generation of Vipers* (New York: Rinehart, 1955 [1942]).

39. Wylie, *Generation of Vipers*, 197.

40. Wylie, *Generation of Vipers*, 213–214.

41. Philippe Halsman's photograph from 1974 was, for example, used to illustrate David Freeman's article "The Last Days of Alfred Hitchcock," *Esquire Film Quarterly* 97 (April 1982): 91.

42. Gregg Kilday, "Hitchcock's Triumph of Tension," *Los Angeles Times*, 27 July 1975, R1.

43. Robert Kervin, "Gravely Speaking, Hitch Digs Fright," *Chicago Tribune*, 11 April 1976, E2.

44. Richard Schickel, "We're Living in a Hitchcock World, All Right," *New York Times*, 29 October 1972, SM22.

45. James Monaco, "The Cinema and Its Double: Alfred Hitchcock," *Take One* 5, no. 2 (May 1976): 7.

46. Stanley Handman, "Alfred Hitchcock Murders a Blonde," *Ottawa Citizen*, 30 May 1958 (*Weekend Magazine* 8, no. 22), 6.

47. "An Old Master Opposes Sink-to-Sink TV," *TV Guide* 7, no. 7 (14 February 1959): 19.

48. Truffaut here seemingly emulates a bit of advice Hitchcock gave a young boy seeking career shortcuts to becoming a film director: "Grow older, sardonic, and somewhat more robust." *Alfred Hitchcock's Mystery Magazine* 3, no. 11 (November 1958): 77.

49. François Truffaut, *Hitchcock*, rev. ed. (New York: Simon and Schuster, 1984).

50. Pat Hitchcock O'Connell and Laurent Bouzereau, *Alma Hitchcock: The Woman behind the Man* (New York: Berkley Books, 2003), 2.

51. "The Elderly Cherub That Is Hitchcock," 18.

52. Hollis Alpert, "Hitchcock as Humorist," in *The Dreams and the Dreamers* (New York: Macmillan, 1962), 168–177; Monaco, "The Cinema and Its Double"; Thomas Elsaesser, "The Dandy in Hitchcock," in Richard Allen and S. Ishii-Gonzales, eds., *Alfred Hitchcock: Centenary Essays* (London: BFI, 1999), 3–13.

53. "The Elderly Cherub That Is Hitchcock," 18.

54. Hedda Hopper, "Hitchcock Speech Too Good to Keep," *Los Angeles Times*, 22 April 1965, C17.

55. The full commencement address was published in *The Santa Claran* (summer 1963): 3–6.

56. Bob Hull, "T.V.-Talk: Hitch Hates Eggs but Loves Relish," *Los Angeles Herald and Express*, 22 September 1959, B2.

57. Truffaut, *Hitchcock*, 320.

58. Dick Stromgren, "Now to the Banquet We Press: Hitchcock's Gourmet and Gourmand Offerings," in Paul Loukides and Linda K. Fuller, eds., *Beyond the Stars: Studies in American Popular Film*, vol. 3: *The Material World in American Popular Film* (Bowling Green, OH: Bowling Green University Popular Press, 1993), 38–50.

59. "People of the TIMES," *Corpus Christi Times*, 2 June 1975, A4.

SELECTED BIBLIOGRAPHY

"The Alfred Hitchcock Dinner Hour." *Look*, 27 August 1963, 42–44.

"Alfred Hitchcock—Director, TV or Movies, Suspense Is Golden." *Newsweek*, 11 June 1956, 105–108.

"Alfred Hitchcock England's Best Director Starts Work in Hollywood." *Life*, 19 June 1939, 66–70.

"Alfred: The Great Shocker." *TV Guide* 9, no. 12 (25 March 1961): 17–18.

Allen, Richard. "Hitchcock, or the Pleasures of Metaskepticism." *October*, no. 89 (summer 1999): 69–86.

———. *Hitchcock's Romantic Irony*. New York: Columbia University Press, 2007.

Alpert, Hollis. "Hitchcock as Humorist." In *The Dreams and the Dreamers*, 168–177. New York: Macmillan, 1962.

Anderson, Christopher. *Hollywood TV: The Studio System in the Fifties*. Austin: University of Texas Press, 1994.

"Arrived." *Newsweek*, 6 September 1937, 25.

Auiler, Dan. *Vertigo: The Making of a Hitchcock Classic*. [1998.] New York: St. Martin's Griffin, 2000.

Bakhtin, Mikhail. "Freudianism: A Critical Sketch." In Katerina Clark and Michael Holquist, eds., *Mikhail Bakhtin*, 134–135. Cambridge, MA: Belknap Press of Harvard University Press, 1986.

———. *Rabelais and His World*. Translated by Hélène Iswolsky. Bloomington: Indiana University Press, 1984.

Barbas, Samantha. *The First Lady of Hollywood: A Biography of Louella Parsons*. Berkeley: University of California Press, 2006.

Barr, Charles. *English Hitchcock*. Moffat: Cameron and Hollis, 1999.

Barrell, John. *English Literature in History 1730–1780: An Equal, Wide Survey*. New York: St. Martin's, 1983.

———. *The Infection of Thomas De Quincey: A Psychopathology of Imperialism*. New Haven, CT: Yale University Press, 1991.

Barthes, Roland. "From Work to Text." Translated by Stephen Heath. In Philip Rice and

Patricia Waugh, eds., *Modern Literary Theory: A Reader*, 191–197. New York: Arnold, 1996.

Behlmer, Rudy, ed. *Memo from David O. Selznick: The Creation of* Gone with the Wind *and Other Motion Picture Classics, as Revealed in the Producer's Private Letters, Telegrams, Memorandums, and Autobiographical Remarks*. New York: Modern Library, 2000.

Belton, John. "Hitchcock and the Classical Paradigm." In David Boyd and R. Barton Palmer, eds., *After Hitchcock: Influence, Imitation, and Intertextuality*, 235–247. Austin: University of Texas Press, 2006.

Berberich, Christine. *The Image of the English Gentleman in Twentieth-Century Literature: Englishness and Nostalgia*. Hampshire, UK: Ashgate, 2007.

Bochner, Paul. "Someplace Like Home." *Atlantic Monthly*, May 1996, 40–41.

Boddy, William. *Fifties Television: The Industry and Its Crisis*. Urbana: University of Illinois Press, 1993.

Brill, Lesley. *The Hitchcock Romance: Love and Irony in Hitchcock's Films*. Princeton, NJ: Princeton University Press, 1988.

———. "'Love's Not Time's Fool': *The Trouble with Harry* (1955)." In Walter Raubicheck and Walter Srebnick, eds., *Hitchcock's Rereleased Films: From* Rope *to* Vertigo, 271–281. Detroit: Wayne State University Press, 1991.

Brinkley, Alan. *The Publisher: Henry Luce and His American Century*. New York: Knopf, 2010.

"Catch It from the Beginning . . ." *Paramount World* 5, no. 1 (1959): 14.

Chandler, Bob. "Sound and Pictures." *Variety* (daily), 1 April 1960, 10.

Chandler, Charlotte. *It's Only a Movie. Alfred Hitchcock: A Personal Biography*. New York: Simon and Schuster, 2005.

Chopra-Gant, Mike. "Absent Fathers and 'Moms,' Delinquent Daughters and Mummy's Moms: Envisioning the Postwar American Family in Hitchcock's *Notorious*." *Comparative American Studies* 3, no. 3 (2005): 361–375.

Cohen, Paula Marantz. *Alfred Hitchcock: The Legacy of Victorianism*. Lexington: University Press of Kentucky, 1995.

Collingham, Lizzie. *The Taste of War: World War Two and the Battle for Food*. London: Allen Lane, 2011.

Conrad, Peter. *The Hitchcock Murders*. London: Faber and Faber, 2000.

Court, Hazel. *Horror Queen—an Autobiography*. Sheffield: Tomahawk, 2008.

Crawley, Budge, Fletcher Markle, and Gerald Pratley. "I Wish I Didn't Have to Shoot the Picture: An Interview with Alfred Hitchcock." In Albert J. LaValley, ed., *Focus on Hitchcock*, 27. Englewood Cliffs, NJ: Prentice-Hall, 1972. Rpt. of "I Wish I Didn't Have to Shoot the Picture: An Interview with Alfred Hitchcock." *Take One* 1, no. 1 (1966): 14–17.

Creelman, Eileen. "Picture Plays and Players." *Sun* (New York), 15 June 1938, 26.

Crosby, John. "Macabre Merriment." In Albert J. LaValley, ed., *Focus on Hitchcock*, 138. Englewood Cliffs, NJ: Prentice-Hall, 1972.

Cumbow, Robert C. "Of Staircases and Potato Trucks: Fear and Fatness and Alfred Hitchcock." *Movietone News*, no. 25 (September 1973): 6–12.

Daku. "Alfred Hitchcock Hour." *Variety* (daily), 24 September 1962, 12.

Davidson, Bill. "Alfred Hitchcock Resents." *Saturday Evening Post*, 15 December 1962, 62–64.

"Dial Ham for Murder." *Life*, 24 May 1954, 126, 129.

Dick, Bernard F. "Hitchcock's Terrible Mothers." *Literature and Film Quarterly* 38, no. 4 (summer 1978): 238–249.

Drake, Sylvie. "If It's Thursday, It Must Be Hitchcock." *Holiday* 57, no. 4 (summer 1976): 32–33, 50.

Durgnat, Raymond. *The Strange Case of Alfred Hitchcock; or, The Plain Man's Hitchcock.* Cambridge, MA: MIT Press, 1974.

Dyhouse, Carol. "Skin Deep: The Fall of Fur." *History Today* 61, no. 11 (1 November 2011): 26–29.

Elsaesser, Thomas. "The Dandy in Hitchcock." In Richard Allen and S. Ishii-Gonzales, eds., *Alfred Hitchcock: Centenary Essays*, 3–13. London: BFI, 1999.

Erish, Andrew A. "Reclaiming *Alfred Hitchcock Presents.*" *Quarterly Review of Film and Video* 26, no. 5 (October 2009): 385–392.

Fallaci, Oriana. "Alfred Hitchcock: Mr. Chastity." [1963.] Rpt. in Sidney Gottlieb, ed., *Alfred Hitchcock Interviews*, 55–61. Jackson: University Press of Mississippi, 2003.

"The Fat Silhouette." *Time*, 26 December 1955, 46.

Fisher, Richard. "Hitchcock's Figure on the Staircase." *Thousand Eyes* 1, no. 12 (July–August 1976): 3–4.

Flügel, J. C. *The Psychology of Clothes.* London: Hogarth Press / Institute of Psychoanalysis, 1930.

Forth, Christopher E., and Ana Carden-Coyne, eds. *Cultures of the Abdomen: Diet, Digestion, and Fat in the Modern World.* New York: Palgrave Macmillan, 2005.

Foster, Paul. "Alfred Hitchcock—an Expert in Tension." *Sketch*, 2 November 1955, 451.

Foucault, Michel. "Of Other Spaces." Translated by Jay Miskowiec. *Diacritics* 16, no. 1 (spring 1986): 22–27.

Freeman, David. "The Last Days of Alfred Hitchcock." *Esquire Film Quarterly* 97 (April 1982): 81–105.

Frost, Jennifer. *Hedda Hopper's Hollywood.* New York: New York University Press, 2011.

Gabler, Neal. *Winchell: Gossip, Power and the Culture of Celebrity.* New York: Knopf, 1994.

Gain, James. *Intimate Nights: The Golden Age of New York Cabaret.* New York: Back Stage Books, 2006.

Gehman, Richard. "The Chairman of the Board." *TV Guide* 12, no. 20 (16 May 1964): 10–13.

Genette, Gérard. *Paratexts: Thresholds of Interpretation.* Translated by Jane E. Lewin. New York: Cambridge University Press, 1997.

Goodman, Ezra. "Strange Case of a British Director Who Has Made an Art of Producing 'Penny Shockers.'" *Cinema Progress* 3, no. 2 (May–June 1938): 9.

Gottlieb, Sidney, ed. *Alfred Hitchcock Interviews.* Jackson: University Press of Mississippi, 2003.

———, ed. *Hitchcock on Hitchcock: Selected Writings and Interviews.* Berkeley: University of California Press, 1995.

Grams, Martin, Jr., and Patrik Wikstrom. *The Alfred Hitchcock Presents Companion.* Churchville, MD: OTR, 2001.

Gras, Pierre. "Hitchcock: Eating and Destruction." In Dominique Païni and Guy Cogeval, eds., *Hitchcock and Art: Fatal Coincidences*, 131–136. Montreal: Montreal Museum of Fine Arts, 2000.

Greven, David. "Engorged with Desire: The Films of Alfred Hitchcock and the Gendered Politics of Eating." In Anne L. Bower, ed., *Reel Food: Essays on Food and Film*, 297–310. New York: Routledge, 2004.

Grimonprez, Johan. *Looking for Alfred*. Ostfildern, Germany: Hatje Cantz, 2007.

Hawkins, Joan. "'See It from the Beginning': Hitchcock's Reconstruction of Film History." *Hitchcock Annual* 8 (1999–2000): 13–29.

Hellman, Geoffrey T. "Alfred Hitchcock: England's Best and Biggest Director Goes to Hollywood." *Life*, 20 November 1939, 33–43.

Helm. "The Glass Eye." *Variety* (daily), 8 October 1957, 8.

———. "The Perfect Murder." *Variety* (daily), 23 October 1957, 14.

Hennelly, Mark M., Jr. "Alfred Hitchcock's Carnival." *Hitchcock Annual* 13 (2004–2005): 154–188.

Higham, Charles. "Hitchcock's World." *Film Quarterly* 16, no. 2 (winter 1962–1963): 3–16.

Hitchcock, Alfred. "Alfred Hitchcock Cooks His Own Goose." *Harper's Bazaar* 109, no. 3169 (December 1975): 132–133.

———, ed. *Alfred Hitchcock Presents: Stories They Wouldn't Let Me Do on TV*. New York: Simon and Schuster, 1957.

———. "Directors Are Dead." In Sidney Gottlieb, ed., *Hitchcock on Hitchcock: Selected Writings and Interviews*, 183–185. Berkeley: University of California Press, 1995. Rpt. of "Directors Are Dead." *Film Weekly*, 20 November 1937, 14.

———. "A Lesson in PSYCHO-ology." *Motion Picture Herald*, 6 August 1960, 17–18.

———. "My Recipe for Murder." *Coronet* 48, no. 5 (September 1960): 49–61.

———. "The Role I Liked Best . . ." *Saturday Evening Post*, December 2, 1950, 138.

"Hitchcock Brews Thrillers Here." *House and Garden* 82, no. 2 (August 1942): 34–35.

"Hitchcock Gives Free Rein to THE GENTLE SEX." *TV Guide* 6, no. 19 (10 May 1958): 12–13.

"Hitchcock's World." *Look*, 26 November 1957, 51–54.

Hoffman, Irving. "Tales of Hoffman." *Hollywood Reporter*, 30 August 1937, 3.

"Hollywood Is . . ." *Harper's Bazaar* 96, no. 3014 (January 1963): 82–97.

Houston, Penelope. "The Figure in the Carpet." *Sight and Sound* 32, no. 4 (autumn 1963): 159–164.

Hyman, Gwen. *Making a Man: Gentlemanly Appetites in the Nineteenth-Century British Novel*. Athens: Ohio University Press, 2009.

"Ingrid Bergman—as Played by Alfred Hitchcock." *Pageant* 2, no. 2 (March 1946): 38–41.

"Integrating Programs and Sell." *Printers' Ink*, 1 April 1960, 51–55.

Johnston, Alva. "300-Pound Prophet Comes to Hollywood." *Saturday Evening Post*, 22 May 1943, 12, 56, 59–61.

Jung, Hwa Yol. "Writing the Body as Social Discourse: Prolegomena to Carnal Hermeneutics." In Stephen Barker, ed., *Signs of Change: Premodern, Modern, Postmodern*, 261–279, 394–416. Albany: State University of New York Press, 1996.

Kapsis, Robert E. *Hitchcock: The Making of a Reputation*. Chicago: University of Chicago Press, 1992.

Kaufman, Dave. "Hitch Stitches TV Viewers' Reaction." *Variety* (daily), 6 January 1965, 8.

Klinger, Barbara. "Digressions at the Cinema: Reception and Mass Culture." *Cinema Journal* 28, no. 4 (summer 1989): 3–19.

Kove. "Fog Closing In." *Variety* (daily), 9 October 1956, 11.

———. "Never Again." *Variety* (daily), 24 April 1956, 12.

Kuhns, J. Lary. "Alfred Hitchcock Presents." In Ken Mogg, ed., *The Alfred Hitchcock Story*, 130–135. London: Titan Books, 1999.

Lane, Christina. "Stepping Out from Behind the Grand Silhouette: Joan Harrison's Films of the 1940's." In David A. Gerstner and Janet Staiger, eds., *Authorship and Film*, 97–118. New York: Routledge, 2003.

Leff, Leonard. *Hitchcock and Selznick: The Rich and Strange Collaboration of Alfred Hitchcock and David O. Selznick in Hollywood*. New York: Weidenfeld and Nicolson, 1987.

Leitch, Thomas M. *The Encyclopedia of Alfred Hitchcock: From Alfred Hitchcock Presents to Vertigo*. New York: Checkmark Books, 2002.

———. *Find the Director and Other Hitchcock Games*. Athens: University of Georgia Press, 2008.

———. "The Outer Circle: Hitchcock on Television." In Richard Allen and S. Ishii-Gonzales, eds., *Alfred Hitchcock: Centenary Essays*, 59–71. London: BFI, 1999.

———. "Self and World at Paramount." In Walter Raubicheck and Walter Srebnick, eds., *Hitchcock's Rereleased Films: From Rope to Vertigo*, 36–51. Detroit: Wayne State University Press, 1991.

Lejeune, Anthony, ed. *The C.A. Lejeune Film Reader*. Manchester: Carcanet, 1991.

Lloyd, Norman. *Stages of a Life in Theatre, Film and Television*. New York: Limelight, 1993.

"London Talk." *Hollywood Reporter*, 2 October 1937, 6.

Lyons, Jeffrey. *Stories My Father Told Me: Notes from the "Lyons Den."* New York: Abbeville, 2011.

Mamber, Steve. "The Television Films of Alfred Hitchcock." *Cinema* 7, no. 1 (fall 1971): 2–7.

Martin, Pete. "I Call on Alfred Hitchcock." *Saturday Evening Post*, 27 July 1957, 36–37, 71–73.

Martine, Arthur. *Martine's Hand-Book of Etiquette, and True Guide to Politeness*. New York: Dick and Fitzgerald, 1866.

Maslin, Janet. "Alfred Hitchcock." *Boston after Dark* 3, no. 24 (12–20 June 1972): 1, 12–13, 23.

Mason, Philip. *The English Gentleman: The Rise and Fall of an Ideal*. London: Deutsch, 1982.

McCarty, John, and Brian Kelleher. *Alfred Hitchcock Presents*. New York: St. Martin's, 1985.

McDougal, Dennis. *The Last Mogul: Lew Wasserman, MCA, and the Hidden History of Hollywood*. New York: Crown, 1998.

McGilligan, Patrick. *Alfred Hitchcock: A Life in Darkness and Light*. New York: Regan Books, 2003.

Mili, Gjon. *Photographs and Recollections*. Boston: New York Graphic Society, 1980.

Millington, Richard H. "Hitchcock and American Character." In Jonathan Freedman and Richard Millington, eds., *Hitchcock's America*, 135–154. New York: Oxford University Press, 1999.

Modleski, Tania. *The Women Who Knew Too Much: Hitchcock and Feminist Theory*. 2nd ed. New York: Routledge, 2005.

Monaco, James. "The Cinema and Its Double: Alfred Hitchcock." *Take One* 5, no. 2 (May 1976): 7.

Morley, David. *Home Territories: Media, Mobility and Identity*. London: Routledge, 2000.

Morris, Nathalie. "The Early Career of Alma Reville." *Hitchcock Annual* 15 (2006–2007): 1–31.

Mosher, Jerry Dean. "Weighty Ambitions: Fat Actors and Figurations in American Cinema, 1910–60." PhD dissertation, University of California, Los Angeles, 2007.

"Movie of the Week: Rope." *Life*, 26 July 1948, 57–58, 60.

Mulvey, Laura. "Visual Pleasure and Narrative Cinema." *Screen* 16, no. 3 (autumn 1975): 6–18.

Murray, Susan. *Hitch Your Antenna to the Stars*. New York: Routledge, 2005.

"No Problem for Mr. Hitchcock." *TV Guide* 5, no. 48 (30 November 1957): 17–19.

Nugent, Frank S. "Assignment in Hollywood." *Good Housekeeping* 121, no. 11 (November 1945): 12–13, 290.

O'Connell, Pat Hitchcock, and Laurent Bouzereau. *Alma Hitchcock: The Woman behind the Man*. New York: Berkley Books, 2003.

"An Old Master Opposes Sink-to-Sink TV." *TV Guide* 7, no. 7 (14 February 1959): 17–19.

Olsson, Jan. "Alfred Hitchcock, théoricien de la television." In Gilles Delavaud and Denis Maréchal, eds., *Télévision: Le moment experimental*, 546–558. Rennes: Éditions Apogée, 2011.

———. *Los Angeles before Hollywood: Journalism and American Film Culture, 1905–1915*. Stockholm: National Library of Sweden, 2008.

Pettigrew, Terence. *British Film Character Actors*. Newton Abbot, UK: David and Charles, 1982.

"Phantom Face in the Foliage." *Life*, 11 July 1960, 54.

Phillips, Gene D. "Hitchcock's Forgotten Films, the Twenty Teleplays." *Journal of Popular Film and Television* 10, no. 2 (summer 1982): 73–76.

"Photocrime." *Look*, 20 September 1955, 104–105, 114.

Polan, Dana. "The Light Side of Genius." In Andrew S. Horton, ed., *Comedy/Cinema/Theory*, 131–152. Berkeley: University of California Press, 1991.

Potts, Neill. "'Revenge': Alfred Hitchcock's 'Sweet Little Story.'" *Hitchcock Annual* 9 (2000–2001): 146–162.

"Reviews." *TV Guide* 3, no. 49 (3 December 1955): 18.

Ripley, Harold Austin. *How Good a Detective Are You?* New York: Blue Ribbon, 1934.

Roberts, Katharine. "Mystery Man." *Collier's*, 5 August 1939, 22.

Robinson, Selma. "Alfred Hitchcock in the Hundred-Pound Mystery." *McCall's* 85, no. 7 (April 1958): 58, 150, 152–153.

Ross, George. "So This Is Broadway." *New York World-Telegram*, 8 June 1938, 23.

Rothman, William. *Hitchcock: The Murderous Gaze*. Cambridge, MA: Harvard University Press, 1982.

Schatz, Thomas. *The Genius of the System: Hollywood Filmmaking in the Studio Era*. New York: Pantheon Books, 1988.

Seldes, Gilbert. "The Alfred Hitchcock Hour." *TV Guide* 11, no. 4 (26 January 1963): 14.

Sharff, Stefan. *Alfred Hitchcock's High Vernacular*. New York: Columbia University Press, 1991.

Sieff, Jeanloup. *40 Years of Photography*. Cologne: Taschen, 2005.

Sklar, Robert. "Death at Work: Hitchcock's Violence and Spectator Identification." In David Boyd and R. Barton Palmer, eds., *After Hitchcock: Influence, Imitation, and Intertextuality*, 216–234. Austin: University of Texas Press, 2006.

Smith, H. Allen. *The Compleat Practical Joker*. Garden City, NY: Doubleday, 1953.

Smith, Susan. *Hitchcock: Suspense, Humour and Tone*. London: BFI, 2000.

"Specialty: Murder. Alfred Hitchcock's Protégée Works at Crime 15 Hours a Day." *TV Guide* 6, no. 10 (8 March 1958): 17–19.

Spigel, Lynn. *Make Room for TV: Television and the Family Ideal in Postwar America*. Chicago: University of Chicago Press, 1992.

Spoto, Donald. *The Dark Side of Genius: The Life of Alfred Hitchcock.* New York: Ballantine Books, 1984.

Stearns, Peter N. *Fat History: Bodies and Beauty in the Modern West.* New York: New York University Press, 1997.

Sterritt, David. "The Diabolic Imagination: Hitchcock, Bakhtin, and the Carnivalization of Cinema." *Hitchcock Annual* 1 (1992): 39–67.

———. *The Films of Alfred Hitchcock.* New York: Cambridge University Press, 1993.

Stromgren, Dick. "Now to the Banquet We Press: Hitchcock's Gourmet and Gourmand Offerings." In Paul Loukides and Linda K. Fuller, eds., *Beyond the Stars: Studies in American Popular Film,* vol. 3: *The Material World in American Popular Film,* 38–50. Bowling Green, OH: Bowling Green University Popular Press, 1993.

Taylor, John Russell. *Hitch: Life and Work of Alfred Hitchcock.* Boston: Faber and Faber, 1978.

Truffaut, François. *Hitchcock.* Rev. ed. New York: Simon and Schuster, 1984.

Vest, James M. "Alfred Hitchcock's Cameo in *Vertigo.*" *Hitchcock Annual* 8 (1999–2000): 84–92.

———. "The Controller Controlled: Hitchcock's Cameo in *Torn Curtain.*" *Hitchcock Annual* 7 (1998–1999): 3–19.

Walker, Michael. *Hitchcock's Motifs.* Amsterdam: Amsterdam University Press, 2005.

Weaver, John D. "The Man behind the Body." *Holiday* 36, no. 3 (September 1964): 85–86, 88–90.

Williams, Linda. "Learning to Scream." *Sight and Sound, New Series* 4, no. 12 (December 1994): 14–17.

Winchell, Walter. "How These Celebrities Stay Thin." *Look,* 19 July 1949, 46–49.

Wollen, Peter. "Hitch: A Tale of Two Cities (London and Los Angeles)." In Richard Allen and Sam Ishii-Gonzales, eds., *Hitchcock: Past and Future,* 13–21. London: Routledge, 2004.

Wylie, Philip. *Generation of Vipers.* [1942.] New York: Rinehart, 1955.

INDEX

Page numbers in italics refer to illustrations. "AHP" stands for *Alfred Hitchcock Presents;* "AHH" stands for *The Alfred Hitchcock Hour.*

143–145; early directing career, 17–18; father-daughter relations, 129, 130, 131, 131–133, 135–136, 139; hoaxes and pranks, 38–39, 41, 103–104, 132–133, 237n34; in London, 14, 30; move to Hollywood, 17–18; in New York, 13–17, 15, 30, 207; Paramount contract, 69; private vs. public persona, 101–104, 141; self-image, 21–22, 29, 122–123, 221n5; self-promotion, 4–5, 46, 206; Selznick agency contract, 18–20, 69. See also body of Hitchcock

Hitchcock, Alma, 131, 205; cooking skills, 55, 56, 57, 59, 61–62; Pat's book on, 139–141, 140; on suspense, 100

Hitchcock, Pat, 15, 61–62, 131, 210; book on Alma, 139–141, 140; Ferris wheel incident, 132–133; film and television roles, 129, 130, 131–133, 134, 135–136, 163; on- and offscreen strangulations, 134, 135, 136; role in *Alfred Hitchcock's Mystery Magazine*, 71, 139; surrogacy role, 118, 129, 135–136; work on AHP, 71

Hitchcock Baker Productions Ltd., 18, 96

Hitchcock figure: across media, 6–7, 187; branding of, 6, 8, 10, 12, 24, 41; in cameos, 123–124; food discourse and, 57; the grotesque and, 36, 41; logo of, 121; multiplicity of, 9, 119; narrative and, 122; television and, 77–78, 103, 106, 206

"Hitchcockian" concept, 4, 9, 156–157; body of work and, 117–120; "ludic" term and, 120; promotion of, 139, 187; television shows and, 145, 206; term usage, 5

Hollywood, 31, 36, 73; Hitchcock's relocation to, 16–20, 22, 30, 42; television, 3, 75–76

Holt, Paul, 104, 223n26, 234n82

Hopper, Hedda, 23–26, 50, 69, 79, 224n44

hosts/hosting, 85–86, 239n64; audiences and, 156, 189, 238n45; control, 156; double, 109, 118; identity and, 87–94, 180; in-jokes, 11–12; segments in AHP, 74–75, 78, 83–84, 94–95, 125, 145, 180

House and Garden, 43

Houston, Penelope, 76, 120

Hull, Bob, 101–102, 126, 129, 212

humor: fatness and, 24–25; the grotesque and, 38; Hitchcock body jokes, 13, 15; Hitchcock's approach to, 32–33; in *Psycho*, 185, 186, 189, 191; televisual in-jokes, 11, 240n70

Humphrey, Hal, 86, 232n56

Hyman, Gwen, 38, 79

identity, 87–94, 122, 124; mirrors and, 176–180

"Into Thin Air" (AHP), 132

Jamaica Inn, 20, 42

James, Henry, 120–121

"Jar, The" (AHH), 183–184, 186

Johnson, Georgann, 178–179, 179

Johnston, Alva, 26–27, 127

"Jonathan" (AHP), 90, 178–179, 179

Journey to the Unknown, 143, 193

Jung, Hwa Yol, 35–36

Kapsis, Robert E., 31, 120, 186

Karloff, Boris, 86

Kaufman, Dave, 184

Kelly, Grace, 33, 36

Kervin, Robert, 205

Kilday, Gregg, 205, 207, 210

King, Don, 29–30

kitchen: domesticity and, 198; Hitchcock family, 9–10, 55, 56, 57, 59, 205; Mary Meade, 227n106; Spirro's ("Specialty of the House"), 63–65, 65

Kjellin, Alf, 216, 217

Lady Vanishes, The, 13–14, 19, 221n12

"Lamb to the Slaughter" (AHP), 11, 70, 78, 88, 115, 202; animal imagery in, 124, 196, 199; murder scene in, 193–194, 197; teleplay, 194–196

"Landlady, The" (AHP), 204

Lane, Christina, 238n42

"Last Request, The" (AHP), 25–26

Laughton, Charles, 20, 118, 126

in "Never Again," 170–171, 171; in "Nothing Ever Happens in Linvale," 171–172

39 Steps, The, 21, 32, 104, 240n74

This Week Magazine, 47, 50

"Three Dreams of Mr. Findlater, The" (AHP), 174, 180

Thriller, 86, 173, 215

Time, 83, 94

"Toby" (AHP), 166

Tone, Franchot, 158–159

Torn Curtain, 33, 185

Transatlantic Pictures, 69

Trouble with Harry, The: body disposal in, 172–173, 240n69; criticism of, 31, 32, 76; grave digging in, 207; humor in, 186; surrogacy function in, 126–127, 129

Truffaut, François, 207–208, 212–213, 243n48

TV Guide, 70, 193, 199, 206, 230n18; Hitchcock interviews, 159, 165; on Hitchcock's personality, 210

Twilight Zone, The, 85, 215, 216

"Unlocked Window, An" (AHH), 191

Variety, 50, 52, 85, 165, 184; on Phyllis Thaxter, 170–171

ventriloquism, 3, 158–159, 163–165

Vertigo, 31, 32, 187, 224n50, 226n83; cast, 168, 198, 239n59; doubling in, 121; launch party, 39, 40, 135, 137, 207, 227n104; painted portraits in, 50, 53

victims, 97, 101–102, 200, 237n34; Hitchcock as, 135, 137

violence: audience reaction to, 184; Hitchcock's view of, 101–102, 102, 185–186; on television, 184, 192, 240n3

visibility, Hitchcock's, 4, 42, 157

vision, 159, 164–165, 179–180

Walker, Michael, 225n68

Wasserman, Lew, 69, 73

Watson, Albert, 61

Weaver, John D., 119

"Wet Saturday" (AHP), 200

Williams, John, 74, 161, 174; in "Back for Christmas," 146, 200; in "Banquo's Chair," 146, 148–151, 154–156; in "The Rose Garden," 204–205

Williams, Linda, 191

Winchell, Walter, 4–5, 43, 219n10

Windust, Bretaigne, 11, 217

Wolters, Larry, 81, 86, 96, 102, 228n2

women: cinematic spectatorship of, 200; Hitchcock's attitude toward, 131, 132; mom characters, 201–205; murderers and victims, 115, 199, 199–200, 240n76; older vs. younger, 34

Woodfield, William Read, 53

Woolley, Monty, 46

Wrong Man, The, 32

Wylie, Philip, 201–202, 204

Young, Loretta, 85

Young & Rubicam, 70, 127, 207, 210

Your Favorite Story, 86